Yolan

DISCIPLE

BECOMING DISCIPLES THROUGH BIBLE STUDY

Study Manual • Youth Edition

DISCIPLE

Acknowledgments

DISCIPLE is the story of a dream turned vision and of a group of people who came together at Flower Mound, Texas, for a brief twenty-four hours and were captured by that vision.

We acknowledge our indebtedness to those persons:

Dan E. Bonner
Maxie D. Dunnam
Ira Gallaway
Dick Murray
Albert C. Outler
Julia K. Wilke
Richard B. Wilke

and staff of the General Board of Discipleship and The United Methodist Publishing House: Lynne M. Deming, Duane A. Ewers, Robert K. Feaster, Marc Lewis, Nellie M. Moser, Robert Paul, Donald G. Sherrod, Gary H. Vincent, David L. Watson, Dal Joon Won, and H. Claude Young.

Special mention is due Jim Beal, whose telephone call to Nashville inquiring about Bible study resources set the wheels in motion for the development of a pastor-taught Bible study program.

Bishop Wilke agreed at the outset to direct the development of the project. Following the Flower Mound consultation, he and Julia Wilke accepted the invitation to write the study manual. A bishop's schedule being what it is, the Wilkes gave up holidays, read and studied in car and plane, and worked into the early hours of the morning to accomplish a mammoth task in an unreasonably short time.

We express sincere appreciation to William Power and Leander E. Keck, who generously arranged already crowded schedules to provide the Wilkes several hours of consultation on Old and New Testaments.

Janice Rogers, secretary to Bishop Wilke, typed the manuscript and managed a myriad of details between Little Rock and Nashville.

Cheryl L. Rude and Susan E. Wilke were handed the challenge of adapting DISCIPLE for youth, of making it accessible and pertinent to youth while maintaining its purpose, integrity, and discipline. They came through with flying colors. Their work shows a keen sensitivity to the intention, tone, and content of DISCIPLE and an understanding of the balance of simplicity and complexity necessary to youth.

Nan Duerling and Steve Moore read the youth adaptation and made valuable comments and suggestions.

Credit goes to Katherine C. Bailey, assistant editor, whose language and computer skills contributed greatly to an orderly, readable manual; to Mary M. Mitchell, who created a design and layout to match our request for simplicity and class; and to Linda O. Spicer for efficient handling of all secretarial matters for the project.

Patricia G. Correll and Vincent W. Isner handled the production of the video component of DISCIPLE, enlisting the participation of a distinguished group of teachers, preachers, and scholars in a remarkably short time.

Dick Murray served as consultant to staff in designing the DISCIPLE training events arranged and managed by Wini Grizzle.

Many persons, named and unnamed, have had a hand in shaping DISCIPLE, and it is accurate to say that DISCIPLE has, in an unusual way, shaped us too.

DISCIPLE: BECOMING DISCIPLES THROUGH BIBLE STUDY
Study Manual • Youth Edition

An official resource for The United Methodist Church prepared by the General Board of Discipleship through the Division of Church School Publications and published by Graded Press, the curriculum publishing department of The United Methodist Publishing House; 201 Eighth Avenue, South; P.O. Box 801; Nashville, Tennessee 37202. Printed in the United States of America.

For more information about DISCIPLE or DISCIPLE training events, call toll free 800-251-8591 or 800-672-1789.

Illustrations by **Mitch Mann**; maps and diagrams by **Ron Martin**; cover design by **Mary M. Mitchell**.

Orion N. Hutchinson, Jr., Editor of Church School Publications; Howard E. Walker, Managing Editor of Church School Publications; Nellie M. Moser, Editor of DISCIPLE; Katherine C. Bailey, Assistant Editor; Linda O. Spicer, Secretary; Mary M. Mitchell, Designer.

Contents

As You Begin DISCIPLE

You are committing yourself to at least two hours a week of independent study and preparation, plus two hours each week for thirty-four weeks in the weekly group meeting.

To establish a disciplined pattern of study, choose and stick to a particular time and location for daily reading and writing, study, and prayer.

Choosing a Bible

This study manual is based on the *Good News Study Bible: The Bible in Today's English Version.* We recommend that you also have a Revised Standard Version of the Bible handy for comparing verses and passages. *The New Oxford Annotated Bible With the Apocrypha*, Revised Standard Version, would be particularly useful because the notes in it are so helpful.

Another excellent translation is the New International Version.

Study Manual Format

This study manual is a discipline. It is a plan to guide your private study and preparation for the weekly group meeting.

Common elements appear throughout the lessons. The theme word, Scripture verse(s), and title at the beginning of each lesson suggest the subject and direction of the lesson. Together, they can help you remember the sequence of the biblical story.

"Our Human Problem" expresses a common human experience and provides a starting point from which to read and listen to Scripture.

Daily Bible reading assignments are listed in the "Assignment" section, and space is provided on the second page of each lesson for making notes about the Scripture—key ideas, persons, events, new insights, geographic or historical information, the meaning of particular words, questions you have about the Scripture that you want to raise in the group meeting. Daily assignments also indicate when to read and respond to "The Bible Teaching" and "Marks of Discipleship" sections of the lesson. The day on which you will do this work will vary depending on the content of the lesson. "Marks" identifies particular characteristics of disciples and invites you to think about ways your life and the life of your congregation reflect those characteristics. Don't rush through this part of your work. It will be a valuable source of insight and discussion for you and members of the group.

"If You Want to Know More" suggests additional individual reading and study, memorizing of Scripture, and occasionally preparing a report to the group.

As you begin your daily study, use the prayer psalm from the "Prayer" section. Write down concerns about which you will pray during the week.

Additional Study Resources

Though you need only the Bible and this study manual for successful study of DISCIPLE, these reference books will help you go deeper into study of the Scriptures:

The Illustrated Bible Handbook (Revision of *Abingdon Bible Handbook*), by Edward P. Blair (Abingdon Press, 1987).

Bible Mapbook, by Simon Jenkins (Lion Publishing Corporation, 1985).

How to Get the Most From Reading Scripture

- Read with curiosity. Ask the questions *who? what? where? when? how?* and *why?* as you read.
- Learn as much as you can about the passage you are studying. It will help you hear God speak to you through the Scripture. Try to discover what the writer was saying for the time in which the passage was written. Read the surrounding verses and chapters to establish the setting or situation in which the action or teaching took place. Pay attention to the form of the passage, because meaning is found not only in what is said but in the form in which it is said. How you read and understand poetry or a parable will differ from how you read and understand the story of an event. Don't force your interpretation on the biblical text. Let the Scripture speak for itself.
- Question the Scripture, but also learn to read Scripture so you find answers to your questions in the Scripture itself. The biblical text itself will solve some of the problems you have with a particular passage. Some problems additional reference material will solve, and some will remain a mystery.
- Come to the Bible with an eagerness to listen to Scripture as the Word of God and a willingness to hear and obey it. Trust the Scripture to teach you and give you power.

THE OLD TESTAMENT

AUTHORITY

"All Scripture is inspired by God and is useful for teaching the truth, rebuking error, correcting faults, and giving instruction for right living, so that the person who serves God may be fully qualified and equipped to do every kind of good deed."

—2 Timothy 3:16-17

1 Introduction

OUR HUMAN PROBLEM

Inside me is this persistent longing to reach out to Someone; this desire to know if God has anything to do with me, to say to me; this need to know if the Bible has any power to offer me.

ASSIGNMENT

Each day throughout the DISCIPLE study, you will be reading Scripture. We urge you to follow the daily pattern of reading and study. During each week you must find time for reading the Bible passages and the study manual. As you read Scripture, make notes in the appropriate space on the adjoining page. The goal of DISCIPLE is to develop disciples of Jesus Christ who know and love God's Word.

Day 1 Hold the Bible in your hands, remembering that it is many books by many writers who were inspired by God. Study the listing of the books of the Bible to "feel" the titles. Look through the entire Bible, paying attention to the content headings. Locate study aids provided in your Bible: preface and introductions, notes at the foot of the page, maps, charts, and supplementary articles. Read portions that interest you.

Day 2 Read and respond to "The Bible Teaching" and "Marks of Discipleship."

Day 3 Taste different styles of biblical literature by random reading. Today, read poetry aloud. Read Psalm 84; Hosea 11:1-4; Exodus 15:1-18.

Day 4 History. 1 Chronicles 22; Acts 9.

Day 5 Law. Exodus 20 (Ten Commandments); Deuteronomy 6 (6:4-9 is called the *Shema,* which means "Hear"). Prophets. Micah 4.

Day 6 Letters. Philemon (a personal letter from Paul). Gospels. Luke 15 (a parable of Jesus).

Day 7 Rest and prayer.

PRAYER

Pray daily before study:

"Treat me according to your constant love,
and teach me your commands.
I am your servant; give me understanding,
so that I may know your teachings" (Psalm 119:124-125).

Prayer concerns for this week: Brad. Joey, MJ, Goddard. (Growth). leaders. Baley hurting people. natural things.

* note—when reading Day 1 try to get the feel of the bible.

AUTHORITY

Day 1 An inspired book, Bible study aids

Day 4 History

- David wanted to build the tempale, but God told him his son Solomon (1 Chr 22)
- Saul becomes Paul. Ananias baptizes Saul. Saul preaches. escapes death. Church grows. Aeneas healed. Dorcas brought back to life.

Day 2 "The Bible Teaching"

Day 5 Law, Prophets

- love the Lord with all your heart, Soul, and strenghth.

Day 3 Poetry

Selah means "to "consider"

Day 6 Letters, Gospels

the letter is about Christian love. Paul offers to pay onesimus's debt. (Philemon)

THE BIBLE TEACHING

The word *Bible* literally means "book." It is *the* book. All others pale beside it. Yet it is not a single book but a library of sixty-six books, written over a period of a thousand years. But the experiences that are recalled, analyzed, evaluated, and celebrated occurred over a period of two thousand years. Stories were told around campfires; songs and psalms were sung in countless worship settings; histories were written and rewritten; laws received by inspiration were codified and interpreted; prophecies were proclaimed, written down, fulfilled. Visions of a kingdom of justice and peace kept circulating through the people's minds.

The Hebrew people were a unique people, unique in that they were called to be a revealing people, struggling always to be God's people, from about 2000 B.C. when Abram and Sarai heard the Lord call them to go forth. God spoke in and through the experiences of this called people. Later, in the life, death, and resurrection of Jesus, God made full revelation and continued to show mysteries of truth in the new covenant people.

The Bible, inspired by God, is both human and divine. You may be surprised at how human the Bible is when you read of violence, rape, betrayal, adultery, sickness, and death. Nothing is hidden. You will also be overwhelmed at how divine the Bible is when you see repentance and faith, just and compassionate laws, acts of devotion and self-sacrifice, and the unending love of the forgiving, covenant God.

Not only are the experiences a mixture of human and divine, but so are the actual writings. Oral tradition was finally put into writing, then edited and reedited, copied, translated, and recopied; the whole process is a tribute to the marvelous inspiration of God. Even the canonizing, setting the standards for what is Scripture, was inspired.

When we speak of Scripture as being inspired, we are recognizing that the Scriptures were written by particular persons under particular circumstances. We are saying that the Scriptures are connected to God and because of that connection, the Scriptures have power to bring about an encounter between God and the one who reads Scripture. The authority of Scripture, then, lies in its ability to cause encounter. When we read the Bible and God speaks to us, we hear the Bible as God's Word.

How Was the Bible Put Together?

Canon means "rule" or standard. Canon here means the list of religious writings considered authoritative.

The Hebrew canon at first simply defined Torah, the Law, the first five books in the Old Testament (the Pentateuch). Torah was not only the central document of Jewish faith but also the fundamental law of the Jewish

NOTES, REFLECTIONS, AND QUESTIONS

nation. It was established between the sixth and fourth centuries B.C.

By the first century A.D., most Jews accepted alongside the Torah a second, less authoritative canon called the Prophets. This group included Joshua through Second Kings (excluding Ruth), plus the Prophets. Other books are known as the Writings. The Hebrew canon of Torah, Prophets, and Writings was finalized at Jamnia on the western coast of Palestine around A.D. 90.

The Hebrew Scriptures, known to Christians as the Old Testament, were originally written in Hebrew; but as early as the third century B.C., the Old Testament was translated into Greek.

A New Testament canon developed gradually. By A.D. 367 a canon identical to our present New Testament had been formed.

The Roman Catholic Church included the Apocrypha as a part of the Scriptures, but Protestants have held to the thirty-nine Old Testament books and the twenty-seven New Testament books as standing alone in inspiration.

How Do We Read the Bible?

Just as God's Spirit guided those who remembered, interpreted, wrote, edited, and copied, God guides the reader today.

Our goal is not to learn the Bible as we learn algebra. Nor do we read a book of Scripture as we would read a detective story or novel. Rather, we listen as we read to the Holy Spirit helping us understand eternal, universal truths. We watch for unexpected insights that are personal, just for us. We savor a promise, thrill to a story that rings true in our experience, or agonize over a law or principle that could change our lives.

As our spiritual understanding grows, we see new truth. Also, as we live through such experiences as sickness, sin, trial, and tragedy, we come to understand what we could never fathom before.

You are beginning a fascinating journey of biblical discovery. The plan of study in this manual; your teacher and fellow students; and the preachers, teachers, and scholars who will instruct you through videotape will aid you on your journey. But most important of all, the Holy Spirit will lead and guide you as you study. Jesus said, "The Helper, the Holy Spirit, . . . will teach you everything and make you remember all that I have told you" (John 14:26).

What Forms of Writing Are in the Bible?

Scripture simply means "writing." But the writing is of every conceivable variety: poetry, laws, historical narratives, liturgies, songs, prophetic utterances, wise sayings, short stories, Gospels, letters, sermons, apocalypses.

Therefore, your reading style must vary. Some poems, such as the Psalms, ought to be read aloud. Stories and

NOTES, REFLECTIONS, AND QUESTIONS

historical narratives can be read rapidly. Law, like a law book, must be read with attention to detail. Reading the prophets requires listening for the message under the words. Proverbs might be memorized. Gospels are such powerful presentations of faith in Christ that they command acceptance of him or rejection.

As you read random samples of Scripture this week, do not try to understand the message yet. Just enjoy the variety in style and begin learning how to read different material.

Why Study the Bible?

What do you bring to the Bible? Your humanity. Nothing you have ever thought, done, experienced, or agonized over is more than the Bible can deal with. Every human emotion is expressed there.

What does the Bible bring to you? God's authoritative guidance and counsel. The Bible has to express humanity in order to reach us; it has to express divinity in order to save us.

Once persons gain familiarity with the Bible and are touched by God's Spirit, they hunger and thirst for more of God's Word. What starts out as hard work turns into satisfaction and joy. The psalmist declared that study of the ordinances of God are

> "sweeter . . . than honey
> and drippings of the honeycomb" (Psalm 19:10, RSV).

Perhaps the Scriptures themselves say it best. Read again 2 Timothy 3:16-17, the verses at the beginning of this lesson.

The words in John's Gospel are even more powerful. Look up John 20:31 and copy that verse here.

but these are written that you may believe that Jesus is the Christ, Son of God, and that believing you may have life in His name.

MARKS OF DISCIPLESHIP

The disciple places himself or herself under the power and authority of Scripture. Under "Marks of Discipleship," we will be asking ourselves how the Word of God is shaping our Christian discipleship.

Right now answer these questions: Why am I participating in DISCIPLE? Why am I planning to study the Bible with intensity, faithfulness, and serious inquiry?

because I want to learn more about God.

NOTES, REFLECTIONS, AND QUESTIONS

IF YOU WANT TO KNOW MORE

Memorize the titles of the thirty-nine Old Testament books so you can locate biblical passages easily and quickly.

The Hebrew Canon

TORAH (LAW)
- Genesis
- Exodus
- Leviticus
- Numbers
- Deuteronomy

PROPHETS

FORMER PROPHETS
- Joshua
- Judges
- 1 and 2 Samuel
- 1 and 2 Kings

LATTER PROPHETS
- Isaiah
- Jeremiah
- Ezekiel

MINOR PROPHETS
- Hosea
- Joel
- Amos
- Obadiah
- Jonah
- Micah
- Nahum
- Habakkuk
- Zephaniah
- Haggai
- Zechariah
- Malachi

WRITINGS

WISDOM
- Psalms
- Proverbs
- Job

FIVE SCROLLS
- Song of Solomon
- Ruth
- Lamentations
- Ecclesiastes
- Esther

- Daniel
- Ezra-Nehemiah
- 1 and 2 Chronicles

The Christian Old Testament Canon

LAW
- Genesis
- Exodus
- Leviticus
- Numbers
- Deuteronomy

HISTORY
- Joshua
- Judges
- Ruth
- 1 and 2 Samuel
- 1 and 2 Kings
- 1 and 2 Chronicles
- Ezra
- Nehemiah
- *Tobit**
- *Judith*
- Esther *(long version)*
- *1 and 2 Maccabees*

WISDOM
- Job
- Psalms
- Proverbs
- Ecclesiastes
- Song of Solomon
- *The Book of Wisdom*
- *Ecclesiasticus*

PROPHETS
- Isaiah
- Jeremiah
- Lamentations
- *Baruch*
- Ezekiel
- Daniel *(long version)*
- Hosea
- Joel
- Amos
- Obadiah
- Jonah
- Micah
- Nahum
- Habakkuk
- Zephaniah
- Haggai
- Zechariah
- Malachi

New Testament Canon

THE GOSPELS
- Matthew
- Mark
- Luke
- John

Acts of the Apostles

LETTERS TO CHURCHES
- Romans
- 1 Corinthians
- 2 Corinthians
- Galatians
- Ephesians
- Philippians
- Colossians
- 1 Thessalonians
- 2 Thessalonians

LETTERS TO INDIVIDUALS
- 1 Timothy
- 2 Timothy
- Titus
- Philemon

Letter to the Hebrews

GENERAL LETTERS
- James
- 1 Peter
- 2 Peter
- 1 John
- 2 John
- 3 John
- Jude

The Revelation

*Titles in italics are not in the Protestant Old Testament. They are from the Apocrypha and are in the Roman Catholic Old Testament.

NOTES, REFLECTIONS, AND QUESTIONS

WONDER

"So God created human beings, making them to be like himself. He created them male and female."

—Genesis 1:27

2 The Creating God

OUR HUMAN PROBLEM

I wonder who made me and my world. If there is a Creator, what is this Creator like? Why was I made? Geologists point to rocks that are billions of years old. Astronomers speak of stars that are millions of light years away. In a universe so big, surely I am only a speck of dust.

ASSIGNMENT

Read Genesis 1–2 and the psalms aloud. This week's preparation is designed for celebration and praise and to establish the habit of daily study and devotion.

Day 1 Genesis 1:1–2:4 (Creation); 2:4-25 (second Creation story)
Day 2 Psalm 8 (praise to the Creator)
Day 3 Psalms 19:1-6; 33 (glory of God)
Day 4 Psalm 100; Job 38–39 (eternal love of God)
Day 5 Psalm 150; John 1:1-5 (praise to the Creator, the Word)
Day 6 Read and respond to "The Bible Teaching" and "Marks of Discipleship."
Day 7 Rest, reflection, prayer, and praise.

PRAYER

Pray daily before study:
"You created me, and you keep me safe;
give me understanding, so that I may learn
your laws" (Psalm 119:73).

Prayer concerns for this week: Courtney nelles hip. greg and Jaime. Shelby ann. John canada. goddar/pastors.

Day 1 Creation, second Creation story

tells about

the new creation and the 2nd creation, and what god made.

Day 4 Eternal love of God

Psalms says his love is never ending and Job tells that God is questioning him.

Day 2 Praise to the Creator

It is telling how God put one man in charge of all the animals etc.

Day 5 Praise to the Creator, the Word

Day 3 Glory of God

It telling me that all the heavens tell gods story, but don't use words, or sound. It tells me about the Glory of God.

Day 6 "The Bible Teaching"

THE BIBLE TEACHING

NOTES, REFLECTIONS, AND QUESTIONS

The Hebrew verb for *create* refers to the activity of God, not to human activity (Genesis 1:1). Two ideas are contained in the verb *create*. First, God causes everything to come into being out of nothing. Second, God orders, arranges, and designs that creation.

"The earth was formless and desolate. The raging ocean . . . was engulfed in total darkness" (Genesis 1:2). This verse refers to a cosmic emptiness, a formless darkness, sometimes referred to as a "sea of chaos." The ancients believed that all creation originated from a dark, watery chaos, "the deep." Over the dark emptiness, "the power of God was moving" (1:2).

The Hebrews did not believe that the Creator was simply one of a group of gods. They did not believe that matter came first and God somehow came out of the matter. They did not believe that two gods, one good and one evil, battled to bring creation into existence. Rather, they believed that the one and only Lord of the universe, the One who had created them to be a covenant people and who had delivered them from slavery, was Author and Designer of all that is.

What Is God Like?

Then God *spoke*. The universe was created by a *word* (Genesis 1:3). God spoke, and created order came into being. God creates the universe but does not walk away. God stays close, in contact with that creation.

Later when Jesus Christ came, Christians understood that in him the Word had become a human being. "Word" became a synonym for Jesus Christ. John had Genesis 1:3 in mind when he wrote, "Before the world was created, the Word already existed; he was with God, and he was the same as God. From the very beginning the Word was with God. Through him God made all things; not one thing in all creation was made without him. . . .

"The Word became a human being and . . . lived among us" (John 1:1-3, 14). By God's Word the universe came into being. Later that Word walked among us.

The apostle Paul also wanted Christians to know that the Word God spoke in Creation was the same Word God spoke on the cross. "For through him God created everything in heaven and on earth, the seen and the unseen things. . . . For it was by God's own decision that the Son has in himself the full nature of God. Through the Son, then, God decided to bring the whole universe back to himself. God made peace through his Son's sacrificial death on the cross" (Colossians 1:16, 19-20). Thus Christians came to understand the Creation story.

Wonder

From the beginning, people have pondered the mystery of Creation. Why am I here? Where did the universe come from? People ask, Who made God?

Giraffes and elephants amuse us; the Rocky Mountains and the Milky Way amaze us; a newborn baby fills us with wonder. With the psalmist we ask,

"What is man, that you think of him;
mere man, that you care for him?" (Psalm 8:4).

We can only respond with wonder as we listen in as God confronts Job (Job 38–39). Those two chapters lay before our eyes the order, majesty, and mystery of Creation. They sing of the glory and goodness of the Creator.

In Job, as you will see in a later lesson, faith and suffering are the issue, and these chapters record God's response to Job's questioning God's purpose and rule.

But the point of Job for us here is

- that the wonders of God's creation are beyond the grasp of our minds;
- that human understanding and divine understanding are vastly different;
- that human values and God's values are worlds apart;
- and above all else, that this Creator cares, that is, loves the creation.

What response can we make? Only wonder. Only worship.

The Bible does not try to prove the existence of God. Rather, the Bible explodes in praise. The stories and the songs portray a vibrant creation and a loving and gracious God. The Bible answers the questions of the heart by celebrating God's creativity and pointing toward human response.

Not a scientific account of some "big bang" theory, not a newspaper reporter's interview with Adam and Eve, the Bible expresses a testimony of trust in a generous and merciful Creator.

Creation

Genesis is a Greek word that means "beginning." Literally, the Hebrew means "in the beginning." The first Creation account is the opening of the Bible (Genesis 1:1–2:4). It is a carefully worded poem of praise to God, containing the accumulated faith of the covenant people.

The second (and the older of the two) Creation story (2:4-25) is a very ancient story, told long ago around campfires, under a star-studded sky. It was recited for centuries before it was written down.

The Creation psalms are songs of worship that spanned the centuries and are as comfortable for us today as they were for ancient Israel. These psalms chant songs of beauty and order and wonder.

NOTES, REFLECTIONS, AND QUESTIONS

“How clearly the sky reveals God’s glory!
How plainly it shows what he has done!
Each day announces it to the following day;
each night repeats it to the next.
No speech or words are used,
no sound is heard;
yet their message goes out to all the world
and is heard to the ends of the earth”
(Psalm 19:1-4).

The symbol of seven days is a faith statement. To take the imagery of “first day” or “second day” as twenty-four-hour periods is to miss the essential point. In understanding “the first day,” “the second day,” and so on, we need to remember that

“A thousand years to you are like one day;
they are like yesterday, already gone,
like a short hour in the night” (Psalm 90:4).

But more, seven days are poetic symbols to show form and to remind us to order our lives as God has ordered the universe.

Some people have trouble with science and the Bible. They either say the Bible is not true, or they separate their study of science from their faith as if God does not understand how mountains are formed or how babies are born. But have you wondered why so many scientists are women and men of faith? Because they know how much they do not know, how many questions they cannot answer except by faith. They see that the Creation poems and stories and songs are statements of faith, not geology or biology. They know that in Creation God acted and is continually acting to create and to bring order.

The wise father or mother responds to the child’s question, Who made God? by answering, “Nobody. That’s who God is—the One who started it all, the One who made you and me and everything.” Bible scholars can do no better. They say God created out of nothing. The Bible simply says, “In the beginning, when God created.”

But what shall we think about this created universe? The biblical refrain gives us a hint: “And God saw that it was good” (Genesis 1:4, 10, 12, 18, 21, 25, RSV).

Some religions have taught that the material world is evil, that the physical body is bad. Not so in Judaism and Christianity. Everything God made—knee joints and sex organs, flying fish and monkeys, the law of gravity and the changing seasons—everything created by God and untouched by sin is called good. God was pleased.

Think what that says about the character of the Creator. Everything that is made is good; therefore God must be very good.

NOTES, REFLECTIONS, AND QUESTIONS

Look at the power in the Creation accounts: After mentioning the sun to light the day and the moon to light the night, the Scripture says, "He also made the stars" (1:16). Imagine, the Bible flings off the infinite galaxies of the heavens in a simple phrase, "He also made the stars." Our God is a great God!

A believer might ask a rabbi, "Why did God give us this mighty poem of Creation?" The rabbi's answer? "To teach us to rest on the sabbath." Why? Because God observed sabbath, and that makes it sacred. And because when we stop our work, we remember that we are God's creatures and that God will take care of us even when we rest for a while. The loving God wants us to trust, to relax, to enjoy.

Stewards

"Then God said, 'And now we will make human beings; they will be like us and resemble us. They will have power over the fish, the birds, and all animals, domestic and wild, large and small' " (Genesis 1:26).

We are to be stewards of the entire universe. The biblical world was before pesticides and pollutants, but the understanding is there.

We are to keep the air clean.

We are to keep water pure.

We are to save the topsoil and replenish the forests and protect the animals, for we are stewards of the environment. We have been given a trust to maintain the balance of nature.

Now consider the older of the two Creation stories (2:4-25). Here the order of Creation is different from that in the other story. But like the first Creation account, this account is a story of faith. Notice the dramatic symbols.

NOTES, REFLECTIONS, AND QUESTIONS

What do you think is the meaning of God's forming man of the soil from the ground (2:7)?

What does the Scripture mean by continuing "he breathed life-giving breath into his nostrils and the man began to live" (2:7)?

What does Eden symbolize to you?

What do you think is the symbolic significance of "the tree that gives knowledge of what is good and what is bad" (2:9)?

MARKS OF DISCIPLESHIP

We are God's creatures. As Christian disciples, we know we belong to God. God has claim on us. How do we show by our actions that we belong to God?

Describe a time when you felt such wonder at the majesty of creation that you could only praise God.

If God created the world for our benefit, what does that intention of God say about the character of God?

NOTES, REFLECTIONS, AND QUESTIONS

Clearly, the Creation stories give us responsibility for caring for the earth, for plants and animals, for birds and fish, for air and water. Read again Psalm 8:6-9. What are you doing right now to exercise this stewardship of all creation?

Describe your day of rest. How does it reflect a quiet trust in the great, good, and loving God who has created you and who will sustain you? How could you rest more creatively on your sabbath?

IF YOU WANT TO KNOW MORE

Take a walk in a park or the out-of-doors and sensitize yourself to the sky, the trees, the water. Take time to watch and listen and feel. Try to see something you have never seen before. From time to time say, "Thank you, God."

NOTES, REFLECTIONS, AND QUESTIONS

SIN

"I recognize my faults;
  I am always conscious of my sins.
I have sinned against you—only against you—
  and done what you consider evil."

—Psalm 51:3-4

3 The Rebel People

OUR HUMAN PROBLEM

Because we have a mind, a will, the power to choose, we want to be in control. We become self-centered. We rebel against our Creator in our attempt to take control. Yet we know that things in the world and in ourselves are terribly wrong, but we don't know why.

ASSIGNMENT

In preparation, read thoughtfully these passages about sin. Try to become a character in the Genesis stories. Imagine yourself in the garden of Eden, on Noah's ark, or helping to build the tower of Babylon. Notice that in Jeremiah the prophet grieves over the sins of a whole society. In Second Samuel the prophet Nathan throws a blinding spotlight on David's sin. Psalm 51 might be David's confession, or your own.

Day 1 Genesis 3–4 (the Fall, Cain and Abel)
Day 2 Genesis 6:5–9:28 (Noah and the Flood)
Day 3 Genesis 11:1-9 (the tower of Babylon)
Day 4 Jeremiah 8:18–9:11 (a lament for Judah and Jerusalem)
Day 5 2 Samuel 11:1–12:12 (David's sin and Nathan's reproof); Psalm 51 (confession)
Day 6 Read and respond to "The Bible Teaching" and "Marks of Discipleship."
Day 7 Rest; reflect on your thoughts and actions of the week.

PRAYER

Pray daily before study:
"Turn to me and have mercy on me
  as you do on all those who love you"
  (Psalm 119:132).

Prayer concerns for this week:

SIN

Day 1 The Fall, Cain and Abel

Day 2 Noah and the Flood

Day 3 Tower of Babylon

Day 4 Lament for Judah and Jerusalem

Day 5 David's sin and Nathan's reproof, confession

Day 6 "The Bible Teaching"

THE BIBLE TEACHING

NOTES, REFLECTIONS, AND QUESTIONS

When did you first rebel and demand your own way? You can't remember? It must have been early in your life. So it was with the human race. When ancient Hebrews asked, How did sin come into the world? an elder would begin to tell the story of the first man and the first woman and the snake. When the story was over, the people would nod their heads knowingly; for they then understood something about themselves and about the human race. Or someone would ask, Why can't people get along with one another? And the elder would tell the story about the building of the great tower and how everybody wanted to be like God. Again the people would nod with understanding.

The Bible is more concerned about *what is* than *what was*. The Bible wants us to understand who God is and who we are.

Sin and its many forms are found everywhere in the Bible. We will study sin in relation to freedom, relationship, temptation, rebellion, alienation, wickedness, and grace. For sin is not merely a topic. Sin is a scarlet thread running through the pages of the Bible from beginning to end.

Freedom

God breathed into men and women the power to think, to decide. This will or soul, this spark of divine freedom, makes us different from rocks, plants, and animals. We have a will so that we can make choices. We are not totally determined by forces inside us or outside us. God wants children, not puppets.

When God said, "You may eat the fruit of any tree in the garden, except the tree that gives knowledge of what is good and what is bad" (Genesis 2:16-17), God appealed to man and woman's freedom of choice. They will be held accountable.

Like Adam and Eve, we have choices to make and are held accountable by God. What are you being held accountable for by God?

____

____

Relationship

Sin makes no sense apart from relationship. If there is no God, there is no sin. We might violate social customs or stumble over the natural order, but sin is an offense against Someone. Sin changes our relationships with other people. Sin scrambles our inner person so that we experience feelings such as shame and guilt. The man and the woman disobeyed God, so they hid. They broke the innocent relationship of love and trust.

Temptation

Some people say, "The Devil made me do it." That attitude is a sidestepping of responsibility. Nevertheless, human experience testifies to a "whisper in the ear." The cunning snake symbolizes an evil power that tempts us. Jesus was tempted (Matthew 4:1-11). Which one of us does not know the tug and pull of temptation?

When you are tempted, what are the words the snake speaks to you?

____

____

Rebellion

Deeper than any individual act of wrongdoing is the human tendency to rebel. From the beginning, people have tried to break out of divine boundaries, grab control of their own lives, and ignore what they knew to be right. Human beings, in selfish striving, seek to be independent of God. We dislike being limited. A kind of pride sweeps over us. The story of the tower of Babylon shows our desire to be like God. Paul said, "They exchange the truth about God for a lie; they worship and serve what God has created [that is, themselves] instead of the Creator" (Romans 1:25).

Rebellion includes disobedience (or transgression) and self-centeredness. We turn from God when we want to do things our way. This rebellion is complete and universal:

"They have all gone wrong;
  they are all equally bad.
Not one of them does what is right,
  not a single one" (Psalm 14:3).

NOTES, REFLECTIONS, AND QUESTIONS

The tower of Babylon is usually pictured as a *ziggurat,* a kind of temple tower in the form of a terraced pyramid. Such *ziggurats* were built by the ancient Babylonians and Assyrians.

NOTES, REFLECTIONS, AND QUESTIONS

Alienation

The woman and the man lived in blissful innocence, naturally trusting and loving God. The earth was their paradise. In childlike wonder, they did not know there was such a thing as evil. But with their disobedience came knowledge of wrongdoing, shame, guilt, alienation. They immediately covered themselves and went into hiding.

David tried to hide his adulterous and murderous actions from the nation, and even from his own conscience, until the prophet Nathan beamed the spotlight of truth on his soul.

How are you experiencing anger, guilt, alienation? How are you hiding in some dark corner?

One way to hide is by rationalizing. The man said, "The woman you put here with me gave me the fruit, and I ate it" (Genesis 3:12). And the woman countered, "The snake tricked me into eating it" (3:13).

When have you found yourself rationalizing and blaming others?

Wickedness

From the rebellious, self-centered heart, all sorts of wickedness spring forth. We can talk about the Ten Commandments, about cheating on income tax or in school, about nuclear armaments or the drug traffic or child abuse or pornography or gossip. The disease is widespread. The whole human race is infected.

Grace

With evil so pervasive, sin so vile, we wonder why God does not destroy us all. The Bible speaks of God's temptation to do so (Genesis 6:5-7). But when the destruction comes, there is always a restraining side to the action: Noah and his family gave humankind a chance to start again.

Remember, in the Fall (Genesis 3 and 4), the touch of God's grace even amid the rebellion. God did not abandon the woman and the man. God came to them, questioned them, but did not destroy them. Their punishment was a form of grace: The man would produce food by sweat; yet work is one of life's great blessings. The woman would bear children with pain; yet children are usually so welcome that the pangs of childbirth are soon forgotten.

Did God lie when he said they would die? Did the snake tell the truth when he said they would not? Both told their own truth. Life to God means fulfillment, joy, a relationship of unblemished love. Life to Satan means eating and sleeping and physically going on. When the woman and the man rebelled, something beautiful died. Innocence was destroyed. A relationship was broken. Pure love of God and one another was violated, mixed forever with guilt and spiritual separation. We can never go home again.

Yet God did not abandon his people. Even as God drove woman and man out of the land of innocence, he took the time and tenderness to make clothes for them and help them dress themselves (3:21). Notice also that the "mark on Cain" (4:15) was to protect him, not to persecute him as is commonly thought. The grace of God permeates the Bible. God's mercy accompanies people even in their wickedness. That grace culminates in the cross of Jesus Christ.

MARKS OF DISCIPLESHIP

As disciples, we acknowledge our human rebellion, accept our personal responsibility for sin, and repent, placing ourselves back under the authority of God.

We all try to hide our sinfulness, don't we? Even from ourselves. Recall a time when some person or some event caused you to realize your own sin.

____

____

____

Because we tend to go against God and take life into our own hands, how do we go about putting ourselves back under God's authority? Read again Psalm 51.

____

____

____

IF YOU WANT TO KNOW MORE

In Romans Paul says in sentences what Genesis says in stories. Read Romans 1:18–2:1.

NOTES, REFLECTIONS, AND QUESTIONS

COVENANT

"I will give you many descendants, and they will become a great nation. I will bless you and make your name famous, so that you will be a blessing."

—Genesis 12:2

4 The Called People

OUR HUMAN PROBLEM

We are confused. Overwhelmed. We don't know what to do. We don't know how to begin. We long for a purpose that will take us beyond ourselves.

ASSIGNMENT

In preparation, read in great sweeps the patriarchal stories of the Bible: Abraham and Sarah; Isaac and Rebecca; Jacob, Rachel, Leah, and Jacob's twelve sons from whom descended the twelve tribes of Israel; and Joseph, the great provider. Read rapidly, being concerned not about detail but about gaining a sense of history, a feeling for a people called for a special mission.

Day 1 Genesis 12–13; 14:17–17:27 (the call of Abram and the covenant with God)
Day 2 Genesis 18–23 (birth of Isaac, testing of Abraham); Genesis 24–27 (Isaac and Rebecca)
Day 3 Genesis 28–33; 35 (Jacob, Rachel, Leah, and the twelve sons)
Day 4 Genesis 37; 39–41 (Joseph in Egypt)
Day 5 Genesis 42–45 (Joseph's brothers in Egypt)
Day 6 Genesis 47–50 (Jacob's move to Egypt); read and respond to "The Bible Teaching" and "Marks of Discipleship."
Day 7 Rest and reflection. Think about the variety of people God uses to achieve God's purposes.

PRAYER

Pray daily before study:

"You have done many things for us, O LORD
our God;
there is no one like you!
You have made many wonderful plans for us"
(Psalm 40:5).

Prayer concerns for this week:

COVENANT

Day 1 Call of Abraham, covenant with God

Day 4 Joseph in Egypt

Day 2 Birth of Isaac, testing of Abraham, Isaac and Rebecca

Day 5 Joseph's brothers in Egypt

Day 3 Jacob, Rachel, Leah, and the twelve sons

Day 6 Jacob's move to Egypt, "The Bible Teaching"

THE BIBLE TEACHING

NOTES, REFLECTIONS, AND QUESTIONS

The stories and oral traditions recorded in Genesis 1–11 have set the stage for us to begin following the historical journey of God's chosen people. The account of Abraham's life is dated approximately 2000 B.C.

Picture the Near Eastern world in 2000 B.C. In Egypt people worshiped the sun and Pharaoh. In Canaan the Canaanites worshiped on the high places, celebrating fertility with sexual orgies and drunkenness. Peoples of Mesopotamia, including the Amorites, also a highly developed people, still served many gods.

Into this world God called his people. God's purpose was to reveal the one true God, Creator of all that is, and to show a way of life compatible with God's holiness and helpful for human wholeness.

God wants a people who trust, a people who will leave their familiar surroundings (gods, culture, land) and go forth in obedience to a fresh place in order to be a blessing to all the families of the earth. As an integral part of this call, God will multiply Abram and Sarai into a great nation with a land of their own.

Covenant

Covenant is not contract. Contract is an agreement between two parties. Covenant is a binding relationship between God and God's people. God initiates covenant and specifies all the provisions. People have the choice of accepting or rejecting, but not of offering alternative plans or conditions. Blessing comes from obedience.

The hinge verse is "When Abram was seventy-five years old, he started out from Haran, as the LORD had told him to do" (Genesis 12:4). On that verse hangs the history of Israel. No wonder the Jews refer to "our father Abraham." The Muslims call him "friend of God," and Christians honor him as the father of the faithful.

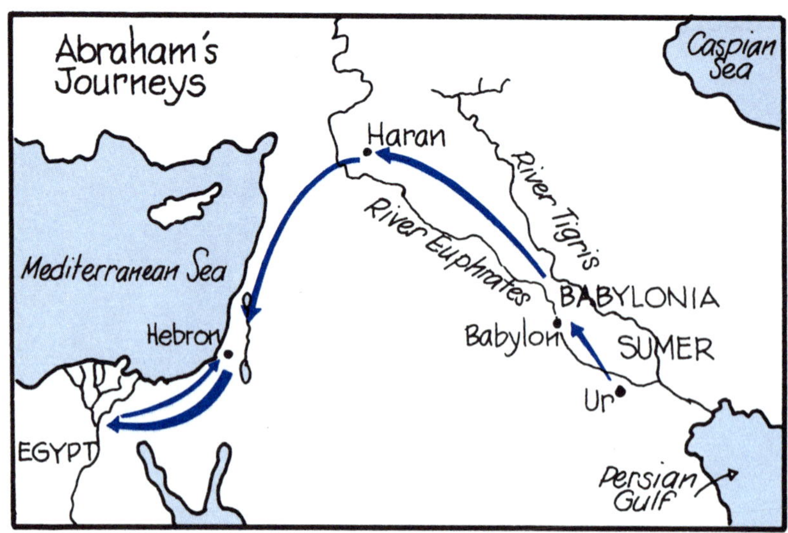

Abram and Sarai (later called Abraham and Sarah; 17:5, 15-16) left the Mesopotamian region where the Tigris and Euphrates Rivers had rocked the cradle of civilization. Early peoples in Mesopotamia had invented writing, designed cities, established government, and established an organized religion of moon god and fertility rites. But Abram and Sarai were called to become nomads in the rough and rugged terrain of Canaan.

God does not reveal God's will to the curious but to the obedient. Faith is not belief without proof; faith is obedience without reservation.

But what a foolish choice God made! Abram was seventy-five years old, past the age of retirement, when he left Ur. God wanted to procreate a great people, and Abram was an old man. His wife Sarai was beyond the age of bearing children. No wonder she laughed (18:12). Here we get a clue that God picks unlikely people to carry the colors: Moses, a stutterer to speak the law; Rahab, a prostitute to open the Promised Land; David, a shepherd boy to be king; Jesus, a Jewish carpenter to be the Savior of the world. The Bible says God purposely chooses "what the world considers nonsense in order to shame the wise" (1 Corinthians 1:27).

NOTES, REFLECTIONS, AND QUESTIONS

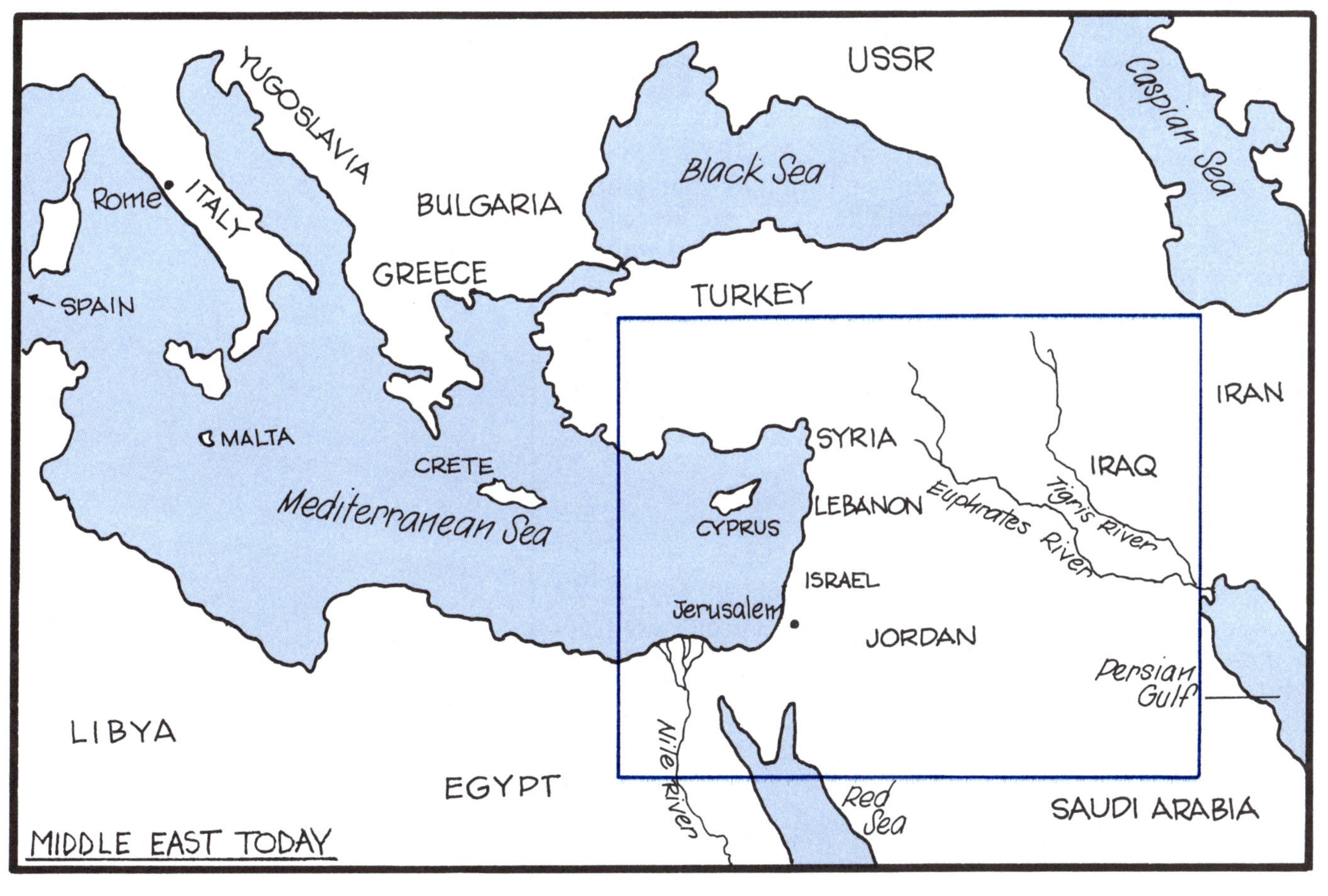

Consider for a moment some surprising (by worldly standards), even limited, people whom God has used in a mighty way. Jot down their names.

Melchizedek, a priest of the Most High God, seems to drop right out of heaven, bringing bread and wine (Genesis 14:18). No wonder early Christians saw him as a forerunner of Jesus, the great high priest of God (Hebrews 6:19–7:3). Abram took the bread and wine and gave a tithe to Melchizedek (Genesis 14:18-20).

Marks of the Covenant

The tithe became an essential part of the covenant. Old and New Testaments emphasize the tithe as the standard of faithful worship. Read what the prophet Malachi said about the tithe (Malachi 3:6-12). The tithe emphasizes first fruits, proportionate giving (ten percent), regular offerings, and joyous worship. The tithe is a mark of discipleship for the people of God.

Another mark of belonging to the covenant people was circumcision (Genesis 17:9-14). No one can understand biblical history without understanding that Jewish males since the time of Abraham have been circumcised as the mark of belonging to the covenant people. Later the religious leaders would call for and promise a circumcision of the heart, recognizing that the physical symbol was not enough. "The LORD your God will circumcise your heart and the heart of your offspring, so that you will love the LORD your God with all your heart and with all your soul, that you may live" (Deuteronomy 30:6, RSV; see 10:16). Paul argued that Christians, if their hearts are filled with Jesus' spirit, do not need physical circumcision in order to belong to the new covenant people (Galatians 5:6; 6:15). But among the Jews, circumcision is the sign of belonging to the people of God—Abraham, Isaac, and Jacob.

At times when the continuity of the covenant could have been broken, God acted in strong ways. Consider God's action:

The Testing of Abraham

God wanted to test Abraham's faith. God wanted him to be willing to offer up Isaac, thc child of promise. (Sometimes in Canaan, worshipers of Canaanite gods did sacrifice their first-born sons.) But God intervened, providing Abraham a ram for the sacrifice instead. Light came to the whole world that God did not want infant sacrifice. (See also Leviticus 18:21, RSV.) Abraham passed God's test; he proved faithful.

NOTES, REFLECTIONS, AND QUESTIONS

Reaffirmation by Isaac

If Isaac had gone back to Mesopotamia, or if he had married a Canaanite woman, then all would have been lost. The arrangement of Isaac's marriage was essential to the continuity of the covenant (Genesis 24). Notice how the servant saw God's hand in the whole affair (24:27).

Later Isaac carried on the tradition and faith of his father. Look at this powerful symbol: Isaac "dug once again the wells which had been dug during the time of Abraham" (26:18). Then he dug his own well, "Well of the Vow," showing his own personal commitment to the call of God (26:25, 32-33).

Esau and Jacob

God can do more with a rascal than with a fool. Jacob was a conniving, cheating scoundrel. But he *did* care about the covenant. His name literally meant "heel grabber." His older twin Esau, as first-born, should have carried on the covenant. But he was more concerned about hunting and fishing and eating. God went to work on Jacob, an unlikely prospect.

When Jacob was running for his life, God met him in a dream. When we sing "We are climbing Jacob's ladder," we remember the angels going up and coming down. Jacob named the place *Bethel,* meaning "house of God." Notice that he confirmed his meeting with the God of Abraham and Isaac by pledging the tithe (Genesis 28:22).

Yet Jacob was not really changed until he was on his return journey to the homeland, the land of promise. Genesis 32:22–33:20 portrays one of the great wrestling matches of history and one of the Bible's most beautiful reconciliations. If you have ever wrestled all night with God and been blessed, then you, like Jacob, have a new name, Israel (meaning "one who struggles with God"), and you too will never be the same.

The two brothers were reconciled when Jacob limped up the hill, bowing low, and "Esau ran to meet him, threw his arms around him, and kissed him" (33:4). The reconciliation was cemented with the death of their father. These are precious words: "Isaac lived to be a hundred and eighty years old and died at a ripe old age; and his sons Esau and Jacob buried him" (35:28-29).

Think about your own family relationships. Do you need to wrestle with God so you can "go home again"?

Joseph the Provider

Four sets of half brothers, a blended family conceived in bitterness because of jealousy among the mothers, a younger brother adored by his father because he was born when his father was old—no wonder the other sons felt anger

NOTES, REFLECTIONS, AND QUESTIONS

toward the favored one. But years later, long after the brothers had thrown Joseph into the pit, after Potiphar's prison, after dreams and harvests and famine, Joseph looked back over his life. He exclaimed to his brothers who were then forgiven and reconciled, "You plotted evil against me, but God turned it into good" (Genesis 50:20). What an awareness of the strange providence of God!

In looking back over your life, where do you sense the shaping or guiding of God's providence?

Recall an experience in your life when God turned evil into good.

So the covenant community is called, shaped, tested, converted, watched over by God. Imperfect people—doubting, conniving, arrogant people—are molded into a message: God is God of all creation. God is to be obeyed; children are to be respected; brothers are to be reconciled; food is to be shared; elderly are to be honored; God can be trusted. The light is beginning to shine for the whole world to see. And we are beginning to sense there is meaning to life, a direction to travel, a people of faith to whom we can belong. We are beginning to know what to do and whom to trust.

MARKS OF DISCIPLESHIP

The disciple responds to God's call to enter the covenant community of faith.

What are some marks by which we Christians can tell we are a part of God's community of faith?

NOTES, REFLECTIONS, AND QUESTIONS

The tithe is one response to God's call that helps persons reach beyond themselves. Do you tithe? Why? Or why not?

Are you willing to tithe during the remainder of this study, linking yourself to the covenant community of faith?

So much emphasis in American Christianity is personal and individual. What helps you feel that you belong to the called corporate people of God?

IF YOU WANT TO KNOW MORE

Chart biblical history. Here are some dates and events to start with. Others will be suggested throughout the study. You may want to break the periods down further or include other events within the time periods.

Chart of Biblical History

2000 B.C. **Patriarchal period**
Abraham, Isaac, Jacob, Joseph
1700 B.C. **Joseph's family enters Egypt**

Both Arabs and Jews are descendants of ancient Semitic people, and both greatly respect Abraham. Study the story of Hagar and Ishmael (Genesis 16; 21:9-21; 25:12-18) to understand some of the background of the tension between Jews and Arabs.

NOTES, REFLECTIONS, AND QUESTIONS

DELIVERANCE

"I have seen the affliction of my people who are in Egypt, and have heard their cry because of their taskmasters; I know their sufferings, and I have come down to deliver them."

—Exodus 3:7-8, RSV

5 God Hears the Cry

OUR HUMAN PROBLEM

We are humiliated, taken advantage of, and trapped in situations beyond our control. We want someone to rescue us. We want a deliverer. We beg for help. Does anybody care?

ASSIGNMENT

As you read, remember that the entire Old Testament is to be seen through "post-Exodus glasses" as the New Testament is to be understood through "post-Resurrection glasses." The Hebrews' understanding of who they were, who God is, and how God acted in history was shaped by the Exodus experiences. Those experiences influenced and shaped the life and faith of the Hebrew people in the same way the Resurrection influenced and shaped the life and faith of Christians.

Day 1 Exodus 1–4 (the oppression of the Hebrews and the call of Moses)
Day 2 Exodus 5–7 (Moses confronting Pharaoh, beginning of the plagues)
Day 3 Exodus 8–11 (remaining plagues)
Day 4 Exodus 12–14 (explanation of Passover Festival, death of the first-born, escape from Egypt)
Day 5 Exodus 15–18 (song of Moses, moving into the desert)
Day 6 Read and respond to "The Bible Teaching" and "Marks of Discipleship."
Day 7 Rest, worship, and reflection.

PRAYER

Pray daily before study:

"Listen to my words, O LORD, and hear my sighs.
Listen to my cry for help,
my God and king!

I pray to you, O LORD;
you hear my voice in the morning;
at sunrise I offer my prayer
and wait for your answer"
(Psalm 5:1-3).

Prayer concerns for this week:

Deliverance

Day 1 Oppression of the Hebrews, call of Moses

Day 4 Explanation of Passover Festival, death of the first-born, escape from Egypt

Day 2 Moses confronting Pharaoh, beginning of the plagues

Day 5 Song of Moses, moving into the desert

Day 3 Remaining plagues

Day 6 "The Bible Teaching"

THE BIBLE TEACHING

Four hundred and thirty years had passed since Joseph stored grain for Pharaoh, the king of Egypt. The Hebrews had prospered on the good land called Goshen on the Nile Delta in northeastern Egypt. The descendants of Jacob's twelve sons had become, as God had promised Abraham, as many as the "grains of sand along the seashore" (Genesis 22:17), hundreds of thousands of people by the time of Moses.

But the politics of Egypt took a downward turn for the Hebrews. "Then, a new king, who knew nothing about Joseph, came to power in Egypt" (Exodus 1:8). The Hebrews were seen as a foreign people who lived on the border and did not worship Egyptian gods.

The powerful central government of the Nineteenth Dynasty of Egypt developed strong armies and constructed huge buildings. The Egyptian pharaohs Seti I and Rameses II built gigantic tombs and temples with mammoth statues. In the Nile Delta, they constructed the great storage cities of Pithom and Rameses. Hebrew men as well as Egyptian peasants were forced into day labor. The work was hard, and the conditions oppressive. Slowly the kings turned the economic screw tighter and tighter. The Hebrews became slaves and so many in number that those in power began to fear them. Human life was cheap.

The king, with a paranoid mentality, was so unreasonably distrustful that he decided to kill the Hebrew boy babies. First he appealed to the midwives; and when that ploy did not work, he demanded that the baby boys be thrown into the Nile. Wailing was heard in the streets. Daily life was reduced to subhuman existence. Freedom gradually slipped away. The Hebrews were intimidated, resigned, helpless. The promises God had made to Abraham seemed far away and long ago.

Then one woman resisted. Moses' mother slipped her baby into the Nile as the king commanded, but in a tar-covered basket. The princess, the king's daughter, drew the baby out, hired a Hebrew woman, not knowing she was Moses' mother, to nurse him. The king's daughter adopted Moses as her own son.

The name *Moses* carried two meanings. It is similar to the Egyptian word for "child" or "son," a son for the princess. But Israel understood *son* to stand for God's people. "I . . . called him out of Egypt as my son" (Hosea 11:1). *Moses* in Hebrew meant "drawn forth." He was drawn forth from the water, but later he drew forth the people through the water.

The boy was nurtured on his mother's Hebrew faith, listening to the lullabies of Israel. Yet he was trained in the ways of the Egyptian king's court, educated by the finest scholars in the known world. When God said to Moses, "What is that in your hand?" (Exodus 4:2, RSV), Moses saw only a stick that stood as a symbol of himself—a

NOTES, REFLECTIONS, AND QUESTIONS

A statue of Rameses II that probably once stood in the temple at Karnak. Rameses II is thought by many to have been the pharaoh of the Exodus. *Pharaoh* is the Hebrew word for the title held by the king of Egypt.

Hebrew slave raised as an Egyptian, a runaway murderer, a stutterer living in the desert as a shepherd. But God saw a different man—a compassionate man who had drunk in the stories of Abraham and Sarah, Isaac and Rebecca, and Jacob and Rachel along with his mother's milk and who had sharpened his mind on the mathematics and astronomy of the pyramids.

Moses had deep concern for the oppressed. He was furious when an Egyptian killed a Hebrew (Exodus 2:11-12), offended when a Hebrew struck another (2:13), and quick to drive away troublemakers from Jethro's daughters (2:17).

When Moses took off his shoes and threw down his stick, he was ready to listen to God.

Moses objected to the call. The impossibility of the task seemed clear to him. He said in effect, "Bring it to pass, Lord, but not through me." Moses felt inadequate. Describe any reluctance you have felt about responding when God called you to a difficult task.

____

____

"I Am Who I Am"

Moses needed to know who his adversary was. Like Jacob wrestling with God at Jabbok, Moses demanded to know. "Tell me your name." Usually to know someone's name is to have power over that person. Hence, most pagan gods did not reveal their names. God did reveal his name because God cannot be controlled. But God's revelation was surrounded by mystery. God's name both revealed and hid. God's people would know God by what he did. Learning God's name still kept Moses in awe and under authority. The name can be translated "I AM" or "I am who I am" or "I will be who I will be." Tell the people, said God, that "I AM" has sent you. Not the fertility gods of the Nile or of the high places of Canaan, not the sun god of Egypt or the moon god of Mesopotamia, but the God of Israel—the same who created the stars and the seas, the same who breathed into men and women the breath of life, the one who inspired your mother to place you in a basket and a childless woman to draw you forth, the God of Abraham, Isaac, and Jacob—"I AM" has sent you.

Moses asked the king's permission for the Hebrews to make a three-day journey into the desert to make sacrifices to God. The king rightly suspected the Hebrews would never return.

Moses and Aaron, struggling with the king, used miracles; but the king's magicians countered. Then the struggle began in earnest. Faith wrestled with unfaith; freedom fought against bondage. Ten plagues occurred—plagues not unknown to Egypt but occurring with severity, rapidity, and preannounced by Moses—pollution of the Nile, frogs, gnats, flies, animal disease, boils, thunderstorms with hail, locusts,

NOTES, REFLECTIONS, AND QUESTIONS

thick darkness, and finally death of the first-born. Until the last plague the king refused to let the people go; he remained stubborn.

In Exodus 4:21, we read that God had warned Moses that the king would not listen and that God would "make the king stubborn." What does this mean? It means that willful resistance to God's intentions makes a person calloused. God has given us the freedom to resist his word. When we make that choice, it is the beginning of a heart closed to God.

A resisting heart, as it continues to encounter the Word of God, becomes even more resistant.

The first miracles failed to impress the Egyptians. Their magicians could stiffen snakes, turn water blood red, and bring frogs out onto the land. But the plague of the gnats confounded them. "God has done this!" they said (Exodus 8:19). Still the king refused to let the people go.

Passover is often misunderstood. The passover is not "passing over" the sea. Rather passover is the plague of death "passing over" or "sparing" the homes of the Hebrews because they had obeyed God and anointed their doorposts with the lamb's sacrificial blood.

If you attend a Passover meal (Seder) with contemporary Jewish people, you eat the unleavened bread (the Hebrews had to leave in a hurry and had no time for bread to rise), roasted lamb (remembering anointing of blood to obtain release and the quick feast in hope of freedom), and the bitter herbs dipped in salt water (remembering the bitter repression and the tears of slavery).

Freedom Costs

Bondage carries a cost, but so does freedom. Most people do not realize the price of justice and freedom. Great leaders do, however, and ultimately are willing to pay that price. Write down the names of some leaders who have led their people to freedom at great cost.

____

____

____

How do people react when they are being delivered from bondage? Moses had great difficulty, not only with the Egyptians but with the Hebrews. They were often afraid, sometimes angry, and many times ready to abandon their dreams. When Moses and Aaron first proposed a three-day journey for a sacrificial feast, the king lashed back with his famous bricks-without-straw speech. The Hebrew foremen turned on Moses and Aaron, accusing them of making their slavery even more painful (Exodus 5:15-23).

NOTES, REFLECTIONS, AND QUESTIONS

Fear of the unknown and anxiety about their future caused the Hebrews to complain again and again. After the plagues, as they stood on the brink of freedom, they panicked. The sea was before them, the chariots behind them. They cried out, "Weren't there any graves in Egypt? Did you have to bring us out here in the desert to die?" (14:11). How human! Once again Moses spoke the word of faith: "Don't be afraid! Stand your ground, and you will see what the LORD will do to save you today" (14:13).

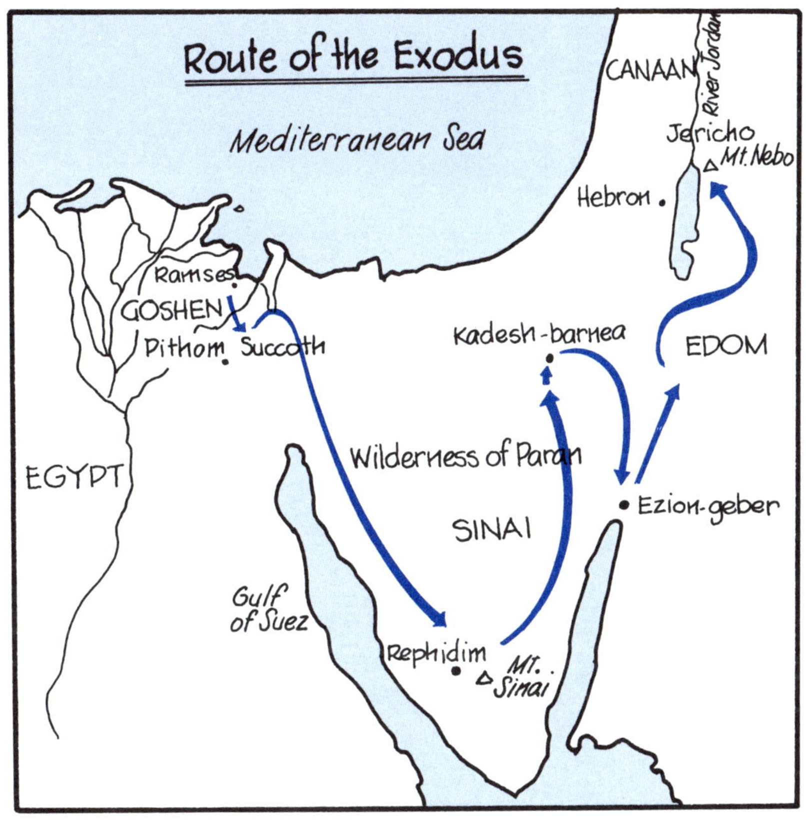

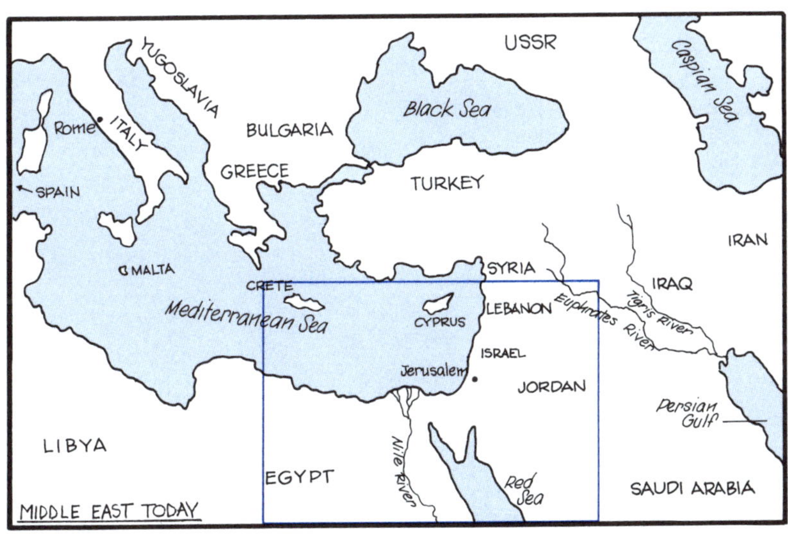

NOTES, REFLECTIONS, AND QUESTIONS

When they complained about food, God provided quails and then manna. Quails still migrate across the Mediterranean Sea and drop exhausted in the desert. The manna was a light, sweet substance gathered early in the morning to be ground and made into bread. The people were to gather enough manna for one day except on the sixth day. Then they were to gather enough to have some left over for the sabbath (16:4-5, 22-26). Notice that the writer of Exodus constantly reinforces the importance of the sabbath.

The message of Exodus is God hears, God sees, God knows, God remembers, God acts. The salvation experience of the Hebrews is repeated throughout the Scripture (for example, Deuteronomy 6:21-25; 26:5-10; Joshua 24:2-14; Hosea 11:1-4).

God's action in the Exodus has eternal and universal implications. When the social systems of humankind become oppressive, God hears the cry of the oppressed and acts. God's covenant with Abraham and his descendants is still valid. God is faithful to his part of the agreement. In the Exodus God fulfills the promise of deliverance. That promise is to everyone who is "in Egypt," to everyone who is in bondage.

MARKS OF DISCIPLESHIP

Weaving its way through the Exodus story (and at times rising above the story itself) is the strong, assuring message that God is faithful to God's promise. God's covenant stands!

God hears the cries of those in bondage and calls them into freedom, using people to help. The faithful disciple hears and obeys God's call to be a bearer of God's message of deliverance.

Think about people today who are trapped by political and economic bondage. Consider ways God is trying to release them.

____

____

____

Every person who has been in bondage as a person or as a people has a deliverance story to tell. Tell a deliverance story.

____

____

____

____

NOTES, REFLECTIONS, AND QUESTIONS

How does personal deliverance differ from the deliverance of the Hebrews from slavery?

In the Passover Haggadah, a Jewish liturgy for Seder, it is written:

"I am a Jew because in every place where suffering weeps, the Jew weeps.

"I am a Jew because every time when despair cries out, the Jew hopes."

Christians have been joined to Abraham's people, and our roots are in the people Israel; so Exodus is our history too. "Some of the branches of the cultivated olive tree have been broken off, and a branch of a wild olive tree has been joined to it. You Gentiles are like that wild olive tree, and now you share the strong spiritual life of the Jews. So then, you must not despise those who were broken off like branches. How can you be proud? You are just a branch; you don't support the roots—the roots support you" (Romans 11:17-18).

What causes the Christian to weep with the suffering and hope with the despairing?

The call of Moses is central to Exodus. Describe any times in your life when you have felt God speaking or calling you.

IF YOU WANT TO KNOW MORE

Chart of Biblical History

1260 B.C. **Moses leads the escape from Egypt**

See what you can discover about the building programs during the time of Seti I and Rameses II. Report your findings to the group.

The salvation experience of the Hebrews is recorded in Joshua 24:2-14. This Scripture would be worth memorizing as a way of summing up the message of Exodus.

NOTES, REFLECTIONS, AND QUESTIONS

ORDER

"People of Israel, listen to all the laws that I am giving you today. Learn them and be sure that you obey them."

—Deuteronomy 5:1

6 God Sends the Law

OUR HUMAN PROBLEM

We cannot live in total disorder and confusion. We want structure. Boundaries give a sense of security. We need order to feel we belong.

ASSIGNMENT

We are studying the Law. It is slow going. In places you will want to read carefully, word for word, as in a law book. Later in this study, you will find references back to these laws.

Day 1 Exodus 19–20 (Israel at Sinai)
Day 2 Exodus 21:1–23:19 (laws concerning slaves, repayment, justice, sabbath, and feasts)
Day 3 Leviticus 11; 17:10–19:37 (cleanness and uncleanness, the law of love); Deuteronomy 6:4-9 (the Shema)
Day 4 Deuteronomy 13 (warning against idolatry); 14:22–15:23 (the tithe); 21–22 (guilt of innocent blood, laws concerning sexual purity)
Day 5 Deuteronomy 24–25 (various unrelated laws); 34 (death of Moses)
Day 6 Read and respond to "The Bible Teaching" and "Marks of Discipleship."
Day 7 Rest and pray.

PRAYER

Pray daily before study:
"Teach me, LORD, the meaning of your laws,
and I will obey them at all times.
Explain your law to me, and I will obey it;
I will keep it with all my heart.
Keep me obedient to your commandments,
because in them I find happiness" (Psalm 119:33-35).

Prayer concerns for this week:

ORDER

Day 1 Israel at Sinai

Day 2 Laws concerning slaves, repayment, justice, sabbath, and feasts

Day 3 Cleanness and uncleanness, the law of love, the Shema

Day 4 Warning against idolatry, the tithe, guilt of innocent blood, laws concerning sexual purity

Day 5 Various unrelated laws, death of Moses

Day 6 "The Bible Teaching"

THE BIBLE TEACHING

NOTES, REFLECTIONS, AND QUESTIONS

Law makes life tolerable. Without law, society explodes into fragments. Traffic lights keep us from crashing into one another at intersections. Law keeps the strong from destroying the weak. Law helps us know who we are. It reassures us that we belong to a given people. The Law helps to hold the covenant people together, to give some sense of social justice, and to provide the light of morality to the world.

Moses is called the lawgiver. Traditionally the first five books of the Bible, the Torah (Law) or Pentateuch (Five Scrolls), have been attributed to Moses. Torah is the heartbeat of Jewish religion. Certainly Moses began the law process with the Hebrew people in the desert. Can you imagine the task of bringing a community of order out of a multitude of newly freed slaves camping out in the desert? Torah was oral for centuries, modified, added to, and codified (arranged systematically) perhaps during the rule of King Josiah in the seventh century B.C.

The Law made the Hebrews a distinct people. That was its purpose. Just as the Hebrew food laws separated the clean animals from the unclean, so the Hebrew people were a "separated" people. "I am the LORD who brought you out of Egypt so that I could be your God. You must be holy, because I am holy" (Leviticus 11:45).

Slowly the covenant people took form and identity. Symbols of Abraham's covenant were circumcision and the tithe. Sabbath, blessed of God in Creation, was honored as a holy and joyous day of rest. The Exodus experience of deliverance shaped the faith community forever. Then God added the most powerful cohesive force of all, the Law given to Moses.

The Law is of one piece and cannot be separated into religious or civil law. All aspects of life and society came under its rule. Still, we will look at different parts of it.

Laws of Social Welfare

When a parent "lays down the law" to a child, the child asks why. Our concern in studying the Hebrew law will be with the why.

"Do not mistreat or oppress a foreigner" (Exodus 22:21). Why? Because "you were foreigners in Egypt" (22:21).

"Do not mistreat any widow or orphan" (22:22). Why? Because "I, the LORD, will answer them when they cry out to me for help" (22:23) as I heard your cries in Egypt.

"If you lend money to any of my people who are poor, do not act like a moneylender and require him to pay interest. If you take someone's cloak as a pledge that he will pay you, you must give it back to him before the sun sets, because it is the only covering he has to keep him warm. What else can he sleep in?" (22:25-27). Notice the reason, for this law goes beyond simple justice: "When he cries out to me for help, I will answer him because I am merciful" (22:27).

Why be compassionate? Because you were once poor, you were once in bondage, you were once widows and orphans, you were once foreigners, you once cried out for help. Don't forget! The same God who heard your cry hears their cry and says,"I am merciful."

Abraham was indeed blessed to be a blessing. What are some examples in our society of providing for the poor, the stranger, the widow, and the orphan?

____

____

Food Laws

Remember the following clean and unclean distinctions: land animals (Leviticus 11:2-8), aquatic animals (11:9-12), fowl (11:13-19), insects (11:20-23), and other food concerns (11:24-45). Just as important was the prohibition against cooking a young sheep or goat in its mother's milk (Exodus 23:19). That concern was so strong that in a kosher kitchen (a kitchen where food is prepared according to Jewish laws) today, meat products and milk products are not cooked in the same utensils or served on the same plates. Drinking blood was prohibited. Today the blood must be drained carefully from the meat, the meat soaked for half an hour, then covered with salt for an hour. In kosher meat the hip tendon is removed to recall how God hit Jacob's hip, causing him to limp.

Why these food restrictions? Many people have speculated on their healthful impact in a primitive culture long before modern knowledge of disease. Without doubt, abstaining from eating contaminated animals was a health factor. Sanitation laws were a health breakthrough. Surely the inspired wisdom of Moses and the priests influenced the food laws to ensure health and well-being.

But from the biblical perspective, health factors were not the point at all. The Hebrews were to be set apart, under special restrictions, deliberately different from other people. The point was not health; it was obedience. They were to be God's people, distinct. These restrictions were holy laws.

You can see that eating with non-Jews became extremely difficult. Before long, a Jew who ate with a Gentile violated covenant, rejected the holy faith, and was considered a sinner.

This study about food may seem unnecessary to contemporary Christians; but it greatly affects our understanding of the New Testament, especially the experience of the sharing of a meal among peoples.

NOTES, REFLECTIONS, AND QUESTIONS

Laws of Justice

Justice in early biblical times was often inconsistent and vengeful. A king could punish with the snap of his fingers. A queen could snuff out a life over a minor offense. Retribution between families or tribes often meant retaliating with double measure. In contrast, the law of Moses demanded uniformity and fairness. Witnesses were required; false testimony was a grave offense. Judges were expected to be just. People in power were guided by the law that stood above them. The concept that no one is above the law is a biblical concept.

Phrases such as "eye for eye, tooth for tooth" seem severe to us. But they were designed to stop the taking of a life in repayment for the loss of an eye and to stop the murder of a man who had knocked out a tooth.

False weights and measures are offensive to God. "Use true and honest weights and measures, so that you may live a long time in the land that the LORD your God is giving you. The LORD hates people who cheat" (Deuteronomy 25:15-16).

Later, the prophets of Israel would chastise the people for cheating, for lying, for using scales that were false and measurements that were unjust. Why? Because God is a just God. God wants fair dealings in the marketplace.

In your life, can you think of any place where you falsify or mislead?

____

____

The law of Moses has a deep sense of fairness, of justice. Why? Because God is a just God.

Family Life

The Law builds in deep respect for parents. In the Ten Commandments, honor for father and mother preceded even the commandments on murder and adultery. The family was of utmost importance to the Hebrews.

"Whoever hits his father or his mother is to be put to death" (Exodus 21:15). A capital offense!

In our day of democracy within the family, how do you think children can be taught to honor their parents?

____

____

Sexual relationships are heavily regulated by the law of Moses. Homosexuality is forbidden. So are sexual relations with animals. Adultery carries a death penalty. Even though men had more than one wife throughout much of Old Testament history, fidelity (sexual faithfulness) was required. In the New Testament church, adherence to many

NOTES, REFLECTIONS, AND QUESTIONS

Stone weights of this kind, dating from about the seventh century B.C., were used to determine the value of gold and silver. The Hebrew characters inscribed on them indicate their weight or value. Usually, they were carried in a small bag or pouch. Weights were sometimes altered by chiseling the bottom off, which allowed the dishonesty often referred to by the prophets and Jesus.

Jewish laws was not required by the council at Jerusalem (Acts 15:19-20), but morality and fidelity were clearly required in the behavior of the Christian.

In a society where sexual promiscuity and adultery are widespread, what can you do to encourage faithfulness within marriage?

What can the church do?

MARKS OF DISCIPLESHIP

The message of Deuteronomy 27:26 to the disciple is to "confirm the words of this law by doing them" (RSV). Identify some of the words of the law that, through your obedience, bring order to your life and give you a sense of belonging.

Can you recall times in your life when failure to obey God's law resulted in chaos?

Describe who the disciple is according to the Scripture you read for this lesson.

IF YOU WANT TO KNOW MORE

Memorize the Ten Commandments and Deuteronomy 6:4-9.

Read the familiar blessing in Numbers 6:24-26.

NOTES, REFLECTIONS, AND QUESTIONS

Atonement

"And he shall bring to the priest his guilt offering to the LORD, a ram without blemish out of the flock, . . . and the priest shall make atonement for him before the LORD, and he shall be forgiven."

—Leviticus 6:6-7, RSV

7 When God Draws Near

OUR HUMAN PROBLEM

When God draws near to us, we feel guilty and ashamed because of our sin. We are overwhelmed by our need when we are in the presence of God. What are we to do?

ASSIGNMENT

In the Scripture, pay particular attention to how the Hebrew people remembered their deliverance from slavery, how they were reconciled to God, and how they gave thanks for what God had done for them.

Day 1 Exodus 24–26 (God's covenant with Israel, the Covenant Box, the Tent)
Day 2 Exodus 34:29–36:1 (commandments and offerings); 40 (dedicating the Tent)
Day 3 Leviticus 1:1–4:12; 5:1-6 (laws for offerings)
Day 4 Leviticus 16–17 (Day of Atonement)
Day 5 Deuteronomy 16 (appointed feasts); 18 (Levites)
Day 6 Read and respond to "The Bible Teaching" and "Marks of Discipleship."
Day 7 Rest. Praise God.

PRAYER

Pray daily before study:
"O God, I will offer you what I have promised;
I will give you my offering of thanksgiving" (Psalm 56:12).

Prayer concerns for this week:

ATONEMENT

Day 1 God's covenant with Israel, the Covenant Box, the Tent

Day 2 Commandments and offerings, dedicating the Tent

Day 3 Laws for offerings

Day 4 Day of Atonement

Day 5 Appointed feasts, Levites

Day 6 "The Bible Teaching"

THE BIBLE TEACHING

Why were the worship rules so complex and so specific? To us they seem ridiculous. But in that time, many worship practices of other peoples were offensive to the Lord. Such practices included witchcraft, astrology and magic divinations, cult prostitution and Baal worship on the high places. Other peoples worshiped moon or sun or graven images. These practices were strictly forbidden to the Hebrews. For Israel belonged to God, totally and completely.

The people of Israel were trying to be a unified people, living under the rule of God. So the rules for worship and for all of life were intermingled. The people were so tied to the soil that animals and crops were their life. Naturally their worship flowed from their daily livelihood. The work of their hands was represented in their sacrifices and worship.

Focus now on three aspects of early Hebrew worship.

Remembrance

The people of freedom can never forget their deliverance. The "passover" from Egypt symbolizes every experience of salvation, historical and personal. Celebration of Passover today is a family celebration, a remembrance designed for intimacy. That is why relatives and close friends are often included. Passover is especially designed to teach children. "As we read in the Torah: You shall tell your son on that day." Jews call the Passover ceremonial feast the Seder. It is a serious but joyful observance. "That night was different from all other nights."

Remember

- that miraculous deliverance of the children of Israel in the face of impossible odds;
- divine sustenance (manna and quails);
- divine wisdom (the Law at Mount Sinai);
- freedom and the Promised Land.

The service ends not only in joy but in clarification: Worshipers understand what they have not known or have forgotten, what they have misunderstood or have neglected.

Jesus transformed the Passover meal for Christians. If the Last Supper was a Passover meal as supposed, the bread used by Jesus was *matzah*. In many Christian denominations the bread used for Holy Communion must be unleavened. The earliest Christians, who were Jews, associated the death of Jesus with the sacrifice of the Passover lamb. Jesus' sacrifice, which freed persons from slavery to sin, gave new meaning to the celebration of freedom from slavery. The remembrance of deliverance from Egypt became the remembrance of deliverance from sin. Easter was originally called "the Pascha," from the Hebrew word *Pesach,* meaning "Passover." Sometimes Holy Communion is called the *Eucharist,* the feast of thanksgiving.

NOTES, REFLECTIONS, AND QUESTIONS

Homes are prepared for the seven days of Passover by removing all leaven (yeast) from the house and by baking unleavened bread (*matzah*). A dramatic search of the house for leaven is fun for children. Elements on the table include a roasted lamb shankbone, scorched, representing the ancient sacrifice; a roasted egg, representing the offering that accompanied the sacrifice; parsley, representing springtime and rebirth; horseradish root, representing bitterness, the lot of all who are enslaved; a mixture of apples, nuts, cinnamon, and wine, representing the clay the Hebrews used to make bricks for Pharaoh; four cups of wine, representing separate acts of redemption or liberation. Also on the table is a cup of wine for the prophet Elijah, foreteller of messiah's coming. The cup represents hope for the fulfillment of the promise of the messianic age.

What are some of the remembrances you experience when eating the bread and drinking the cup?

____

____

____

Atonement

Do you remember what we said about sin? Deeper than acts of wrongdoing, sin is broken relationships. God is offended. Barriers are erected. Life is fouled up. Guilt and shame come rushing in. Friend is alienated from friend. The soul of a man or a woman begins to fight a civil war within itself. Adam and Eve hid from God. Today unresolved guilt is widespread and often repressed, resulting in emotional, mental, and social illness.

The ancient Hebrews ritualized their expressions of guilt with carefully prescribed worship experiences. They expressed their guilt and shame as a corporate community of faith. They made amends directly to the One who was offended—their Creator, Redeemer God.

Leviticus 16 helps us understand the Day of Atonement (Yom Kippur) and atonement sacrifices. Once a year the chief priest (Aaron) cleansed himself, put on holy garments, and killed a bull as an offering. The blood sacrifice was a sin offering for himself and his house. Then Aaron chose two goats to bear symbolically the sins of the people. The one he offered as a blood sacrifice for atonement. Aaron then laid both his hands on the head of the second goat, confessing "all the evils, sins, and rebellions of the people of Israel." He put their sins upon the head of the goat and sent the goat into the desert (Leviticus 16:21). The goat carried the sins away and freed the people from their guilt and shame. Hence the name "scapegoat."

Many preachers have explained atonement as *at-one-ment.* Through atonement humankind is reconciled to God, made at one with God. People are freed to be in fellowship, and persons need no longer carry the load of guilt.

Explain whether or not your church's rituals (and which rituals) are helping you feel freed of guilt and shame.

____

____

Thanksgiving

When the Pilgrims wanted to express gratitude for surviving their first winter and growing their first American crops, they had a biblical model in the Festival of Shelters. In Leviticus 23:33-43 and Deuteronomy 16:13-15, the outline

NOTES, REFLECTIONS, AND QUESTIONS

According to tradition, a cord of red wool was tied around the horns of the scapegoat to represent the sins of the people.

was clear: seven days of feasting and worship when the autumn harvest was over; a time of joy, thanksgiving, and celebration; no laborious work; and invitations to "the Levites, foreigners, orphans, and widows who live in your towns" (Deuteronomy 16:14).

A significant element of Hebrew worship was the offering of gifts to God and God's acceptance of those gifts. Through the celebrative days prescribed in the festival calendar of the Law, the Hebrews relived the story of how their ancestors became bound to God in covenant and expressed their thanksgiving by offering gifts to God.

- New Year (festival of trumpets), in September-October at the beginning of the religious calendar;
- Day of Atonement (Yom Kippur) ten days later, the climax of purification rites;
- Feast of Booths (*shelters* in Today's English Version, *tabernacles* in the King James Version), began two weeks after the New Year and five days after Yom Kippur, celebrated the autumn harvest, the thanksgiving festival used as a model by the Pilgrims;
- Passover, commemorated the Hebrews' deliverance from slavery in Egypt, eight days in the spring that began with the Feast of Unleavened Bread and concluded with the offering of first fruits of the barley harvest;
- Pentecost (meaning "fiftieth"), also called the Feast of Weeks because this feast day fell on the fiftieth day after Passover (a week of weeks, or seven weeks, had passed), celebration of the offering of first fruits of the wheat harvest (waving the sheaf), the day of the Holy Spirit experience recorded in Acts 2.

Today most people have jobs unrelated to agriculture. How can we offer the fruit of our hands in worship and thanksgiving?

MARKS OF DISCIPLESHIP

When God draws near, it seems as if someone has turned on a light in the dirty, dusty rooms of our hearts. In the dark we pretended we were clean. In the light our failures stand out boldly. That is why we run and hide from God, lest truth and pure love find us out.

So in worship we not only discover God drawing near to us, but we find our lives inadequate. Close to God, we recognize that we are in need of prayer. Our need cries out. Our guilt screams for forgiveness.

The most striking characteristics of the aspects of Hebrew worship discussed above are these:

- They are corporate.
- They are mandatory.
- They are prescribed.

NOTES, REFLECTIONS, AND QUESTIONS

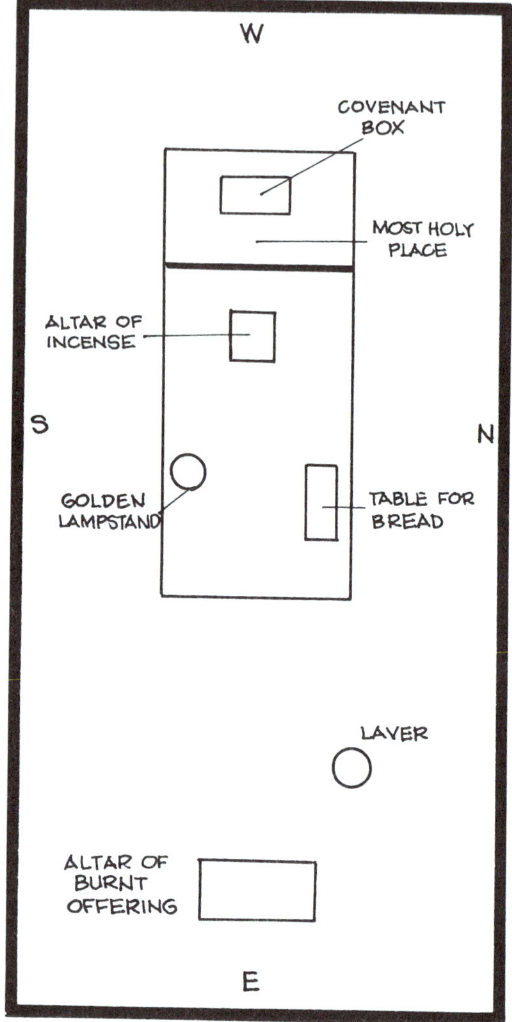

The Tent, also called the Tabernacle, was a portable place of worship symbolizing the presence of God with the people. It was used in the desert to house the Covenant Box (ark of the covenant) and was the pattern for the Temple built by Solomon.

So many Christians take worship lightly, worshiping occasionally or as they feel like it. Others understand faith as a private matter, as if their religion were solely between themselves and God. Still others find form, tradition, and ritual a restriction on their free spirits. But biblical worship is heavily corporate and based on habits and patterns. Individual feelings, preferences, and subjective influences are not allowed to destroy the sacred traditions. Corporate worship teaches children, youth, and adults
to remember,
to ask for forgiveness, and
to give thanks.

Christian disciples commit themselves to corporate worship for the same reasons. The Letter to the Hebrews in the New Testament draws heavily on atonement imagery: "We have, then, my brothers, complete freedom to go into the Most Holy Place by means of the death of Jesus. . . . We have a great priest in charge of the house of God. So let us come near to God with a sincere heart and a sure faith, with hearts that have been purified from a guilty conscience and with bodies washed with clean water. . . . Let us be concerned for one another, to help one another to show love and to do good. Let us not give up the habit of meeting together, as some are doing. Instead, let us encourage one another all the more, since you see that the Day of the Lord is coming nearer" (Hebrews 10:19-25).

Disciples of Jesus should be drawn to communal worship with excitement and joy.

Describe your reaction to these words:
"I was glad when they said to me,
'Let us go to the LORD's house' "
(Psalm 122:1).

Do they ring true for you? Why?

In terms of worship, which element do you find most meaningful: remembrance or atonement or thanksgiving? Why?

IF YOU WANT TO KNOW MORE

Try to discover when in Israel's history animal sacrifice came to an end, and why. Tell the group what you learned.

NOTES, REFLECTIONS, AND QUESTIONS

LEADERSHIP

"Then the LORD gave the Israelites leaders who saved them from the raiders."

—Judges 2:16

8 The People Without a King

OUR HUMAN PROBLEM

We cannot tolerate political disorder and confusion. We swing between wanting someone to direct us and wanting to "do our own thing." We need leadership. Please, somebody give us a sense of direction.

ASSIGNMENT

The Book of Joshua stresses what occurs when the people "trust and obey," when the leadership is faithful, and when the people are united.

The Book of Judges stresses what happens when the people do not "trust and obey," when they act individually rather than as a united people.

Day 1 Joshua 1–3 (entering the land, Rahab and the spies)
Day 2 Joshua 4–6 (fall of Jericho); Joshua 24 (covenant at Shechem, death of Joshua)
Day 3 Judges 1–2 (effects of the death of Joshua); 4 (Deborah)
Day 4 Judges 6–8 (Gideon)
Day 5 Judges 13–16 (Samson)
Day 6 Read and respond to "The Bible Teaching" and "Marks of Discipleship."
Day 7 Rest.

PRAYER

Pray daily before study:
"Come, O God, and rule the world;
all the nations are yours" (Psalm 82:8).

Prayer concerns for this week:

LEADERSHIP

Day 1 Entering the land, Rahab and the spies

Day 4 Gideon

Day 2 Fall of Jericho, covenant at Shechem, death of Joshua

Day 5 Samson

Day 3 Effects of the death of Joshua, Deborah

Day 6 "The Bible Teaching"

THE BIBLE TEACHING

NOTES, REFLECTIONS, AND QUESTIONS

The Book of Joshua is transitional. The return to Canaan fulfills the promise of land made to Abraham and Sarah. Joshua, as Moses' successor, completes the story of faith: Trust God's promises, and God will bring victory. The Book of Joshua stresses obedience to the covenant.

So the term *transitional* applies to the book that records the deeds of Joshua because he came between the time of Moses and the time of the judges, between the time of the Exodus and the time of tribal government under the judges.

Joshua completed Moses' work of deliverance. In faithfulness to God, he led the people into the land of promise. The name *Joshua* means "God is salvation" and has the same Hebrew root as the name *Jesus*.

After forty years of desert wandering, the generation of pessimists has died, the people have been tempered by forty years of discipline, and Moses is buried. Joshua, God's faithful leader, takes over Moses' leadership role and crosses the Jordan. Notice the parallels between Moses and Joshua:

Moses	**Joshua**
Spies to Hebron area (Numbers 13)	Spies to Jericho area (Joshua 2)
Crossing the Red Sea (Exodus 14)	Crossing the Jordan River (Joshua 3)
Circumcision (Exodus 4:24-26)	Circumcision again (Joshua 5:2-7)
Passover (Exodus 12:1-36)	Observe Passover (Joshua 5:10)
"Take off your sandals," burning bush (Exodus 3:1-5)	"Take your sandals off," man holding a sword (Joshua 5:13-15)
The gesture of strength, "Moses held up his arms" (Exodus 17:8-13)	"Point your spear" (Joshua 8:18-21)
Law to be given on stone at Mount Sinai (Exodus 24)	Law written again on stone at Mount Ebal (Shechem) (Joshua 8:30-35)
Cities of refuge, anticipated by Moses (Numbers 35:9-15)	Cities of refuge, appointed and named (Joshua 20)
Covenant at Sinai (Exodus 24:7-8)	Covenant at Shechem (Joshua 24:15, 24-25)

Looking back on Joshua and his time, Israel understood the meanings hidden in the dramatic and often bloody events. God fought for Israel. The constant theme was "out of Egypt . . . into the land of promise." The continual assumption, using various stories and strains of history, was *to violate the covenant meant chaos in the life of the people; to keep the covenant was to fulfill Israel's purpose with order and meaning.*

Joshua's words ring clear: "If you are not willing to serve him [the LORD], decide today whom you will serve. . . . As for my family and me, we will serve the LORD" (Joshua 24:15).

NOTES, REFLECTIONS, AND QUESTIONS

The fascinating account of the distribution of the land among the tribes of Israel is in Joshua 13–21. Read it with a Bible atlas at hand.

Judges

Many of the judges were not judges as we think of judges today, but some were. All were tribal leaders—men and women who were raised up by the Lord in time of crisis and confusion to call Israel back to obedience, to unify the people, and to lead them in battle against an assortment of enemies. "The LORD gave the Israelites leaders who saved them from the raiders" (Judges 2:16).

Deborah, Gideon, and Samson were three of those raised up as judges. They served for a time and then disappeared without forming any permanent central government. They were not noted for their great spiritual qualities but for their willingness to hear and respond to the call of God. They were not so much heroes as they were instruments of the Lord.

The covenant people, under the leadership of Moses and Joshua, were governed by the direct authority of God. No president, no pharaoh, no king ruled them. The spiritual leaders wanted *God* to be their king. Gideon said, "I will not be your ruler, nor will my son. The LORD will be your ruler" (Judges 8:23). Until the time of the kings, all the leaders were temporary. They were prophets, military leaders, and priests who served for a brief moment.

Psalm 24 identifies God as Israel's King:

"Fling wide the gates,
open the ancient doors,
and the great king will come in.
Who is this great king?
He is the LORD, strong and mighty,
the LORD, victorious in battle" (Psalm 24:7-8).

Later on, Israel would demand a king. Their enemies would seem better organized, more unified, better equipped for war. But during the period of the judges, about 1220 B.C. to 1020 B.C., from the time of Joshua's death until the rise of the monarchy (King Saul), various judges insisted that the Lord was Israel's true ruler. Imagine farmers and herdsmen, people under periodic attack and conflict, trying to maintain their land, herds, and family and tribal life without a central government.

During these conflicts they were continually influenced by and often caught up in pagan Canaanite religious practices. Thus we read in Judges of frequent apostasy (abandonment of faith), divine disapproval, urgent appeals to God in time of crisis, the raising up of leaders to throw off oppressors. After the victories, they returned to their family lands and to peace again. The chaos was not totally unrelieved. The recurring pattern during the period of the judges was *apostasy, punishment, repentance,* and *peace.*

Now consider as examples these judges:

NOTES, REFLECTIONS, AND QUESTIONS

Deborah

Picture the situation: Jabin had "ruled the people of Israel with cruelty and violence for twenty years" (Judges 4:3). His general Sisera commanded nine hundred iron chariots. The Canaanites had a tremendous military advantage because their iron weapons were vastly superior to the Israelite weapons. The Israelites were frightened by superior weapons, in confusion and disarray, incapable of united action, and lacked the courage to face the enemy.

Enter two women: Deborah (the name means "bee") and Jael (the name means "mountain goat"). Deborah was a prophet and judge, and Jael a homemaker. Barak, the Israelite general, pleaded with Deborah, "I will go if you go with me, but if you don't go with me, I won't go either" (4:8). She replied, "All right, I will go with you, but you won't get any credit for the victory, because the LORD will hand Sisera over to a woman" (4:9).

With great faith, Deborah said to Barak, "Go! The LORD is leading you!" (4:14). She chose for the battle the Valley of Jezreel. It seemed perfect for maneuverability of the enemy chariots. The Israelites waited on Mount Tabor. Then the heavens poured (5:4). The Kishon River flooded the plain, and the chariots became stuck in the mud. (Remember the Egyptian chariots that also got stuck in the mud?) Israel won a great victory.

The defeated general Sisera found refuge in the tent of Jael, a Kenite woman. While he slept, Jael drove a tent spike through Sisera's head. The mighty chariots of iron were defeated by a "bee," a "mountain goat," some mud, and God. Now there would be forty years of peace.

Gideon

"Once again the people of Israel sinned against the LORD" (Judges 6:1). Israel was in disarray. The Midianites raided them continually. Pagan practices pervaded Hebrew society, and all around them Canaanite peoples practiced Baal worship. *Baal* refers to the gods of the various fertility cults. The Bible condemns their worship on the "high places" (hill shrines). The Hebrews continually intermingled their worship with these neighborhood fertility religions. Prophets and judges condemned Baal worship because it involved sexual orgies, including sex with animals and sacred prostitutes; human sacrifice; drinking of animal blood; drunkenness; and worship of animal images, sexual organs, trees, and other idols.

Now the Lord called Gideon.

Where was he? In a wine press. Separating wheat from chaff! Why wasn't he outdoors where the wind could blow the chaff away? Because he was hiding from the Midianites; he was afraid. Notice the irony when the angel of the Lord said to Gideon, "The LORD is with you, brave and mighty man!" (6:12). Mighty indeed! He was hiding. Do you ever feel like hiding from your enemies?

NOTES, REFLECTIONS, AND QUESTIONS

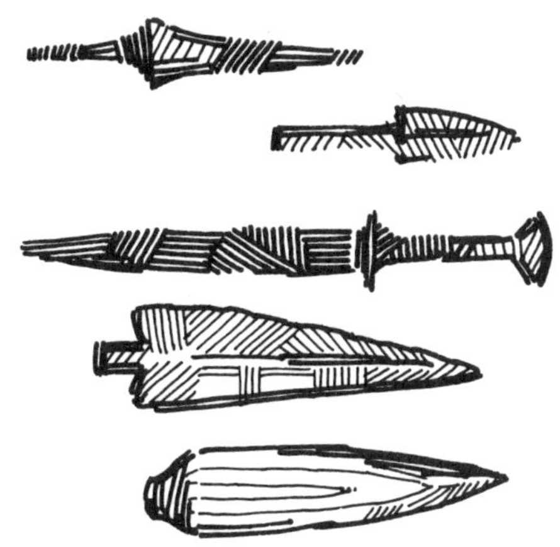

Weapons typical of the time of the judges

Baal of the Lightning from ancient Ugarit. *Baal* means "lord" and refers to the most important of the Canaanite gods, the weather god. Good harvests depended on the weather god who controlled the rain, the dew, and the mist.

Why Gideon? In a society where the oldest son was the most important and in a tribal system where the largest tribes provided the most soldiers, Gideon was the youngest ("least") son of an insignificant ("weakest") family in an unimportant tribe. Like Moses, he tried to get out of it. Why did God choose an insignificant, frightened soldier-farmer?

How much faith did Gideon have? Not much. After his dramatic religious experience (6:19-24), he still demanded signs. Some people think that putting out the wool was a sign of faith (6:36-40). It was just the opposite. It was a sign of lack of faith. Recall that Jesus, when urged by Satan to jump from the highest point of the Temple, said, "Do not put the Lord your God to the test" (Matthew 4:7).

God was amazingly patient with Gideon.

The selection of three hundred men always intrigues readers and scholars. Some interpret those three hundred who lapped water, putting their hand to their mouths, as tough mountain men with eyes flashing about, always alert. But the biblical point is that God wanted a small group to show that the victory belonged not to humans but to God. Perhaps the divine-human mixture is the way God often works.

Samson

Samson was scarcely a judge. He did not call his people to corporate action. Rather, he pranked his way through the enemy ranks, amusing his friends and dumbfounding his enemies. Samson captures our imagination with his unusual strength, his romantic exploits, and his mischievous pranks.

Why did God use Samson? Perhaps to help us understand a devout set of parents who set aside their son to be a special person, a Nazirite who neither cut his hair nor drank wine. Perhaps to help us laugh, since so much of the Bible is serious. Who can resist smiling at riddles about lions and honey? Perhaps to teach us, in sadness, how a powerful person can be brought low by "selling out" that holy vow that makes him or her set apart and special.

Probably God used Samson because Samson dramatically symbolizes the people of God—so human, so quick to act without thinking, so prone to folly. We are set apart to be a holy people, capable of great strength against formidable foes, weakened by sin, blinded by the enemy, yet able through the power of God to experience forgiveness and rise from the ashes to strike a blow for freedom once again.

NOTES, REFLECTIONS, AND QUESTIONS

MARKS OF DISCIPLESHIP

God calls leaders to give people a sense of direction and purpose. When the leaders are godly, they give sound direction; when they are disobedient or undecided, they lead people astray.

What kind of people does God choose as leaders?

Who are your spiritual leaders?

What does it mean to place yourself under the authority of your spiritual leaders?

Describe a time God called you to be a leader.

IF YOU WANT TO KNOW MORE

Chart of Biblical History

1220 B.C. **Joshua leads the people into Canaan**
1210 B.C. **Beginning of the period of the judges**

Read the poetic version of the story of Deborah and Barak in Judges 5.

Read one of the most beautiful stories ever written, the Book of Ruth, a love story about David's great-grandmother during the time of the judges, but quite unlike the Book of Judges.

NOTES, REFLECTIONS, AND QUESTIONS

SECURITY

"All will go well with you if you honor the LORD your God, serve him, listen to him, and obey his commands, and if you and your king follow him. But if you do not listen to the LORD but disobey his commands, he will be against you and your king."

—1 Samuel 12:14-15

9 The People With a King

OUR HUMAN PROBLEM

We demand leaders, hoping they will bring security and peace. We want our leaders to make decisions for us, to tell us what to do so we won't have to take responsibility for ourselves and our actions. But power tends to corrupt; and we discover that our leaders, like us, have faults.

ASSIGNMENT

This week we read fascinating narratives of explosive human emotions and human and divine interactions. The characters are some of the most colorful in Scripture, people like Hannah, Samuel, Saul, David, Bathsheba, Absalom, and Solomon. You must read rapidly to cover so much story material.

Day 1 1 Samuel 1:1–2:11; 2:18-21; 3; 7 (Samuel)
Day 2 1 Samuel 8–10; 12 (Samuel anoints Saul)
Day 3 1 Samuel 14:47–19:24; 31 (Saul, death of Saul)
Day 4 2 Samuel 7; 11–12; 16:15–18:33 (David)
Day 5 1 Kings 1:1–2:12; 3; 4:20-34; 5:1–6:14; 7:1-12; 8 (Solomon)
Day 6 1 Kings 11:1-13, 26-43; 12 (Solomon's apostasy, division of the kingdom); read and respond to "The Bible Teaching" and "Marks of Discipleship."
Day 7 Rest.

PRAYER

Pray daily before study:

"I will thank you, O Lord, among the nations.
I will praise you among the peoples.
Your constant love reaches the heavens;
your faithfulness touches the skies.
Show your greatness in the sky, O God,
and your glory over all the earth" (Psalm 57:9-11).

Prayer concerns for this week:

Day 1 Samuel

senent of god.
Prophet.

Day 2 Samuel anoints Saul

Day 3 Saul, death of Saul

Day 4 David

Wasn't at the
right place.

Day 5 Solomon

Day 6 Solomon's apostasy, division of the kingdom, "The Bible Teaching"

THE BIBLE TEACHING

Did God's people want a king? Yes and no. Samuel was ambivalent. He actually anointed both Saul and David, yet he argued against the idea of kingship.

The Bible does not back away from ambivalence. Confusion clouds all human experience. The Bible records that confusion. On one hand, a king might bring cohesiveness and greater security. On the other hand, as Samuel stated (1 Samuel 8:10-18), a king could increase taxes, draft an army, and restrict personal liberty. A faithful king might lead the people along a righteous path, but a disobedient king could lead them to tragic ends.

Even more important was the question of the people's relationship to God. The religious ideal of the people was to obey God and to live together in harmony. Leaders like Moses, Gideon, and Samuel had hoped that God would be King of the Hebrews. Their security would rest in God.

But the people were like Adam and Eve—disobedient, afraid, vulnerable, and alienated. They were like Cain—hostile and jealous. They were like those who built the tower of Babylon—proudly wanting to be like gods. They went off in all directions: "There was no king in Israel at that time. Everyone did whatever he pleased" (Judges 21:25).

The people cried to Samuel, "Appoint a king to rule over us, so that we will have a king, as other countries have" (1 Samuel 8:5). Samuel prayed, and God said, "You are not the one they have rejected; I am the one they have rejected as their king. . . . So then, listen to them, but give them strict warnings and explain how their kings will treat them" (8:7, 9).

The pressure for unity intensified with the coming of the Philistines. The loose union of Hebrew tribes had fought fairly well against Canaanites and neighboring groups such as the Amorites, the Moabites, and the Midianites. But around 1200 B.C. a powerful group called Philistines settled along the coastal plain. They used advanced technology, including iron weapons and chariots. Under strong leadership, living in five tightly coordinated city states (Ashkelon, Ashdod, Gath, Ekron, and Gaza), the Philistines raided practically at will. In their temples they worshiped many fertility gods—the god Dagon (chief god of the Philistine city states) in Ashdod and Gaza, the goddess Ashtoreth in Ashkelon, and Baal-zebub in Ekron. Israel thus faced a unified and powerful enemy.

Samuel

The story begins with a childless couple, Elkanah and Hannah. Hannah prayed so fervently for a child that the priest presumed she was drunk. The Lord answered Hannah's prayers, and she gave birth to Samuel.

Samuel was God's man. He was the last of the great judges and the first of the great prophets. Like Moses, he

NOTES, REFLECTIONS, AND QUESTIONS

The term *Palestine* came from the Philistines, enemies of Israel who settled the southern coast of the country in the twelfth century B.C. Originally, the name applied only to the Philistine territory. Herodotus, the fifth-century B.C. Greek historian, was the first to apply the name to the entire region.

was nursed on his mother's faith but raised by another. In this case Samuel was raised by Eli the priest, who after failing with his own sons, Hophni and Phinehas, tried extra hard to instill dedication in the young boy entrusted to his care. Hannah gave him the name *Samuel,* which probably meant "name of God," though Hannah explained its meaning as "I asked the LORD for him" (1 Samuel 1:20).

Three kings are described in these Scriptures.

Saul

Saul physically stood head and shoulders above other men (1 Samuel 9:2). He experienced intense religious emotion (19:18-24). He earned the respect and love of brave men, including David (2 Samuel 1:19-24).

Samuel anointed Saul to be king but gave him a continual stream of divine commands. There was no room for error. Samuel gave mixed support to Saul, revealing an old man's unwillingness to yield his long-term power.

Saul spent his entire reign struggling to keep his authority intact. He became increasingly anxious about his throne, slipped into depression, and finally descended into paranoia.

When David said, "How are the mighty fallen" (2 Samuel 1:19-27, RSV), he could have been referring to Saul's personality deterioration as well as to Saul's defeat and death in battle.

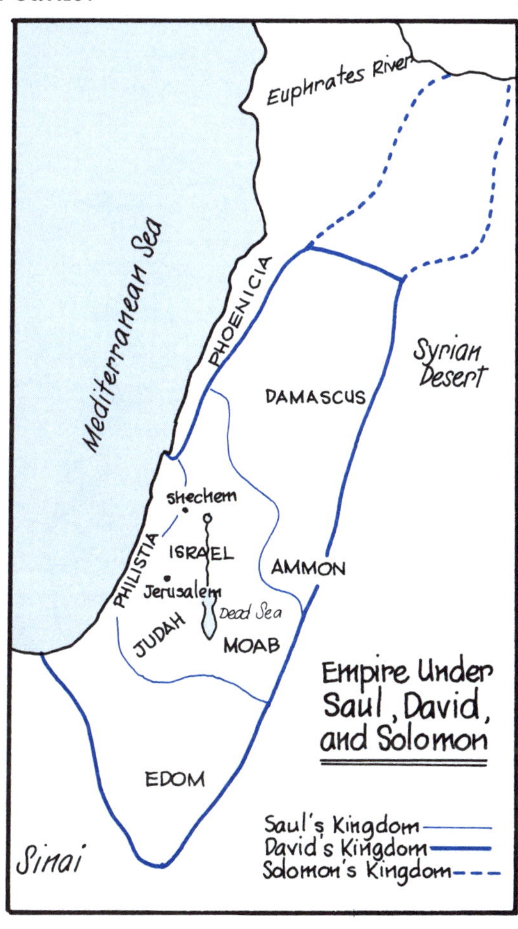

NOTES, REFLECTIONS, AND QUESTIONS

Saul was the first king to rule the tribes of Israel. David expanded the boundaries of the kingdom to include the territories of Philistia, Edom, Ammon, and Syria (Damascus). Solomon kept intact the territory controlled by David and expanded the kingdom to its greatest extent.

NOTES, REFLECTIONS, AND QUESTIONS

David

In April, Jerusalem bursts forth in beauty. Perfume is in the air on a spring evening. April is also a time for war, after the cold winter and the spring rains have ended (2 Samuel 11:1). The troops of Israel were in the field. But David, mighty warrior, commander-in-chief, had chosen not to go but to run the war from the comfort of the capital.

King David, now middle-aged, took a walk on his roof and saw in the courtyard below the strikingly beautiful wife of one of his elite soldiers, bathing in the late afternoon sun.

The rest of the story reads like the morning newspaper. An evening romance, an unwanted pregnancy, an anxious conversation, and a frantic search for a cover-up plan.

The cover-up seemed to have worked. Then, in one of the Bible's most dramatic encounters, David listened to the prophet Nathan tell a simple story of a grave injustice. The prophet pointed his finger at the king and said, "You are that man" (12:7).

David had so much to offer. A natural-born leader, an athlete, and a soldier, he also became a skilled politician who unified Israel.

David was God's man. His faith was strong, his loyalty to God was sure, and his personal ambition blended well with the needs of his nation.

But he sinned. He shattered the commandments of Moses as if he had broken the tablets into fragments:

You shall not covet Uriah's wife.

You shall not commit adultery with Bathsheba.

You shall not kill your faithful soldier-companion.

You shall not bear false witness to the nation.

In one act of passionate rebellion against God, David betrayed his divinely anointed leadership.

David was God's man. Even in his sin and repentance he was God's man, and Israel would always remember "the kingdom of David" as a golden era of unity and strength.

To say "I'm sorry" removes guilt but not consequences. The kingdom was shaken by family unfaithfulness. David did not feel worthy to build the Temple. The line to Solomon was marred.

Like Saul, David failed God, his people, and himself.

Solomon

Solomon would have made a good American. He was born rich. He was as crazy about wheels as any sixteen-year-old kid. He bought his chariots from Egypt, his horses from Arabia. His stables sported forty thousand stalls. Solomon maintained a jet-set image—swimming pools, summer homes, winter palaces. Wives were a status symbol, and Solomon had seven hundred wives and three hundred concubines. Many marriages were political, personalizing foreign alliances. Even the Queen of Sheba came to visit and gaze at the riches of Solomon's court. Solomon needed

one hundred sheep and thirty head of cattle a day to feed his family and court.

During Solomon's reign, Israel buzzed with activity. Trade flourished. Construction boomed. The "Gross National Product" soared. Wise men from all over the kingdom established a school of wisdom. After Solomon built the Temple, he got the fever for government building programs. He pressed men into labor camps. He raised taxes (Samuel had warned that this would happen). King Solomon enlarged the army. He even developed a Jewish navy. He stripped Lebanon of its trees so that cedar in Jerusalem became as common as sycamore.

Before the bubble burst, the splendor of Solomon's kingdom was the talk of the world. Later, Jesus spoke of Solomon "with all his wealth" (Matthew 6:29). But when the country crumbled, the fall was faster than the rise. Men were weary of forced labor, tired of the huge bureaucracy, annoyed by the arrogance in the capital. Solomon's majestic palace made the Temple seem insignificant.

Solomon's big trouble, according to Scripture, was with God. He had prayed for wisdom (1 Kings 3:6-9), and God had granted it. Solomon *was* wise. He was a skilled engineer and a philosopher. But he forgot. He forgot that he stood in a line with Abraham and Joseph, Moses and Samuel, Saul and David. He forgot that he and his people were slaves whom God had delivered from Egypt. In his old age he worshiped the gods of his foreign wives, and the integrity of the covenant people was compromised. Solomon's sin was apostasy. He forgot who he was. He forgot who God is.

At Solomon's death the kingdom came crashing down. It broke into northern and southern kingdoms, destroying its unity, both spiritual and political, and one day would be trampled by the great armies of the world.

Moses had warned, "Make certain that you do not forget the LORD your God. . . . When you have all you want to eat and have built good houses to live in and when your cattle and sheep, your silver and gold, and all your other possessions have increased, be sure that you do not become proud and forget the LORD your God who rescued you from Egypt, where you were slaves. . . . So then, you must never think that you have made yourselves wealthy by your own power and strength" (Deuteronomy 8:11-14, 17).

Solomon forgot.

Saul, like Adam and Eve, disobeyed, and the kingdom was taken from him.

David, like Cain who killed his brother Abel, passionately rebelled, so that God and Uriah's blood cried, "You are that man."

Solomon, like the builders of the tower of Babylon, arrogantly tried to be like God. He wanted to build a city and a name for himself. He was apostate, and the kingdom came tumbling down.

NOTES, REFLECTIONS, AND QUESTIONS

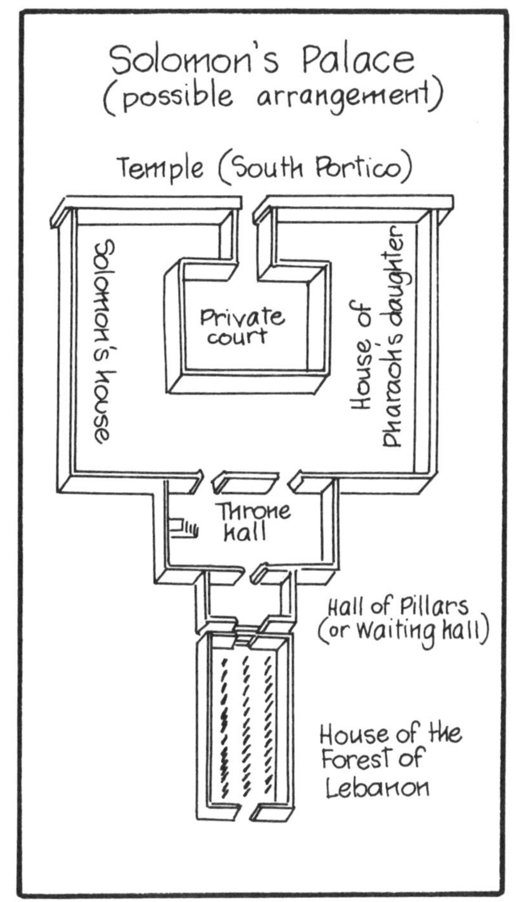

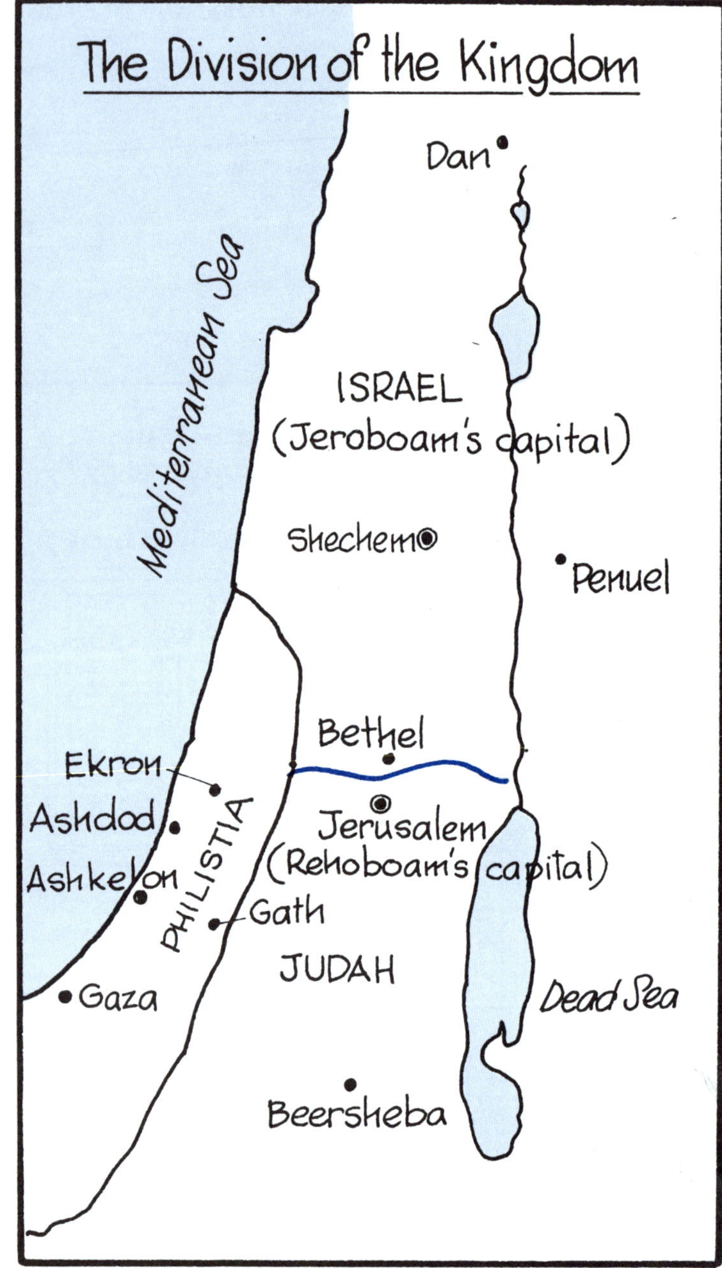

The fortunes of the people went from bad to worse. Rehoboam, Solomon's son, now had the throne. The northern tribes came to King Rehoboam pleading for more lenient work conditions. Rather than granting their wishes, King Rehoboam chose to increase the already heavy burden his father Solomon had laid on the people. In response, the ten northern tribes withdrew from King Rehoboam and made Jeroboam their king.

Under King Jeroboam's rule, the ten northern tribes, Israel, were not faithful to the Lord. King Rehoboam was now the ruler over only the Southern Kingdom, Judah. He and his people were also unfaithful to the Lord.

NOTES, REFLECTIONS, AND QUESTIONS

The United Kingdom, held together largely by the strength of the personalities of David and Solomon, fell apart at Solomon's death. No later king had the strength to unite the tribes again. After the division of the kingdom Judah became more self-contained, and Israel became increasingly open to outside influences.

MARKS OF DISCIPLESHIP

The disciple keeps a proper perspective on human leadership, giving respect and support to godly leaders but true allegiance only to God.

Why do people put such high hopes in political leaders?

Sometimes people contribute to a leader's downfall without knowing it. Describe how this might happen.

Right now, in what ways are people counting on you to be a leader?

List some ways you can give support and encouragement to civil and church leaders right now, helping them avoid tragedy.

IF YOU WANT TO KNOW MORE

Chart of Biblical History

1020 B.C. **Beginning of the monarchy**
Saul, David, Solomon
935 B.C. **Division into Northern and Southern Kingdoms after death of Solomon**
North—Israel (capital: Samaria)
South—Judah (capital: Jerusalem)

The biblical tradition puts considerable emphasis on Solomon's construction and dedication of the Temple (1 Kings 6–8). Bible dictionaries and handbooks often have drawings of what the Temple and its furnishings might have looked like. Prepare a report for the group using the biblical text and visuals you can locate.

Solomon was a wise man. Many of his sayings are recorded in Proverbs. Read Proverbs 1–3; 5–6; 10–11 for a taste of Solomon's wisdom.

NOTES, REFLECTIONS, AND QUESTIONS

WARNING

"He [the Lord] asked me, 'Amos, what do you see?'

" 'A plumb line,' I answered.

"Then he said, 'I am using it to show that my people are like a wall that is out of line. I will not change my mind again about punishing them.' "

—Amos 7:8

10 God Warns the People

OUR HUMAN PROBLEM

Generally we do not pay attention to warnings until too late. We hate to be told we are doing wrong. We don't really believe that severe punishment will come to us. Let us alone. We are getting along fine. We will call you when we need you.

ASSIGNMENT

This week we will read about some of the many prophets. The prophets delivered God's word to the people. They often spoke the word of warning. Different prophets, different times, different sins, yet always the same theme: Because of your disobedience and unfaithfulness to your covenant God, punishment is coming to Israel. Some of the prophets whose warnings you will be reading are Elijah, Amos, and Isaiah.

Day 1 1 Kings 16:29–19:18 (Elijah and Ahab)
Day 2 1 Kings 21:1–22:40 (Ahab, Naboth's vineyard)
Day 3 Amos 2:6–4:13 (repeated warnings)
Day 4 Amos 5; 7:1-9; 9 (visions of Amos, a plumb line in Samaria)
Day 5 Isaiah 1; 3–6 (rebellious Judah, Isaiah's call)
Day 6 Read and respond to "The Bible Teaching" and "Marks of Discipleship."
Day 7 Rest and prayer.

PRAYER

Pray daily before study:

"LORD, don't be angry and rebuke me!
Don't punish me in your anger!
I am worn out, O LORD; have pity on me!
Give me strength; I am completely exhausted
and my whole being is deeply troubled.
How long, O LORD, will you wait to help me?" (Psalm 6:1-3).

Prayer concerns for this week:

WARNING

Day 1 Elijah and Ahab

Day 4 Visions of Amos, a plumb line in Samaria

Day 2 Ahab, Naboth's vineyard

Day 5 Rebellious Judah, Isaiah's call

Day 3 Repeated warnings

Day 6 "The Bible Teaching"

THE BIBLE TEACHING

NOTES, REFLECTIONS, AND QUESTIONS

The prophets understood the tension that existed between Israel's religion and the pagan practices of neighboring peoples. Also, the prophets clearly discerned the difference between a righteous, faithful people and a popular, comfortable practicing of religion. In their finest moments, the prophets called the people of God to remember their deep roots: "The LORD has told us what is good. What he requires of us is this: to do what is just, to show constant love, and to live in humble fellowship with our God" (Micah 6:8).

Early prophets were "seers" who peered into the future and gave signs, warnings, and predictions. But in addition to peering into the future, another dimension of prophecy developed. Great prophets felt a deep moral righteousness. They saw God interacting with history. A classical prophet may be defined as "one who is called" or "one who announces." The prophet clearly believes that God enters decisively into human history. The prophet "sees," "hears," or "understands" what God is doing or is going to do and, often at great personal risk, announces that reality to the people.

Prophets may be speaking to kings, as Nathan spoke to David about Uriah (2 Samuel 12) and as Elijah spoke to Ahab about Naboth's vineyard (1 Kings 21), or to people and nations as Amos spoke to the Northern Kingdom. But they all have a sense of *being called to announce God's actions.*

Paganism

The prophets were opposed to two things—*paganism* and *injustice*. Paganism meant *not putting God first in their lives.* It meant flirting with the gods of other tribes and nations, forgetting their unique covenant community. If they ate unclean foods, neglected the sabbath, intermarried with foreign peoples, worshiped at the high places, then they were "living with prostitutes." If Israel was to be God's chosen people, then they must be a separate people. Israel was to be an alternative community if the people were to be a "light to the nations."

King Ahab (873–853 B.C.) ruled the Northern Kingdom, called Israel. The prophet Elijah was furious because Ahab married Jezebel, a foreign princess who brought Baal worship into accepted practice in Israel (1 Kings 16:29-33).

Notice that King Ahab accused Elijah of being a troublemaker. People always accuse prophets of being troublemakers because they point out evil. Elijah responded, "I'm not the troublemaker. . . . You are. . . . You are disobeying the LORD's commands and worshiping the idols of Baal" (1 Kings 18:18).

Then came the great contest between Elijah and the priests of Baal on Mount Carmel, which reflected a spiritual crisis, a national watershed. Was Israel to be God's people or not? Everything was at stake, as far as Elijah was concerned. The priests of Baal were killed, and Queen Jezebel vowed revenge.

Jezebel threatened to kill the prophet. Why didn't King Ahab make the threat? Because the Hebrews had an amazing willingness to allow the prophet's word to take place in their midst. Can you imagine a king in another culture permitting severe criticism like Nathan gave David over Uriah or like Elijah gave Ahab over Naboth's vineyard?

Elijah warned Israel about paganism.

Injustice

The second cause of sin was *injustice*. When Israel and Judah did not put God first in their lives, they began to put themselves first. (We do the same.) As a result, they lacked consideration for neighbor and compassion for the weak. The prophets, sensing destruction was coming, first from Assyria and then from Babylonia, announced these disasters as punishment. The Hebrew people, they warned, would be destroyed and exiled because of their refusal to take seriously their responsibility for one another.

Religious responsibilities, political responsibilities, and economic responsibilities—all of life was included in the divine perspective. God's vision was a new social community in which everyone would be an integral part. A radically free God was trying to form a radically just and caring people! God wanted the covenant people to model justice to the world.

"Not one of your people will be poor if you obey him and carefully observe everything that I command you today. The LORD will bless you, as he has promised. . . .

" . . . There will always be some Israelites who are poor and in need, and so I command you to be generous to them" (Deuteronomy 15:4-6, 11).

But Israel failed. Self-interest prevailed. Love of God declined; so did love of neighbor. Remember the social wickedness described in Amos. Remember that *transgression* or *sinning again and again* is not just failing or forgetting. It is aggressive rebellion, active revolt against the established authority of Almighty God.

"The LORD says, 'The people of Israel have sinned again and again, and for this I will certainly punish them. They sell into slavery honest men who cannot pay their debts, poor men who cannot repay even the price of a pair of sandals. They trample down the weak and helpless and push the poor out of the way. A man and his father have intercourse with the same slave girl, and so profane my holy name. At every place of worship men sleep on clothing that they have taken from the poor as security for debts. In the temple of their God they drink wine which they have taken from those who owe them money' " (Amos 2:6-8).

In Amos's vision, the Lord drops a plumb line on Israel

NOTES, REFLECTIONS, AND QUESTIONS

(7:8). Israel does not line up with God's will. Look at the greed, the materialistic fever in 8:4-6.

"Listen to this, you that trample on the needy and try to destroy the poor of the country. You say to yourselves, 'We can hardly wait for the holy days to be over so that we can sell our grain. When will the Sabbath end, so that we can start selling again? Then we can overcharge, use false measures, and fix the scales to cheat our customers. We can sell worthless wheat at a high price. We'll find a poor man who can't pay his debts, not even the price of a pair of sandals, and we'll buy him as a slave.'

" ' . . . I will turn your festivals into funerals and change your glad songs into cries of grief. I will make you shave your heads and wear sackcloth, and you will be like parents mourning for their only son. That day will be bitter to the end' " (8:4-6, 10).

Describe in your own words this burning desire for money. How do you see this desire expressed in our fast-paced economic system?

Of special importance, Amos, like other prophets, preferred justice to religious ceremony. Amos expressed this preference with intense feeling:

"I hate your religious festivals" (5:21).

"Stop your noisy songs; I do not want to listen to your harps. Instead, let justice flow like a stream, and righteousness like a river that never goes dry" (5:23-24).

The warnings are proclaimed. They do not come from human beings. They come from God with a roar through the "one who announces": through Amos, a shepherd from the little village of Tekoa in Judah (Amos 1:1); through Jeremiah, a youth (Jeremiah 1:4-9); through Isaiah, a sophisticated adviser in the king's court (Isaiah 6:1-8).

They preached, sometimes by running naked through the streets (Isaiah 20), sometimes by naming their children (Isaiah 8:1-4; Hosea 1:4-9), sometimes with symbolic actions (Jeremiah 19:1-11); but the nation would not listen. Some of the hardest words were given to Isaiah:

"So he told me to go and give the people this message: 'No matter how much you listen, you will not understand. No matter how much you look, you will not know what is happening.' . . .

"I asked, 'How long will it be like this, Lord?'

"He answered, 'Until the cities are ruined and empty—until the houses are uninhabited. . . . I will send the people far away and make the whole land desolate' " (Isaiah 6:9, 11-12).

The people were warned about injustice, but they would not listen.

NOTES, REFLECTIONS, AND QUESTIONS

A plumb line was used to check the vertical line of a wall or building. The tool consisted of a string with a lead cone on one end and a piece of wood of the same diameter on the other end. If the wall was straight, the lead cone would barely touch the wall when the wooden piece was held against the top of the wall. The plumb line became a symbol of God's measuring a nation or a people.

MARKS OF DISCIPLESHIP

Prophets do warn us. In different ways.

Doctors explain our physical future if we do not change our habits.

Evangelists show a heavenly path and a hellish path and plead for decision.

Social prophets point to racial injustice and are called troublemakers, point to massive military armaments and are called peaceniks, point to environmental pollutants and are called antibusiness.

Is someone you recognize, right now, saying something prophetic in the biblical sense for our nation? How are we listening to the warning?

Describe a time you felt God's Spirit placing in your mouth a holy warning that you felt called upon to give to others.

IF YOU WANT TO KNOW MORE

We did not read the prophet Hosea. Hosea's wife Gomer ran off to be a prostitute, and Hosea bought her back as God will buy back a bedraggled people. If you have time, read Hosea's dramatic social witness.

NOTES, REFLECTIONS, AND QUESTIONS

CONSEQUENCES

"Israel, you brought this on yourself!
You deserted me, the LORD your God,
while I was leading you along the way."
—Jeremiah 2:17

11 God Punishes the People

OUR HUMAN PROBLEM

We think we can sidestep the consequences of our actions, but we cannot. We fool ourselves. We think religious practices will save us. We think wealth or prestige will protect us. But we are held accountable. We usually respond to punishment with denial, blame on others, anger, depression, and despair.

ASSIGNMENT

The Scriptures you will be reading this week are action packed. The main characters are the kings, the prophets, and God. Israel and Judah are on a judgment course. No words or no actions will change that course. But pay attention to the presence and action of God. Watch as God both judges and holds out the offer and hope of redemption.

Day 1 2 Kings 17; 22:1-2; 23; 25 (fall of Samaria, King Josiah's reforms, fall of Jerusalem)
Day 2 Jeremiah 8 (warnings and judgment on Judah)
Day 3 Jeremiah 37–39 (Jeremiah imprisoned)
Day 4 Isaiah 28:1–30:18 (warnings to Jerusalem, God's grace)
Day 5 Lamentations 1–3 (sorrow over Jerusalem)
Day 6 Read and respond to "The Bible Teaching" and "Marks of Discipleship."
Day 7 Rest and prayer.

PRAYER

Pray daily before study:
"Keep your promise, LORD, and forgive my sins,
for they are many" (Psalm 25:11).

Prayer concerns for this week:

Church / Pastors.
Building
Elizabeth.

CONSEQUENCES

Day 1 Fall of Samaria, King Josiah's reforms, fall of Jerusalem

Day 2 Warnings and judgment on Judah

Day 3 Jeremiah imprisoned

Day 4 Warnings to Jerusalem, God's grace

Day 5 Jeremiah's sorrow over Jerusalem

Day 6 "The Bible Teaching"

THE BIBLE TEACHING

NOTES, REFLECTIONS, AND QUESTIONS

The destruction actually came: to the Northern Kingdom (Israel, capital city Samaria) by the Assyrians in 722 B.C. and to the Southern Kingdom (Judah, capital city Jerusalem) in 587 B.C. by the Babylonians. What took place personally for Ahab and Jezebel now befell the entire nation.

Moses' plea for obedience in Deuteronomy now rings true: "Even when you have been in the land a long time and have children and grandchildren, do not sin by making for yourselves an idol in any form at all. This is evil in the LORD's sight, and it will make him angry. I call heaven and earth as witnesses against you today that, if you disobey me, you will soon disappear from the land. You will not live very long in the land across the Jordan that you are about to occupy. You will be completely destroyed. The LORD will scatter you among other nations" (Deuteronomy 4:25-27).

In 2 Kings 17 you read of the destruction of the Northern Kingdom and in 2 Kings 25 of the destruction of the Southern Kingdom, particularly the destruction of the Temple and the fall of Jerusalem.

The prophets made two points when interpreting these events:

First, the people of God brought it on themselves. They had been warned by a God "who is not easily angered." They could not blame somebody else. Nor could they blame foreign gods more powerful than their own. The one true God of the universe called them into accountability.

Near the end, the people made several "last-ditch" efforts to no avail. The sickness was too deep: "Israel, your head is already covered with wounds, and your heart and mind are sick. From head to foot there is not a healthy spot on your body" (Isaiah 1:5-6).

So prayers and feasts were "too little too late." They could not substitute "churchiness" for social responsibility: "It's useless to bring your offerings. I am disgusted with the smell of the incense you burn. . . . I hate your New Moon Festivals and holy days; they are a burden that I am tired of bearing" (1:13-14).

Second, the search for salvation took the form of a desperate desire for military alliances with other nations.

With armies coming down from the north, the leaders decided to put their trust in the Egyptians. Prophets warned them: Egypt was a weak reed to lean upon (36:6). They should trust God alone and not alliances with foreigners. They had more chance of survival as an independent nation with integrity than as a wavering ally of the enemy of Assyria and Babylonia.

The prophet Isaiah denounced alliances as a further form of apostasy: "The LORD has spoken: 'Those who rule Judah are doomed because they rebel against me. They follow plans that I did not make, and sign treaties against my will, piling one sin on another. They go to Egypt for help without asking for my advice. They want Egypt to protect them, so they put their trust in Egypt's king' " (30:1-2).

That ploy will bring "neither help nor profit, but shame and disgrace" (30:5, RSV).

The Tears of the Prophets for Israel and Judah

Do not think the prophets were eager to announce the calamity. The message they gave broke their hearts. They loved the Lord, the covenant, the Temple, the people, and their homeland.

> "My sorrow cannot be healed;
> I am sick at heart. . . .
> My heart has been crushed
> because my people are crushed;
> I mourn; I am completely dismayed" (Jeremiah 8:18, 21).

Nothing, not even the tears of the prophets, could stop the dreadful consequences of apostasy and rebellion, infidelity and social injustice. Institutions would topple. Kings and princes would be led away in chains. The brightest and best would be tied to chariots and led like animals into captivity. The government, established by God, would go down in ruins. The land of promise, flowing with "milk and honey," would be burned and made desolate. The economy would be destroyed. The Temple, built by Solomon on the site chosen by David, would be demolished. All would be lost.

The Takeover of the Northern Kingdom (Israel)

Sure enough, in the eighth century B.C., following the preaching and prophesying of Amos, Hosea, and Isaiah, the Assyrians marched down the coastline. Based in their capital, Nineveh, the Assyrians ambitiously set out to rule the world and quickly created an empire that unified most of the ancient Near East. By 722 B.C., when the Northern Kingdom (Israel) fell to Assyria, pure political independence by small neighboring states was impossible.

In Israel, as predicted, many leading citizens and skilled people were taken captive to various regions of the Assyrian Empire. In exchange, several thousand people from throughout the empire were transported into Israel. That political process was designed to break down national pride and help unify the Assyrian kingdom. In time the conquered peoples brought into Israel intermarried with the remaining Israelites and became the people known as the Samaritans.

What does God use as the instrument of punishment? God is Lord of the nations, as the prophets understand clearly. Israel is special, a covenant people, blessed to be a blessing; but all the nations are under God's providential power too. Therefore, God can use a foreign king, a "secular" people to perform the task of chastisement.

NOTES, REFLECTIONS, AND QUESTIONS

Captive Israelites being taken to Assyria

Listen:

"The LORD said, 'Assyria! I use Assyria like a club to punish those with whom I am angry. I sent Assyria to attack a godless nation, people who have made me angry. I sent them to loot and steal and trample the people like dirt in the streets' " (Isaiah 10:5-6).

Assyria does not know it, but its army is being used by the Lord. "The Assyrian emperor has his own violent plans in mind" (10:7). Nevertheless, God is using the king of Assyria to perform the punishment. Later Assyria will be punished for arrogance (10:12-16). After all, "Can an ax [the instrument] claim to be greater than the man who uses it?" (10:15).

That powerful Assyrian Empire existed over two hundred years but began to deteriorate in the mid-seventh century B.C. Assyria ended with decisive military defeats in 614 B.C. and 612 B.C.

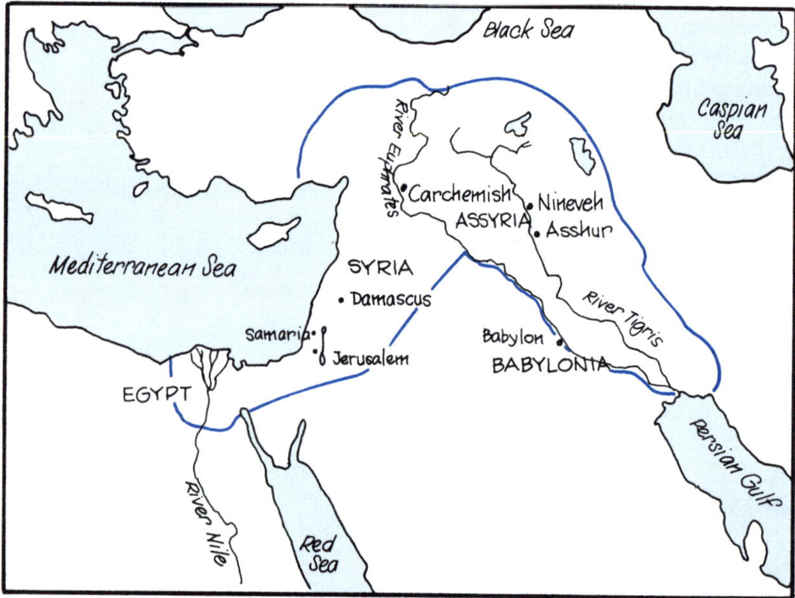

The extent of the Assyrian Empire about 722 B.C., the time of the fall of the Northern Kingdom

NOTES, REFLECTIONS, AND QUESTIONS

The Takeover of the Southern Kingdom (Judah)

The little Southern Kingdom (Judah), barely surviving by paying duty, now had a brief rest. With lessening political pressure from outside, Judah's King Josiah (640–609 B.C.) instituted significant reform. Josiah was so moved on hearing the words of the newly discovered book of the Law (the earliest form of Deuteronomy) that he restored purity in worship, maintained integrity in government, and established social legislation. Josiah abolished cult prostitution and Assyrian and Babylonian practices of star and animal worship. He reestablished Passover and enforced the law of Moses.

But the moment of grace was short-lived. When Josiah died in 609 B.C., Judah fell back into old ways. Repentance is more than reform in worship. Repentance means reorienting your lifestyle, placing the Lord first in all your ways (Deuteronomy 4:25-40).

Jeremiah says clearly that Judah is continually tempted. "Israel, you have had many lovers" (Jeremiah 3:1). (Remember, the focus here is on Judah, but the term *Israel* is often used to refer to Judah as the people of Israel.) Once again, in political intrigue, Israel flirts with foreign allies.

"What do you think you will gain by going to Egypt
to drink water from the Nile? . . .
Your own evil will punish you,
and your turning from me will condemn you"
(2:18-19).

An interesting and terrifying thought develops in the minds of the prophets. Egypt symbolized their earlier slavery during the time of Moses. Now, political alliances that would spell ruin were being made with Egypt. But at a deeper level, Israel was practicing a *spiritual apostasy* that would lead to *slavery*, slavery in which their distinctiveness would be destroyed, their unity fragmented.

Centuries earlier in the desert, the Hebrews yearned to go back to Egypt rather than face the demands of freedom: "We wish that the LORD had killed us in Egypt. There we could at least sit down and eat meat and as much other food as we wanted. But you have brought us out into this desert to starve us all to death" (Exodus 16:3). Now, as punishment, God was permitting them to run back to Egypt and receive their reward—enslavement.

The Babylonians ravaged Jerusalem, demolished the Temple, killed King Zedekiah's sons right before his eyes, then gouged out his eyes and led him and thousands of others into Babylonian captivity in 587 B.C. (2 Kings 25:6-7; Jeremiah 39:6-9).

Hope for Israel and Judah

Yet . . .

" 'Even if one person out of ten remains in the land, he too will be destroyed; he will be like the stump of an oak tree that has been cut down.'

"(The stump represents a new beginning for God's people)" (Isaiah 6:13).

God's purpose is not to destroy but to discipline, not to annihilate but to purify and redeem. Do not read the prophets with unrelieved doom. Even when the punishment is fulfilled, there is a glimmer of hope. For God is not the same as the Temple. Though the Temple is destroyed, God is not dead. Though the Promised Land is ravaged, the God of promise lives and rules. Though most of the people are scattered or dead, a remnant will survive.

"I am placing in Zion a foundation that is firm and strong. In it I am putting a solid cornerstone on which are written the words, 'Faith that is firm is also patient' " (Isaiah 28:16).

But most of us cannot see that ray of hope when our

NOTES, REFLECTIONS, AND QUESTIONS

In the Old Testament *Zion* is sometimes used as a synonym for *Jerusalem* or *city of David*. Often, particularly in the Psalms, the term refers to the Temple Mount: "On Zion, my sacred hill" (Psalm 2:6). In the New Testament *Zion* may be used to speak about the church, the gospel, or the place God dwells.

world caves in around us. We are just like the grieving exiles, thinking revenge rather than repentance.

"By the rivers of Babylon we sat down;
there we wept when we remembered Zion. . . .
How can we sing a song to the LORD
in a foreign land? . . .
Babylon, you will be destroyed.
Happy is the man who pays you back
for what you have done to us—
who takes your babies
and smashes them against a rock" (Psalm 137:1-9).

But there is no turning back. The judgment of God has come upon Israel and Judah.

MARKS OF DISCIPLESHIP

Something human in us all makes us believe we never will be punished. We won't get caught. We'll be let off easy. We'll be given another chance.

Sometimes that is true. List some times when you were not held strictly accountable, when you were "let off easy," when you were given a period of grace or a second chance.

____

____

But second chances run out, even for the disciple. The period of grace is over. The disciple accepts the consequences, asks for forgiveness, and looks for healing and new opportunities for faithfulness.

List some times when you were held strictly accountable and received the consequences for your actions.

____

____

How might an organization suffer the consequences of its actions?

____

IF YOU WANT TO KNOW MORE

Chart of Biblical History

722 B.C.	**Fall of Samaria to Assyria (capital: Nineveh)**
587 B.C.	**Fall of Jerusalem to Babylonia (capital: Babylon)**
	Temple destroyed
	Exile into Babylon

Much can be learned about the Jews in Exile. Look up in a Bible dictionary topics such as Assyrian Empire, Babylonian Empire, Exile, Captivity, destruction of Jerusalem and prepare a brief report to bring to the group.

NOTES, REFLECTIONS, AND QUESTIONS

The Ishtar Gate, main entrance to the ancient city of Babylon

CONSEQUENCES

Kings and Prophets (selected) of the Northern Kingdom—Israel (approximate dates)

KINGS	PROPHETS
Jeroboam I (925–905)	Ahijah
Omri (880–873)	Jehu
Ahab (873–853)	Elijah
Ahaziah (853–852)	Elijah
Jehoram/Joram (852–842)	Elisha
Jehu (842–814)	Elisha
Jehoash/Joash (800–783)	Elisha
Jeroboam II (783–749)	Hosea
	Amos
Pekahiah (740–739)	Micah
Pekah (739–732)	Micah
Hoshea (732–724)	Micah
	Hosea
Fall of Samaria to Assyria (722)	

Kings and Prophets (selected) of the Southern Kingdom—Judah (approximate dates)

KINGS	PROPHETS
Rehoboam (925–914)	Shemaiah
Jehoshaphat (871–849)	Jehu
Jehoram/Joram (849–842)	Elijah
Ahaziah (842 only)	Jehu
Joash/Jehoash (836–798)	Jehoiada
	Joel
	Zechariah
Amaziah (798–780)	(Unnamed)
Uzziah (780–741)	Zechariah
	Amos
	Isaiah
	Hosea
Jotham (741–734)	Isaiah
	Micah
	Hosea
Ahaz (734–715)	Isaiah
	Micah
Hezekiah (715–687)	Nahum
	Isaiah
	Micah
	Hosea
Manasseh (687–642)	(Unnamed)
Josiah (640–609)	Huldah
	Zephaniah
	Jeremiah
Jehoiakim (608–597)	Jeremiah
Zedekiah (597–587)	Jeremiah
Fall of Jerusalem to Babylonia (587)	

NOTES, REFLECTIONS, AND QUESTIONS

COMFORT

" 'Comfort my people,' says our God. 'Comfort them!
Encourage the people of Jerusalem.
Tell them they have suffered long enough
and their sins are now forgiven.
I have punished them in full for all their sins.' "

—Isaiah 40:1-2

12 God Restores the People

OUR HUMAN PROBLEM

In the darkest hour of our misery, our guilt, and our pain, when we experience the consequences of our sins and the sins of others, we angrily blame others, refuse comfort, and deny the possibility of starting over. We think all is lost.

ASSIGNMENT

Comfort is found many places in the Bible, but especially in the Prophets and in the Psalms. In this lesson we will study Isaiah (40–66) as our model of the comforting work of God. Passages from other prophets will add to our understanding of this redeeming, comforting God at work. Isaiah 40–66, often called Second Isaiah, was written by a prophet of the Babylonian exile. Keep in mind as you read Isaiah that Chapters 1–39 are set in the time before the Exile when Judah was threatened by Assyria. Chapters 40–66 relate to the period of the Exile and the return to Jerusalem.

Day 1 Isaiah 40; 42:1–43:21 (words of comfort)
Day 2 Isaiah 44 (idolatry); 49–50 (God's help)
Day 3 Isaiah 51–53 (hope for Zion, the Lord's servant)
Day 4 Isaiah 55 (God's offer of mercy); Ezekiel 37 (valley of dry bones)
Day 5 Jeremiah 31–32 (the new covenant)
Day 6 Read and respond to "The Bible Teaching" and "Marks of Discipleship."
Day 7 Rest and prayer.

PRAYER

Pray daily before study:
"You have changed my sadness into a joyful dance;
you have taken away my sorrow
and surrounded me with joy.
So I will not be silent;
I will sing praise to you.
LORD, you are my God;
I will give you thanks forever" (Psalm 30:11-12).

Prayer concerns for this week:

COMFORT

Day 1 Words of comfort

Day 2 Idolatry, God's help

Day 3 Hope for Zion, the Lord's servant

Day 4 God's offer of mercy, valley of dry bones

Day 5 The new covenant

Day 6 "The Bible Teaching"

THE BIBLE TEACHING

NOTES, REFLECTIONS, AND QUESTIONS

From the beginning God's punishment was never total destruction. God's grace works even amid punishment. Remember, God clothed Adam and Eve even as God drove them from the garden of innocence. The Lord saved Lot and his family from Sodom and Gomorrah. Cain was marked for protection, and Noah and his family were spared from the Flood.

Isaiah of Jerusalem, the writer of Isaiah 1–39, when he was called to be a prophet (Isaiah 6:1-8) knew the people would not listen. God would make the land desolate in spite of his pleas for repentance. Yet, "like the stump of an oak tree that has been cut down," God would still let Israel live. "The stump represents a new beginning for God's people" (6:13). There would be a remnant.

Jeremiah, when the armies of Babylonia were only a few miles from Jerusalem and real estate prices had totally collapsed, bought a farm and had the title registered to show his faith in the future (Jeremiah 32:6-15).

Ezekiel, while still in exile, was swept up in a vision and saw in the "valley of dry bones" a hope that Israel would be a living people again (Ezekiel 37).

In Israel's darkest hour, God spoke a word of consolation (recall that this Isaiah, Isaiah of Babylon, was writing near the end of or after the Exile):

> " 'Comfort my people,' says our God. 'Comfort them!
> Encourage the people of Jerusalem.
> Tell them they have suffered long enough
> and their sins are now forgiven.
> I have punished them in full for all their sins' "
> (Isaiah 40:1-2).

The destruction had been severe, very severe; and everyone had suffered, even the innocent. The punishment had been given. Now was the time for tenderness. He will gather the lambs and carry them in his arms (40:11).

Some are suggesting that foreign gods have prevailed. Isaiah laughs at the idea. He ridicules gods made of gold or silver or wood (40:18-20; 44:9-17). No, the action is God's action:

> "Do you not know?
> Were you not told long ago?
> Have you not heard how the world began?
> It was made by the one who sits on his throne
> above the earth and beyond the sky;
> the people below look as tiny as ants. . . .
> He brings down powerful rulers
> and reduces them to nothing" (40:21-23).

The comfort comes from God just as the punishment came from God. The idols are a laughing matter. We still have to deal with almighty God.

God reaffirms the covenant with his servant Israel. Justice has been reestablished. The price has been paid (42:1-4). Reconciliation has occurred. A cleansing has taken place. God will not forsake the called people of Abraham and Sarah.

Surely countless Jews, when the Temple lay in ruins, the people killed or in exile, cried out with the psalmist, "My God, my God, why have you abandoned me?" (Psalm 22:1).

But God claims eternal kinship.

"Can a woman forget her own baby
and not love the child she bore?
Even if a mother should forget her child,
I will never forget you.
Jerusalem, I can never forget you!
I have written your name on the palms of my hands"
(Isaiah 49:15-16).

What a foretaste of the nails in the hands of Christ!

A Light to the Nations

You would think it enough for Israel to be going home rejoicing. King Cyrus of Persia gave permission for the Temple to be rebuilt and for people to return to Jerusalem. But no, God has more for the servant Israel. They are not finished with their mission. They were called in Abraham to be blessed in order to be a blessing (Genesis 12:2-3). God wants them to take their witness, their sense of justice, their understanding of God, and now their punishment and disciplined experience to benefit the whole world.

Treating Israel as if the nation were a single individual—a servant—God says it is too easy just to return home.

"I have a greater task for you, my servant.
Not only will you restore to greatness
the people of Israel who have survived,
but I will also make you a light to the nations—
so that all the world may be saved"
(Isaiah 49:6).

But how will that be done? In a most perplexing way: by being a servant, a suffering servant. Kings will be speechless to see so unattractive, so disfigured a servant (52:14-15). Israel's remnant suffered for the sins of the whole world. "He took the place of many sinners" (53:12). No wonder this great suffering servant passage astonished Israel. No wonder the Gospel writers and early church saw it as one of the great prophetic messages of Christ's crucifixion.

MARKS OF DISCIPLESHIP

The disciple accepts the comfort of God and begins to look for new beginnings, fresh possibilities, and chooses to serve rather than to despair.

Just as God used the Assyrians and the Babylonians to discipline Israel and Judah, God may have used other persons as the instrument of discipline for you. In the same way that Isaiah and Jeremiah were used as messengers of

NOTES, REFLECTIONS, AND QUESTIONS

comfort, some person may have brought you God's comfort. Write about a time when you felt you were disciplined for your sin and later comforted by God.

___

___

___

___

After suffering the consequences for your sins and after being comforted, how did your behavior change?

___

___

___

IF YOU WANT TO KNOW MORE

Through the prophet Ezekiel, God assured the people that he was with them in their exile. Read Ezekiel 1–5.

One day Ezekiel sat beside the Chebar River in Babylonia. He had been one of those strong, intelligent young men roped to the chariots of Nebuchadnezzar in an exile group before the final fall of Jerusalem. He was lonesome for God and homesick. Did not the God of Abraham reside in Jerusalem? Did not the God of Moses dwell in the Covenant Box in the Temple?

Suddenly the sky opened, and Ezekiel saw four creatures, each with four faces (Ezekiel 1). The faces were like a bull and a lion, an eagle and a human being—the symbols of God: God is strong—powerful like a bull, courageous like a lion, soaring like an eagle, touching the hearts of people. These creatures are cherubim, guardians of God's throne. God is everywhere, even to the four corners of the earth.

Each creature went straight forward. Wherever the Spirit would go, they went, without turning as they went. *Aha,* thought Ezekiel, *no turning, no deviation from God's purpose.* The Lord will carry out whatever the Lord wills!

"As I was looking at the four creatures I saw four wheels touching the ground, one beside each of them. . . . Whenever the creatures moved, the wheels moved with them" (1:15-19).

"I understand!" cried Ezekiel. Those chariot wheels, turning, turning, rolling away from Jerusalem, were not rolling away from God! God was in the wheels. God moved with the movement. The God of the universe was everywhere. Now they could sing a song to the Lord in a foreign land, in any land (Psalm 137:4)!

NOTES, REFLECTIONS, AND QUESTIONS

The impact of this understanding on Judaism was tremendous. Jews began to gather beside the Chebar River and beside the rivers in a hundred other cities to sing the songs of Zion. They studied the law of Moses and debated and discussed it. They tried to keep certain sabbath rules and many of the food laws. They prayed together.

From these gatherings the synagogue was born. Far from the Temple, dispersed throughout the known world, the people of Israel moved from an emphasis on animal sacrifice and Temple worship to being a people of the law and of prayer. Even in exile, even in punishment, even in Babylon, God was with them.

From Ezekiel's vision, we understand better the synagogue of New Testament times. We see how the Jews began to focus on the law and how they preserved their distinct identity. Most of all, we understand a dynamic spiritual truth: God is with us no matter how far we travel geographically, no matter how far we go away from God spiritually, no matter how severe the tragedy, no matter how salty the tears.

As the psalmist declared,

"Where could I go to escape from you?
Where could I get away from your presence?"
(Psalm 139:7).

NOTES, REFLECTIONS, AND QUESTIONS

WORSHIP

"LORD, you have examined me and you know me.
You know everything I do;
from far away you understand all my thoughts."
—Psalm 139:1-2

13 Songs of the Heart

OUR HUMAN PROBLEM

We hide parts of ourselves, certain feelings and thoughts from God, ourselves, and others. To be whole, we need to express our true selves before God and within the worshiping community of faith.

ASSIGNMENT

The Psalms mirror human emotions. They are songs, chants, prayers, liturgies, and responses. Most are meant to be used in corporate worship. They are poetry. To savor the feelings, the depth of emotion, read each psalm aloud.

Day 1 Psalm 136 (history of salvation); Introduction and Day 1 of "The Bible Teaching"
Day 2 Psalms 90; 137 (lament as community); Psalm 42 (individual lament); Psalm 22 (Passion psalm); Day 2 of "The Bible Teaching"
Day 3 Psalm 51 (David's confession); Psalm 130 (penitence); Day 3 of "The Bible Teaching"
Day 4 Psalm 65 (community thanksgiving); Psalm 116 (personal thanksgiving); Day 4 of "The Bible Teaching"
Day 5 Psalm 104 (hymn of praise, nature); Psalm 23 (trust and meditation); Day 5 of "The Bible Teaching"
Day 6 Psalm 73 (wisdom and meditation); Day 6 of "The Bible Teaching"; read and respond to "Marks of Discipleship."
Day 7 Rest.

PRAYER

Pray daily before study:
"O LORD, I will always sing of your constant love;
I will proclaim your faithfulness forever.
I know that your love will last for all time,
that your faithfulness is as permanent as the sky" (Psalm 89:1-2).

Prayer concerns for this week:

WORSHIP

Day 1 History of salvation

Day 4 Community thanksgiving, personal thanksgiving

Day 2 Lament as community, individual lament, Passion psalm

Day 5 Hymn of praise, nature; trust and meditation

Day 3 David's confession, penitence

Day 6 Wisdom and meditation

THE BIBLE TEACHING

NOTES, REFLECTIONS, AND QUESTIONS

Introduction

Jews and Christians of all persuasions and all ages claim the Psalms or Psalter. People delight in the Psalms for various reasons and approach them from different perspectives. The form and arrangement of the Psalms are classical Judaism. Psalm 1 lifts up the importance of studying the Law (Torah), and Psalm 2 refers to God's choice of a king, literally the messiah. Thus two central beliefs of the Jewish people are quickly established: revelation of God's will in Torah and the concept of messiah, the chosen one to carry out God's purposes.

The Book of Psalms is divided into five "books" to pattern after the five books of the Pentateuch. The Psalter was coming into being from the beginning of the Hebrew nation. Some psalms were written before the Exile, some during the Exile, and some after the Exile. The present form of the Psalms comes from the time of the building of the Second Temple (520–515 B.C.) when Haggai and Zechariah were prophets.

The Psalter may also be called the prayer book of the synagogue. As the synagogues sprang up where Jews were dispersed all over the known world, the hymnbook helped them keep faith and tradition alive.

The early Christians took the whole Old Testament as their own, but the Psalms were especially precious. Jesus quoted most often from three sources: Deuteronomy (Moses and the Law), Isaiah, and the Psalms. The New Testament writers quoted most frequently from Psalms and Isaiah.

The earliest Christian disciples met in synagogues, singing psalms. Undoubtedly they sang them in prison, feeling at one with the community of faith: "About midnight Paul and Silas were praying and singing hymns to God, and the other prisoners were listening to them" (Acts 16:25). The writer of Ephesians encouraged believers to "be filled with the Spirit. Speak to one another with the words of psalms, hymns, and sacred songs; sing hymns and psalms to the Lord with praise in your hearts" (Ephesians 5:18-19).

This week the study hopes not to teach you *about* the Psalms as much as to *guide you into* the Psalms. If you can let them help you express your inexpressible thoughts and feelings, they will become your prayers. Athanasius, a Christian leader in the fourth century A.D., said that most Scripture speaks *to* us; but the Psalms speak *for* us. They are "songs of the heart," mirroring the totality of our human experiences.

The songs are corporate in nature, even when they are expressed in lonely agony. Always the one in prayer or song is aware of the historic covenant community, the faithful worshiping fellowship, and the encompassing arms of the Almighty. We learn to praise God, not just in times when we feel God's presence, but also in times when we experience God's absence. We sing while undergoing the severest of trials, when separated from the visible support of the Christian fellowship, but we are never alone.

Day 1: Salvation History

Psalm 136 recalls the salvation history of the Jews. Notice the corporate experience, the plural language, the sense of unity in Israel. Feel the beat from the powerful response, "his love is eternal." Are we afraid, troubled, anxious, oppressed? Remember, "his love is eternal." God loved us in creation (136:4-9), in history (136:10-22), and with divine care (136:23-25).

Since this "salvation history" poem ends thousands of years ago, try adding events from your own personal, family, or national pilgrimage to which you could respond "his love is eternal."

____

____

____

Day 2: Lament

Read carefully Psalm 90. Ask yourself what feelings come to you as you consider these verses of this psalm of sorrow:

90:1-2 ______________________________

____

90:4-6, 9 ______________________________

____

90:12 ______________________________

____

90:17 ______________________________

____

Day 3: Confession

Psalm 51 is David's prayer for forgiveness after his sin with Bathsheba. Pause as you read the following verses to recall times you have felt as David felt. Describe your memories.

51:3 ______________________________

____

51:7 ______________________________

____

NOTES, REFLECTIONS, AND QUESTIONS

51:10 ______________________

____

51:12 ______________________

____

Day 4: Thanksgiving

Psalm 65 expresses thankfulness as a community of faith. For what are the people thanking God?

____

For what might your congregation thank God?

____

Day 5: Praise

Read Psalm 104. Write down new ideas of ways to praise God in prayer.

____

____

Day 6: Wisdom

Psalm 73 is a meditative "wisdom" psalm.

In 73:2-3, how do you feel when things go well for the wicked?

____

In 73:16-18, what did the psalmist come to understand?

____

In 73:25-26, finally, what really matters?

____

____

MARKS OF DISCIPLESHIP

The disciple, seeking constant connectedness and openness with God, trusts God with all her or his thoughts and feelings. The Psalms and the psalmists set us an example in their bold expression of the full range of human emotion—from love to hate, from joy to despair, from blessing to cursing. Sometimes we cringe as we read and want to avoid or explain away these psalms that call on God to curse and destroy others. Better that we read them for what they are and admit that we too have similar feelings and wishes.

NOTES, REFLECTIONS, AND QUESTIONS

Growing in willingness and ability to boldly express to God any thought or emotion can enable a person to begin to trust others with his or her hidden self.

What feelings can you easily express to God?

What feelings are difficult for you to express to God?

Our Lord, on the cross, murmured these words: "My God, my God, why did you abandon me?" (Matthew 27:46). In agony he seems to have been praying Psalm 22. Nothing in Scripture could have been more in keeping with the pain of the Crucifixion experience. It is a holy thing to have a psalm on our lips when we die.

IF YOU WANT TO KNOW MORE

Memorize Psalm 23 from your favorite version of the Bible.

Countless hymns have been inspired by the Psalms. Most hymnbooks contain hymns that derive from specific psalms. You might enjoy taking a hymnbook and looking up these hymns and comparing them with a psalm.

"The King of Love My Shepherd Is"	Psalm 23
"Savior, More Than Life to Me"	Psalm 51
"O God, Our Help in Ages Past"	Psalm 90
"All People That on Earth Do Dwell"	Psalm 100
"O Worship the King"	Psalm 104
"Still, Still with Thee"	Psalm 139

NOTES, REFLECTIONS, AND QUESTIONS

RIGHT LIVING

"They find joy in obeying the Law of the LORD,
  and they study it day and night.
They are like trees that grow beside a stream,
  that bear fruit at the right time,
  and whose leaves do not dry up.
They succeed in everything they do."

—Psalm 1:2-3

14 The Righteous Are Like a Tree

OUR HUMAN PROBLEM

We want to be healthy and happy, but on our own terms. Usually we are not willing to pay the price that right living requires.

ASSIGNMENT

As you read, you will be looking for the good life, the righteous life, the way of religious living that causes emotional, physical, and spiritual well-being. You will be looking for individual right living but also for qualities or characteristics that make for healthy families, strong churches, harmonious nations, and a peaceful world.

Day 1 Psalms 1; 19:7-14; 112; 128 (happiness)
Day 2 Proverbs 1–3 (rewards of wisdom, advice to youth)
Day 3 Proverbs 16–18; 31 (life and conduct, warnings, moral lessons)
Day 4 Ezra 1; 3; 4:1-5; 5:1-16; 7:1-10, 25-26 (return of the exiles to Jerusalem, rebuilding the Temple)
Day 5 Nehemiah 1; 2; 8:1–9:3; 10:28-39 (Nehemiah goes to Jerusalem, reading the Law, renewing the covenant)
Day 6 Read and respond to "The Bible Teaching" and "Marks of Discipleship."
Day 7 Rest.

PRAYER

Pray daily before study:
"You are all I want, O LORD;
  I promise to obey your laws.
I ask you with all my heart
  to have mercy on me, as you have promised!
I have considered my conduct,
  and I promise to follow your instructions.
Without delay I hurry
  to obey your commands" (Psalm 119:57-60).

Prayer concerns for this week:

RIGHT LIVING

Day 1 Happiness

Day 4 Return of the exiles to Jerusalem, rebuilding the Temple

Day 2 Rewards of wisdom, advice to youth

Day 5 Nehemiah goes to Jerusalem, reading the Law, renewing the covenant

Day 3 Life and conduct, warnings, moral lessons

Day 6 "The Bible Teaching"

THE BIBLE TEACHING

The ways of God are good for us, and following them leads to a healthy, harmonious life. Evil ways cause great unhappiness, often resulting in sickness, poverty, broken relationships, injury, incapacity, and early death. Because we live in families and in community, individual sins and wickedness often result in disaster and corruption for large groups of people. Also, sin weaves its way through the generations: "I bring punishment on those who hate me and on their descendants down to the third and fourth generation" (Exodus 20:5).

How can we try to walk the godly path? As you work through the following section, you will be looking at some of the proverbs that give guidelines for right living.

Think about integrity. What do the following verses from Proverbs tell us

about truthtelling? (Proverbs 4:24; 6:12-15; 12:19, 22)

---

about honest measurement? (11:1; 16:11)

Think about sex, abstinence in singleness and faithfulness in marriage. What do the following verses tell us

about adultery? (5:1-6; 6:28-35)

---

about how a woman or a man should treat her or his mate? (5:15-19; 31:10-31)

Think about conflict. What do the following verses say

about hot tempers? (14:17; 15:17-18)

---

about arguments? (17:14)

Think about concern for the poor. What do the following verses say

about generosity? (14:21, 31; 22:9)

NOTES, REFLECTIONS, AND QUESTIONS

about care for widows and orphans? (15:25; 23:10-11)

Think about greed. What do the following verses say

about dishonest gain of money? (15:27; 16:8; 20:17)

about extravagant show of wealth? (16:18-19)

Think about care for one's own family. What do the following verses say

about concern for teaching and disciplining children? (4:1-5; 13:24; 22:6)

about respect for elders? (13:1; 20:20)

Think about honest hard work. What do the following verses say

about laziness? (6:9-11; 20:4)

about planning for the future? (21:5, 20)

Think about food and drink. What do the following verses say

about overeating? (23:19-21; 25:16)

about drunkenness? (20:1; 23:29-35)

In Proverbs 1, what happens to people who rob and commit murder?

NOTES, REFLECTIONS, AND QUESTIONS

Read again about wisdom calling out in the streets (Proverbs 1:20-33). What will wisdom do to those who ignore her teachings?

What is required to be wise (9:10)?

The idea that right living would bring divine approval became an obsession. The Jews had experienced exile and were going home to begin again. They wanted to obey perfectly. As some of the Jewish leaders returned to Jerusalem, they wanted to avoid the sins of the past.

They believed

- that God would punish sin and reward righteousness;
- that keeping the law offered great reward;
- that the covenant people must be pure, not intermarried with foreign people who worshiped other gods and ate unclean foods;
- that the Temple and the holy sacrifices were a major part of faithfulness;
- that sabbath laws were essential to righteousness;
- that everything they did must be built on reestablishment of the laws of Leviticus and Deuteronomy;
- that sickness came from sin and that prosperity and health came from right living.

God is just. Right living has great rewards. But as we will see in our next lesson, this is not always the case. Sometimes sickness is not caused by sin. Sometimes the good are cut down. Sometimes the wicked seem to prosper. Job would raise those issues. So, later, would Jesus. But among the Jews a theology emerged that focused on the Temple, the Temple sacrifices, personal holiness, the keeping of the Torah with great care, the separation of Jews (particularly in Jerusalem) from non-Jews, and the observance of holy days.

Therefore, Ezra, under King Zerubbabel and encouraged by the prophets Haggai and Zechariah, rebuilt the Temple. (This was the Second Temple, as Solomon's Temple had been destroyed.) The rebuilding took place between 520 and 515 B.C.

Two emphases of Judaism developed—the Temple, emphasizing sacrifice, and the synagogue, emphasizing study. Synagogues were scattered throughout the world, wherever Jews lived. Jerusalem and other large cities had several synagogues. Jews all over the world, though separated from the Temple, continued to be attached to it, and the people longed for the time when they could again worship there.

So the punishment of Israel and Judah for their disobedience now turned the faith of the Jewish people toward a radical, legalistic obedience. Their experience strengthened the Jews in their belief that the righteous will prosper but the wicked will perish.

NOTES, REFLECTIONS, AND QUESTIONS

MARKS OF DISCIPLESHIP

A disciple strives to live in harmony with God's laws, even though such obedience is costly.

Is it realistic today to expect Christian disciples to abstain from sex in singleness and to be faithful in marriage? What guidance do you find in Proverbs?

With our society built on profit motives and personal ambition, how can Christians avoid greed, overspending, and undergiving?

The body's health is important. Yet we spend billions of dollars on the effects of tobacco smoking, alcohol and drug abuse, overeating. What can we do within the community of faith to strengthen "right living"? What would help you?

In the Bible, God is concerned with the well-being of widows and orphans and the poor. What can we do in our church, community, and nation to show greater concern, and therefore greater righteousness, toward the poor?

IF YOU WANT TO KNOW MORE

Chart of Biblical History

539 B.C. **Persian period**
Jews return to Jerusalem
515 B.C. **Temple rebuilt**

Most of the Jews did not, could not, return to Israel but remained scattered. From time to time, great prejudice erupted in cities where they lived. The Book of Esther is a fascinating account of a brave woman who was used by God to save her people. Her action became the basis for the Jewish celebration of the festival of *Purim*. Look up information about the festival of *Purim*.

NOTES, REFLECTIONS, AND QUESTIONS

SUFFERING

"Instead of eating, I mourn,
  and I can never stop groaning.
Everything I fear and dread comes true.
I have no peace, no rest,
  and my troubles never end."

—Job 3:24-26

15 When Trouble Comes

OUR HUMAN PROBLEM

Life isn't fair. Sometimes the wicked prosper and the good are cut down. Some sick people are healed, and others are not. Suffering puzzles us. Why did this happen to me? we ask. If God is just and good, why do we sometimes suffer so much? Surely it is not always because of our sin. It is easy to become bitter.

ASSIGNMENT

You will enjoy reading the Bible especially this week, for the powerful drama of Job captures the imagination.

Even though the cutting of the drama printed below will be read aloud during the group meeting, take time to read it and make your own notes prior to the meeting. As you read, work on identifying the arguments posed in the drama. Pay attention also to the emotions displayed by Job and others.

Day 1 Job 1–2 (prologue); Introduction in "The Bible Teaching"
Day 2 Job 3–4 (Job and Eliphaz)
Day 3 The Drama in "The Bible Teaching"
Day 4 Job 38–39 (God speaks)
Day 5 Job 40–42 (God speaks, epilogue)
Day 6 Arguments in "The Bible Teaching"; read and respond to "Marks of Discipleship."
Day 7 Rest.

PRAYER

Pray daily before study:
"Be merciful to me, LORD,
  for I am in trouble;
my eyes are tired from so much crying;
  I am completely worn out.
I am exhausted by sorrow,
  and weeping has shortened my life.
I am weak from all my troubles;
  even my bones are wasting away"
    (Psalm 31:9-10).

Prayer concerns for this week:

SUFFERING

Day 1 Prologue, Introduction in "The Bible Teaching"

Day 2 Job and Eliphaz

Day 3 The Drama in "The Bible Teaching"

Day 4 God speaks

Day 5 God speaks, epilogue

Day 6 Arguments in "The Bible Teaching"

THE BIBLE TEACHING

NOTES, REFLECTIONS, AND QUESTIONS

Introduction

Earlier we learned from the Proverbs that right living has great rewards. But sometimes those who live right suffer. In the light of this contradiction, the story of Job is presented here.

This week at the group meeting, persons will read a cutting of the Job drama. The cutting is clear and relatively brief. It contains the major arguments Job's friends used to try to defend the then commonly accepted Jewish belief: The righteous prosper; the wicked suffer and perish.

The group's main task will be to try to identify the different kinds of counsel offered by Job's friends, to observe how their explanations are still used today, and to consider the sense in which they are partly true yet not completely appropriate, and not helpful.

A little more explanation:

The prologue (Job 1–2) describes a real tragedy, a series of terrible disasters. Job loses all his children (seven sons and three daughters).

They were a happy family, sons taking turns giving dinner parties for one another and for their sisters, Job getting up early the next morning to lead family devotions.

Job's unbelievable wealth—seven thousand sheep, three thousand camels, one thousand cattle, five hundred donkeys—is all lost by enemy raids and natural disaster.

Finally Job's own body is afflicted with terrible sores. He sits by the garbage dump, scraping his sores with a piece of broken pottery. All the promises of reward for right living are shattered: Health, wealth, large family, dignity, and honor—all are dramatically taken from God's good man.

The author's use of drama heightens the mystery, the confusion, the conflict in which Job finds himself. Easy answers won't do. Job wants something greater than traditional religion. He wants to meet God, face to face.

Satan is used dramatically as the cause of all the trouble. (*Satan* in the story of Job is a semidivine being who is an opponent of human beings, not of God. This Satan is not the Devil of Christian tradition.) The prologue is a conversation between Satan and God. This is the author's way of setting up the problem. Then the author uses the three friends to present the arguments in support of the idea that right living will be rewarded.

Remember that in Job's day people had no concept of life after death. The drama points out that justice must be proved during *this* life. Fairness, if there is fairness, and God's punishment, if there is God's punishment, must occur before death.

The Drama to Be Read in the Group

(The following dramatic reading is excerpted from the Good News Bible: The Bible in Today's English Version. *It follows the sequence of verses in the Book of Job from Chapter 3 through Chapter 42 but omits much of the book; it includes only speeches necessary to follow the logic of the drama.)*

JOB: O God, put a curse on the day I was born;
put a curse on the night when I was conceived!
Turn that day into darkness, God.
Never again remember that day;
never again let light shine on it. . . .
Keep the morning star from shining;
give that night no hope of dawn.
Curse that night for letting me be born,
for exposing me to trouble and grief.
I wish I had died in my mother's womb
or died the moment I was born. . . .
Instead of eating, I mourn,
and I can never stop groaning.
Everything I fear and dread comes true.
I have no peace, no rest,
and my troubles never end.
ELIPHAZ: Job, will you be annoyed if I speak?
I can't keep quiet any longer.
You have taught many people
and given strength to feeble hands.
When someone stumbled, weak and tired,
your words encouraged him to stand.
Now it's your turn to be in trouble,
and you are too stunned to face it.
You worshiped God, and your life was blameless;
and so you should have confidence and hope.
Think back now. Name a single case
where a righteous man met with disaster.
I have seen people plow fields of evil
and plant wickedness like seed;
now they harvest wickedness and evil. . . .
"Can anyone be righteous in the sight of God
or be pure before his Creator? . . ."
Evil does not grow in the soil,
nor does trouble grow out of the ground.
No! Man brings trouble on himself,
as surely as sparks fly up from a fire.
If I were you, I would turn to God
and present my case to him. . . .
Happy is the person whom God corrects!
Do not resent it when he rebukes you. . . .
JOB: Why won't God give me what I ask?
Why won't he answer my prayer?
If only he would go ahead and kill me!
If I knew he would, I would leap for joy,
no matter how great my pain.
I know that God is holy;
I have never opposed what he commands. . . .
All right, teach me; tell me my faults.
I will be quiet and listen to you.
Honest words are convincing,
but you are talking nonsense. . . .
But you think I am lying—
you think I can't tell right from wrong. . . .
When I lie down to sleep, the hours drag;
I toss all night and long for dawn. . . .
JOB *(to God)*: Remember, O God, my life is only a breath;
my happiness has already ended. . . .
No! I can't be quiet!
I am angry and bitter.
I have to speak. . . .
Why is man so important to you?
Why pay attention to what he does? . . .
Are you harmed by my sin, you jailer?
Why use me for your target practice?
Am I so great a burden to you? . . .
Soon I will be in my grave,
and I'll be gone when you look for me.
BILDAD: Are you finally through with your windy speech?
God never twists justice;
he never fails to do what is right.
Your children must have sinned against God,
and so he punished them as they deserved.
But turn now and plead with Almighty God;
if you are so honest and pure,
then God will come and help you
and restore your household as your reward.
All the wealth you lost will be nothing
compared with what God will give you then. . . .
JOB: Yes, I've heard all that before.
But how can a man win his case against God?
How can anyone argue with him?
He can ask a thousand questions
that no one could ever answer.
God is so wise and powerful;
no man can stand up against him. . . .
Though I am innocent, all I can do
is beg for mercy from God my judge. . . .
If God were human, I could answer him;
we could go to court to decide our quarrel.
But there is no one to step between us—
no one to judge both God and me. . . .
Isn't my life almost over? Leave me alone!
Let me enjoy the time I have left. . . .
ZOPHAR: How I wish God would answer you!
He would tell you there are many sides to wisdom;
there are things too deep for human knowledge.
God is punishing you less than you deserve. . . .
God knows which men are worthless;
he sees all their evil deeds. . . .

Put your heart right, Job. Reach out to God.
Put away evil and wrong from your home.
Then face the world again, firm and courageous. . . .
You will live secure and full of hope;
God will protect you and give you rest. . . .
JOB: Yes, you are the voice of the people.
When you die, wisdom will die with you.
But I have as much sense as you have;
I am in no way inferior to you;
everyone knows all that you have said.
Even my friends laugh at me now;
they laugh, although I am righteous and blameless;
but there was a time when God answered my prayers.
You have no troubles, and yet you make fun of me;
you hit a man who is about to fall. . . .
But my dispute is with God, not you;
I want to argue my case with him. . . .
I am ready to state my case,
because I know I am in the right.
Are you coming to accuse me, God?
If you do, I am ready to be silent and die.
Let me ask for two things; agree to them,
and I will not try to hide from you;
stop punishing me, and don't crush me with terror.
Speak first, O God, and I will answer.
Or let me speak, and you answer me.
What are my sins? What wrongs have I done?
What crimes am I charged with? . . .
ELIPHAZ: Empty words, Job! Empty words!
No wise man would talk the way you do
or defend himself with such meaningless words.
If you had your way, no one would fear God;
no one would pray to him.
Your wickedness is evident by what you say;
you are trying to hide behind clever words.
There is no need for me to condemn you;
you are condemned by every word you speak. . . .
Why, God does not trust even his angels;
even they are not pure in his sight.
And man drinks evil as if it were water;
yes, man is corrupt; man is worthless. . . .
JOB: I have heard words like that before;
the comfort you give is only torment. . . .
(*To God*) You have worn me out, God;
you have let my family be killed.
You have seized me; you are my enemy.
I am skin and bones,
and people take that as proof of my guilt. . . .
BILDAD: You are only hurting yourself with your anger.
Will the earth be deserted because you are angry?
Will God move mountains to satisfy you?
The wicked man's light will still be put out;
its flame will never burn again. . . .
JOB: Even if I have done wrong,
how does that hurt you?
You think you are better than I am,
and regard my troubles as proof of my guilt.
Can't you see it is God who has done this? . . .
You are my friends! Take pity on me!
The hand of God has struck me down.
Why must you persecute me the way God does?
Haven't you tormented me enough? . . .
But I know there is someone in heaven
who will come at last to my defense.
Even after my skin is eaten by disease,
while still in this body I will see God.
I will see him with my own eyes,
and he will not be a stranger. . . .
ZOPHAR: Surely you know that from ancient times,
when man was first placed on earth,
no wicked man has been happy for long. . . .
JOB: My quarrel is not with mortal men;
I have good reason to be impatient.
Look at me. Isn't that enough
to make you stare in shocked silence?
When I think of what has happened to me,
I am stunned, and I tremble and shake.
Why does God let evil men live,
let them grow old and prosper?
They have children and grandchildren,
and live to watch them all grow up.
God does not bring disaster on their homes;
they never have to live in terror. . . .
And you! You try to comfort me with nonsense!
Every answer you give is a lie!
ELIPHAZ: Is there any man, even the wisest,
who could ever be of use to God?
Does your doing right benefit God,
or does your being good help him at all?
It is not because you stand in awe of God
that he reprimands you and brings you to trial.
No, it's because you have sinned so much;
it's because of all the evil you do. . . .
JOB: I still rebel and complain against God;
I cannot keep from groaning.
How I wish I knew where to find him,
and knew how to go where he is.
I would state my case before him
and present all the arguments in my favor.
I want to know what he would say
and how he would answer me. . . .
I follow faithfully the road he chooses,
and never wander to either side.
I always do what God commands;
I follow his will, not my own desires. . . .
I tremble with fear before him. . . .

BILDAD: Can anyone be righteous or pure in God's sight?
In his eyes, even the moon is not bright,
or the stars pure.
Then what about man, that worm, that insect?
What is man worth in God's eyes? . . .

JOB: If only my life could once again
be as it was when God watched over me. . . .
Almighty God was with me then,
and I was surrounded by all my children. . . .
I have always acted justly and fairly.
I was eyes for the blind,
and feet for the lame.
I was like a father to the poor
and took the side of strangers in trouble.
I destroyed the power of cruel men
and rescued their victims. . . .
Why do you attack a ruined man,
one who can do nothing but beg for pity?
Didn't I weep with people in trouble
and feel sorry for those in need?
I hoped for happiness and light,
but trouble and darkness came instead.
I am torn apart by worry and pain;
I have had day after day of suffering. . . .
I swear I have never acted wickedly
and never tried to deceive others.
Let God weigh me on honest scales,
and he will see how innocent I am. . . .

ELIHU: I am young, and you are old,
so I was afraid to tell you what I think.
I told myself that you ought to speak,
that you older men should share your wisdom.
But it is the spirit of Almighty God
that comes to men and gives them wisdom.
It is not growing old that makes men wise
or helps them to know what is right. . . .
Now this is what I heard you say:
"I am not guilty; I have done nothing wrong.
I am innocent and free from sin.
But God finds excuses for attacking me
and treats me like an enemy.
He binds chains on my feet;
he watches every move I make."
But I tell you, Job, you are wrong.
God is greater than any man.
Why do you accuse God
of never answering a man's complaints?
Although God speaks again and again,
no one pays attention to what he says.
At night when men are asleep,
God speaks in dreams and visions.
He makes them listen to what he says,
and they are frightened at his warnings.
God speaks to make them stop their sinning
and to save them from becoming proud.
He will not let them be destroyed;
he saves them from death itself.
God corrects a man by sending sickness
and filling his body with pain. . . .
God does all this again and again;
he saves a person's life,
and gives him the joy of living. . . .
God's power is so great that we cannot come near him;
he is righteous and just in his dealings with men.
No wonder, then, that everyone is awed by him,
and that he ignores those who claim to be wise. . . .

THE LORD *(to Job)*: Who are you to question my wisdom
with your ignorant, empty words?
Stand up now like a man
and answer the questions I ask you.
Were you there when I made the world?
If you know so much, tell me about it.
Who decided how large it would be?
Who stretched the measuring line over it?
Do you know all the answers?
What holds up the pillars that support the earth?
Who laid the cornerstone of the world? . . .
Job, you challenged Almighty God;
will you give up now, or will you answer?

JOB: I spoke foolishly, LORD. What can I answer?
I will not try to say anything else.
I have already said more than I should. . . .

THE LORD: Stand up now like a man,
and answer my questions.
Are you trying to prove that I am unjust—
to put me in the wrong and yourself in the right?
Are you as strong as I am?
Can your voice thunder as loud as mine?
If so, stand up in your honor and pride;
clothe yourself with majesty and glory. . . .

JOB: I know, LORD, that you are all-powerful;
that you can do everything you want.
You ask how I dare question your wisdom
when I am so very ignorant.
I talked about things I did not understand,
about marvels too great for me to know.
You told me to listen while you spoke
and to try to answer your questions.
In the past I knew only what others had told me,
but now I have seen you with my own eyes.
So I am ashamed of all I have said
and repent in dust and ashes.

Arguments

Using the cutting of the Job story, identify who gave the following arguments:

Nobody is perfect. ____________________

____

You have sinned. ____________________

____

Your children have sinned. ____________________

____

Somebody sinned. ____________________

____

You are being corrected. ____________________

____

Trust God; God will help you. ____________________

____

Don't be angry with God. ____________________

____

Shut up; you have no right to complain. ____________________

____

Trouble comes to everybody. ____________________

____

List some of Job's responses. ____________________

____

____

____

____

What happened to Job when God spoke to him?

____

____

____

NOTES, REFLECTIONS, AND QUESTIONS

Finally, not counting the epilogue (42:7-17), which was probably designed to put the drama back in the context of traditional Jewish belief, what gave Job his peace of mind?

MARKS OF DISCIPLESHIP

Mystery often accompanies our suffering. Natural disasters, disease, the actions of others can cause us great pain. In the face of unexplained suffering, the disciple trusts God. God does not always give us answers; God promises to be with us (Psalm 23).

The Christian disciple knows that suffering causes a person to turn away from God or turn to God. Think of some times when you chose to turn away from God during suffering.

Think of some times when you chose to turn to God during suffering.

Sometimes people need a long time to work through their pain. How can we as church people help people during those times?

IF YOU WANT TO KNOW MORE

Read the entire story of Job. Try a different version of the Bible, perhaps the New International Version, the Revised Standard Version, or *The Jerusalem Bible*.

NOTES, REFLECTIONS, AND QUESTIONS

HOPE

"During this vision in the night, I saw what looked like a human being. He was approaching me, surrounded by clouds, and he went to the one who had been living forever and was presented to him. He was given authority, honor, and royal power, so that the people of all nations, races, and languages would serve him. His authority would last forever, and his kingdom would never end."

—Daniel 7:13-14

16 People Hope for a Savior

OUR HUMAN PROBLEM

We swing between two extremes. Either we drift into pessimism, supposing that evil prospers and death ends all. Or we try to convince ourselves that a new government, a change in leadership, some quick fix will save us. Only special people seem to catch the vision of God's final kingdom of peace.

ASSIGNMENT

This week's Scripture will be difficult, for it contains visions, dreams, prophecies, and revelations of end times. The difficulties are increased by ancient images, deliberately concealed symbols, and scholarly problems. So we will read a small amount rather slowly. But notice, as we end our study of the Old Testament, hope is alive, and light shines in the darkness.

Day 1 Daniel 1–3 (young Daniel and his three friends, the fiery furnace)
Day 2 Daniel 4–6 (two kings, the pit of lions)
Day 3 Daniel 7; 12 (Daniel's visions, time of the end)
Day 4 Isaiah 8:21–9:7; 11:1-10; 42:1-9 (future hope of Israel)
Day 5 Zechariah 9:9-17; (God's people restored); Micah 5:2-4; Malachi 3:1-12; Isaiah 55 (God's mercy and promise)
Day 6 Read and respond to "The Bible Teaching" and "Marks of Discipleship."
Day 7 Rest.

PRAYER

Pray daily before study:
"You, LORD, are all I have,
and you give me all I need;
my future is in your hands.
How wonderful are your gifts to me;
how good they are!" (Psalm 16:5-6).

Prayer concerns for this week:

HOPE

Day 1 Young Daniel and his three friends, the fiery furnace

Day 4 Future hope of Israel

Day 2 Two kings, the pit of lions

Day 5 God's people restored, God's mercy and promise

Day 3 Daniel's visions, time of the end

Day 6 "The Bible Teaching"

THE BIBLE TEACHING

NOTES, REFLECTIONS, AND QUESTIONS

Every Bible student should know these words:
Apocalypse—prophetic revelation; to uncover; to reveal what is to come, especially end times. The Book of Revelation is sometimes called "The Apocalypse."

Eschatology—concerned with ultimate or last things, such as death, judgment, heaven, and hell.

Messiah—the anticipated deliverer, the "anointed one" who is to come.

Kingdom of God—different from earthly kingdoms; the concluding time when God will rule in justice, harmony, and peace.

The Book of Daniel

We have not had time to read some other important parts of the Old Testament. Why read a difficult book like Daniel?

Four reasons:

1. Daniel provides a perspective on Jewish people scattered throughout the world, living in a foreign culture rather than in Palestine.
2. Daniel for Jews, like Revelation for Christians, was written to help the faithful "hang on" during persecution.
3. Many Christians see in the Book of Daniel as in other Old Testament passages glimpses of messiah, the anointed one who is to come.
4. A study of Daniel formally introduces us to apocalyptic literature, which takes our thoughts beyond the kingdoms of this world into a concluding kingdom of God, and lays groundwork for much New Testament thought. Understanding apocalyptic literature is necessary to our later understanding the early Christian community.

Before going further, let us identify themes and characteristics of apocalyptic literature:

- Apocalyptic literature reflects the belief that a cosmic struggle is being waged between the forces of good and the forces of evil. This struggle is leading up to a climactic battle in which good will triumph.
- Apocalyptic literature emphasizes eschatology or the study of end times. The "end" usually means the end of a particular age, although it can refer to the end of time as we know it. The basic idea is that the present age is under the influence of evil and that the people of God are suffering persecution. Further, this suffering will increase until God suddenly intervenes on behalf of God's people and brings in a new age of peace and joy.
- Apocalyptic literature often contains images and symbols that at the time of the writing were meant to be unclear and therefore are difficult for readers in later generations to understand. For example, the image of a horn generally represented power; the color white stood for victory or purity.

• Apocalyptic literature is usually pessimistic about the current world order and regards the intervention of God as the only solution to the problems and suffering of God's people.

• Despite its pessimism, apocalyptic literature is designed to give readers a sense of confidence and security. Its primary message is that God is in control of history and God's people will ultimately triumph.

Daniel in Babylon

King Nebuchadnezzar of Babylon destroyed Judah, deported the stronger, younger people in 597 B.C. (Ezekiel was one), and finally destroyed Jerusalem and the Temple in 587 B.C. Apparently Daniel and his young friends were recruited to be trained to serve the empire. They refused to break Jewish food laws and refused to worship Babylonian gods, including images of the kings. Jews in exile have always had to face the difficulty of remaining faithful in a different culture. The Book of Daniel says, Be strong. God will be with you. Just as God was with you in the trials of Egypt, so he was with Shadrach, Meshach, and Abednego in the fiery furnace.

The Book of Daniel delights children yet puzzles scholars. At times the story is as simple as young Jewish men refusing to eat unclean food. At other times the visions and dreams are complex with mighty empires cascading and crashing into one another.

Daniel's message fits any time, but more than any other book in the Old Testament Daniel peers into last days. We see Daniel in broad daylight saying his prayers. Then we stand amazed as he speaks of a kingdom that will never end and of one whose authority will last forever (Daniel 7:14).

Daniel interpreted dreams for Nebuchadnezzar and his successor Belshazzar. Notice that the two kings thought they were all-powerful, but God humbled them. Daniel read the handwriting on the wall. "You have been weighed on the scales and found to be too light" (5:27). Earlier, Isaiah had used a similar image in describing nations:

> "To the LORD the nations are nothing,
> no more than a drop of water" (Isaiah 40:15).

Be strong; the kingdoms of this world come and go. The four beasts are thought to refer to kingdoms: the lion (Babylonian Empire), the bear (Median Empire), the leopard (Persian Empire), and the terrifying dragonlike beast (Greek Empire).

So much of the material in Daniel 7–12 is apocalyptic, visionary, and symbolic that it is difficult to accurately identify. That is for a reason. Either it was written to prepare the people for times of trouble, or it was written to comfort the people during times of trouble by drawing on past courage and wisdom. Most scholars agree that the Book of Daniel was written during the terrible persecution under the rule of Antiochus Epiphanes IV (167–164 B.C.).

NOTES, REFLECTIONS, AND QUESTIONS

Maps showing the extent of the four kingdoms represented in Daniel's vision of the four beasts:

- **Babylonian Empire (defeated Assyria in 612 B.C., sacked Jerusalem, and took the people into exile);**
- **Median and Persian Empires (Persia defeated Babylonia in 539 B.C. and permitted Judean exiles to return home);**
- **Greek Empire (dominated the Middle East during the time between the testaments).**

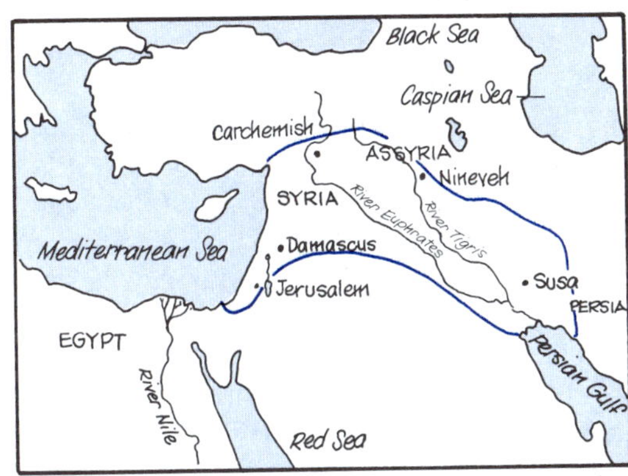

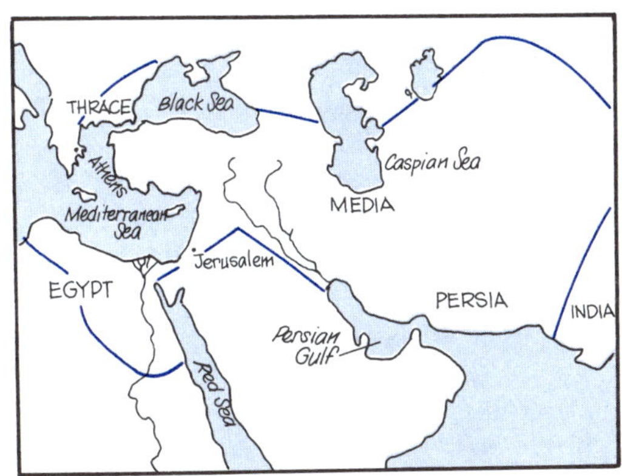

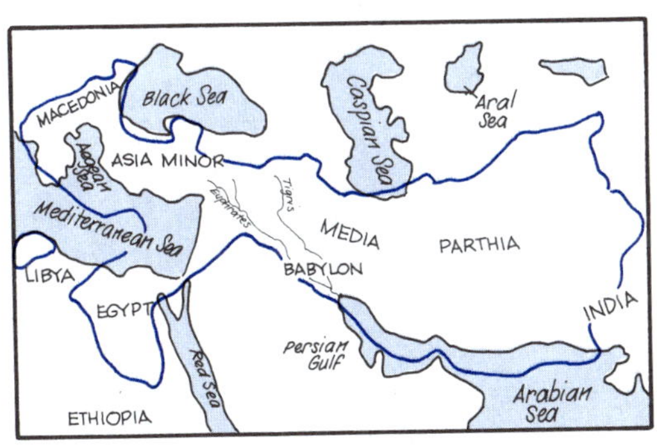

During that time, many people were killed; foreign idols were actually placed in the Temple; Jerusalem was sacked; and Jews were forbidden to observe sabbath and dietary laws, to practice circumcision, or to offer sacrifices in the Temple.

Be strong; do not lose heart; remember whose people you are. Will not the God who rescued Daniel from the pit of lions save his obedient people even from the jaws of persecution?

Apocalyptic Visions

Then the prophet sees even beyond the empires. He sees a kingdom greater than Babylonia or Media or Persia or Greece, a ruler greater than Antiochus Epiphanes IV.

"While I was looking, thrones were put in place. One who had been living forever sat down on one of the thrones. His clothes were white as snow, . . . and the books were opened.

" . . . As I watched, the fourth beast was killed. . . .

"During this vision in the night, I saw what looked like a human being. He was approaching me, surrounded by clouds, and he went to the one who had been living forever and was presented to him. He was given authority, honor, and royal power, ... His authority would last forever, and his kingdom would never end" (Daniel 7:9-14).

The anointed one is anticipated; the kingdom is envisioned. A resurrection of the dead is expected (12:1-3). But the words are now "to be kept secret and hidden until the end comes" (12:9).

The anointed one, or messiah, is foretold by many of the prophets. The one who is to bring in the Kingdom will be "humble and riding on a donkey" (Zechariah 9:9). He will be born in Bethlehem, will rule his people with the strength of the Lord, and will bring peace (Micah 5:2-5). Malachi promised a "messenger to prepare the way," who will be "like a fire that refines metal" (Malachi 3:1-2). Isaiah of Jerusalem wrote:

"A child is born to us!
A son is given to us!
And he will be our ruler.
He will be called, 'Wonderful Counselor,'
'Mighty God,' 'Eternal Father,'
'Prince of Peace' " (Isaiah 9:6).

MARKS OF DISCIPLESHIP

Disciples keep the dream alive. The disciple has a sense of unity with the historic people of God and holds in his or her mind's eye a vision of God's kingdom. People of faith and commitment believe that ultimately God will be victorious and that messiah will reign forever.

NOTES, REFLECTIONS, AND QUESTIONS

As a Christian, when you read about Daniel and his friends refusing foreign foods or declining to worship false idols even though it meant danger of death, what are your thoughts?

What are some ways you stand up for your beliefs?

Describe your vision of God's final kingdom.

IF YOU WANT TO KNOW MORE

Apocrypha means "hidden." Some say "hidden" because the Apocrypha was not included in the Hebrew or Protestant Bibles. It is in Roman Catholic Bibles. Others say "hidden" because it is symbolic and often difficult, apocalyptic. Written during the intertestamental period, the books of the Apocrypha usually depict end times. You might enjoy reading 2 Esdras 1:1–5:20 or portions of Tobit from the Apocrypha. Can you see why these books were not included in our canon?

NOTES, REFLECTIONS, AND QUESTIONS

WAITING

"The LORD Almighty answers, 'I will send my messenger to prepare the way for me. Then the Lord you are looking for will suddenly come to his Temple. The messenger you long to see will come and proclaim my covenant.' "

—Malachi 3:1

17 The Time of Transition

OUR HUMAN PROBLEM

We experience times when, though daily life goes on, we desire something more; something more is necessary. So we wait.

ASSIGNMENT

Sometimes we are confused by the contrast between the Old and New Testaments. Some people talk as if there were two Gods, one of the Old Testament and one of the New Testament, as if one were the God of wrath and one the God of love. There also seems to be a huge gap between the rebuilding of Jerusalem and the coming of Jesus. What happened in those four hundred years?

Read Esther, Jonah, Zechariah, and Malachi, thinking about the situation of the Jewish people and their desire for a political ruler to lead them to independence under the rule of God.

Day 1 Read "The Bible Teaching."
Day 2 Esther 1–4 (to remind us that many Jews were scattered all over the known world)
Day 3 Esther 5–10 (triumph of the Jews over their enemies)
Day 4 Jonah 1–4 (Israel's mission to the world)
Day 5 Zechariah 9; Malachi 2:17–4:6 (desire for a political messiah)
Day 6 Review Lessons 1–16, noting the theme words and how the story of God's chosen people fits the timeline on page 122. Read and respond to "Marks of Discipleship."
Day 7 Rest and prayer.

PRAYER

Pray daily before study:
"O God, you are my God,
and I long for you.
My whole being desires you;
like a dry, worn-out, and waterless land,
my soul is thirsty for you" (Psalm 63:1).

Prayer concerns for this week:

WAITING

Day 1 "The Bible Teaching"

Day 4 Israel's mission to the world

Day 2 Jews scattered over the known world

Day 5 Desire for a political messiah

Day 3 Triumph of the Jews over their enemies

Day 6 The story of God's chosen people

THE BIBLE TEACHING

NOTES, REFLECTIONS, AND QUESTIONS

Remember the fall of Jerusalem in 587 B.C. to the Babylonians. The Jews were taken into exile and remained there for about forty-eight years. In 539 B.C. the Babylonian Empire crumbled under the Persians. Some Jews acted immediately to get back to Jerusalem. This is the beginning of the Persian period.

The Persian Period (539–333 B.C.)

Nehemiah gained permission from Cyrus II, the Persian king, for Jews to go back to Jerusalem. Ezra, a descendant of a priestly family, came from Babylon and gave spiritual leadership in the rebuilding of the Temple. The Temple was completed in 515 B.C.

Nehemiah the layman and Ezra the priest were tough. They had to be, for they rebuilt Jerusalem with opposition from the mixed peoples living in and around Jerusalem and with political tightrope walking with Persia.

As Nehemiah said, they rebuilt the walls of Jerusalem with a weapon in one hand and building materials in the other (Nehemiah 4:17-18).

Although many Jews returned to Israel, the majority did not. This fact is terribly important. Millions of Jews were scattered all over the Mediterranean world. Think for a minute. Some had been exiled from the Northern Kingdom for nearly two hundred years; others, from the Southern Kingdom for two or three generations. They now had jobs, businesses, or were slaves. They had families, often no money, and had become a part of other cultures and climates. Besides, the economic conditions in Israel were bleak indeed. Why go back?

By the third century B.C. an estimated one million Jews lived in Egypt alone.

During this week you will read two magnificent stories, Esther and Jonah. Both were written during the Persian period. Esther barely made it into the canon because the book reveals few religious themes and does not mention God. Yet Queen Esther's courage, the book's explanation of the Jewish festival of Purim, and the political victory put it in the Bible. We are reading it to remind ourselves of the millions of Jews who lived scattered over the known world, often under persecution.

Jonah is a reaction to Ezra. Ezra pulled back from foreigners. Sobered by national tragedy, he determined to be strict. He demanded absolute obedience to the laws of circumcision, sabbath observance, and tithes for Temple support. Most drastic of all, Ezra dictated divorce of all foreign wives (Ezra 9–10). Never had separation been so intense; for now all foreigners, mixed blood, and intermarried people were cut off.

The message of Jonah insists that Israel is to be a light to the Gentiles. A prophet named Jonah was under orders to go to Nineveh (the capital of the old Assyrian Empire, symbolizing the heart of "the enemy") and preach repentance and faith. Like Israel, Jonah resisted. The miracle in the story is that Nineveh repented, something Israel refused to do under the preaching of the prophets. The writer of Jonah, through story, attacks the strict doctrines of separateness that Ezra preached.

Later, when Jesus said, "The only miracle you will be given is the miracle of Jonah" (Matthew 16:4; Luke 11:29-30), he meant that his gospel of repentance and good news would be carried to the Gentiles and, miracle of miracles, they would repent and believe.

The Greek Period (333–199 B.C.)

An important date, and easy to remember, is 333 B.C. Alexander the Great won a decisive victory at Issus over the Persians and began to establish Greek influence throughout the known world. Alexander's goals were cultural. His armies spread Greek language and Greek culture everywhere. Greek money, trade, travel, knowledge, and athletic events spread throughout the Mediterranean lands. New cities, such as Alexandria in Egypt, were established.

The common language in Palestine under the Persians had become Aramaic. But now every educated person could speak and write Greek. People moved about more freely. Trade flourished.

Athletic events, in which athletes participated without clothing, became popular everywhere. The nakedness was strongly opposed by the Jews. Circumcision became an issue. Some Jewish men had surgery to make it appear that they had never been circumcised. They could then compete in the athletic events without being recognized as Jews.

The existence of many Greek gods and philosophies fostered an atmosphere of tolerance and freedom for Jewish religion. Dialogue and debate over philosophical, ethical, and religious matters were common. Many Greeks, like Socrates, were drawn to the idea of one supreme Creator God. Many people under Greek influence studied Judaism and became "God-fearers" or Gentile believers. Some became converts.

The Period of the Seleucids (198–167 B.C.)

After the death of Alexander the Great, the Greek Empire split into several parts governed by his military officers from Egypt to Persia, Babylonia, Syria, Asia Minor and Greece. The area of Palestine and Asia Minor came under the control of an officer named Seleucus and his heirs. This kingdom became the most powerful of all, and its rulers were called Seleucids. When Antiochus IV came to rule (175–163 B.C.), he called himself Epiphanes, "god manifest." This cruel king cracked down hard on the Jews. He forced cultural and religious conformity. He demanded worship of himself as Zeus, built an altar to Zeus in the Temple, and even slaughtered a pig (unclean in Jewish ritual) on the altar.

NOTES, REFLECTIONS, AND QUESTIONS

Alexander the Great (356–323 B.C.), king of Macedonia, conquered Greece, the Persian Empire, and Egypt, and spread Greek culture from Egypt to India. Depicted here in the Battle of Issus.

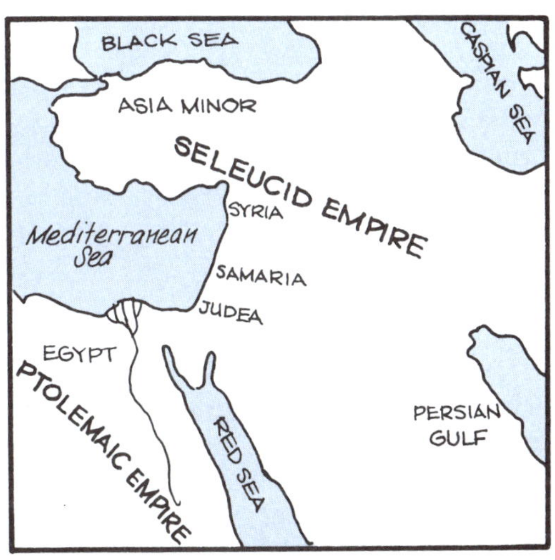

The Seleucid and Ptolemaic Empires during the time between the death of Alexander the Great and the Hasmonean period

He also
- confiscated valuables from the Temple in Jerusalem;
- appointed the office of high priest to the highest bidder;
- rewarded Jews who cooperated with his government;
- called in his troops to put down resistance;
- burned copies of Jewish law;
- outlawed circumcision under penalty of death;
- outlawed sabbath observances and food laws, forcing Jews to eat the flesh of pigs.

The Hasmonean Period (167–63 B.C.)

Under the leadership of the Maccabean family, some Jews took up arms against Antiochus and after violent warfare established a few years of Jewish independence.

Roman Rule (63 B.C. and Beyond)

Roman control over Palestine began in 63 B.C. and flourished under Caesar Augustus, who was emperor from 31 B.C. to A.D. 14. As we read the New Testament, we tend to emphasize Roman brutality because of Herod the Great. But the world experienced the *Pax Romana* (the peace of Rome) for nearly two hundred years. Roman engineers built roads to the farthest reaches of the empire. Later, Christian missionaries like Barnabas and Paul traveled easily because of that peace and those roads, spreading the gospel in a few short years throughout the Mediterranean world.

The Romans took much from Greek culture. They too encouraged trade, often allowed great freedom in religious matters, adopted a universal money system, used Greek language for trade and education, and established regional control with new Roman towns.

Taxation under Greeks, Seleucids, and Romans was a direct taxation plan. Wealthy people (like Zacchaeus in Luke 19:1-10) bid for the right to be "tax farmers." For a price, Rome gave them territories. They hired other people to work as collectors. These "publicans" collected head taxes and property taxes on slaves, cattle, buildings, and so on. They set their rate with few guidelines, paid Rome the required fee, and kept anything else they collected. Tax collectors were considered "sinners" and unclean, not primarily because of their greed but because of their contact with Gentiles.

Religious Life

Jews in exile (the Diaspora) had no Temple, no formal priesthood; they simply met together. So another form of religious life emerged: *synagogue*. *Synagogue* meant "a gathering," but it came to mean "a place of prayer." What happened to the ten lost tribes of Israel? They were not lost at all but were dispersed all over the world, meeting in synagogues in town after town, city after city. Scholars debate about when formal synagogues came into being, but the "gatherings," the assembling for prayer and discussion

NOTES, REFLECTIONS, AND QUESTIONS

Caesar Augustus was the Roman ruler when Jesus was born. Augustus allowed Jews throughout the empire to send money to support the Temple in Jerusalem.

Diaspora is a Greek term that is used to refer to all the Jews who were scattered over the world when the Northern Kingdom was conquered by the Assyrians and the Southern Kingdom was conquered by the Babylonians. After some Jews returned to Judea at the end of the Exile, the term *Diaspora* was still used to describe those Jews who did not return. Now it includes any Jew who does not live in Israel.

were common. As you read Esther, you sense a "networking" for prayer and fasting.

What happened at synagogue? People met daily for prayer. Lay teachers called rabbis emerged. Children were taught. Sabbath worship, consisting of prayer and reading of Scripture with teaching and discussion, was conducted.

The synagogue provided welfare for poverty-stricken Jews and traveling Jews. It was a political center for life in the Jewish community.

As the centuries just before the New Testament time unfolded, the law of Moses became increasingly important. The law sometimes meant Torah (the first five books of the Old Testament), but more often it referred to the entire law with all of the oral traditions and interpretations.

The law was elevated, praised, glorified. Ezra established the law of Moses squarely at the heart of Judaism. So did the rabbis. The goal was to obey the law in every detail and to live perfectly before God. Long before the Temple was destroyed by the Romans in A.D. 70, sacrifice at the Temple was less important than study of the law in the synagogue.

Several religious groups developed within Judaism during the time between the testaments: scribes, Sadducees, Pharisees, Essenes, and Zealots.

The *scribes* were religious lawyers, laymen whose task was to interpret the law, including the oral tradition, sometimes adjusting the law to meet the demands of daily life. Some scribes were Pharisees and some Sadducees, learned men, careful with the law, of whatever party.

The *Sadducees* tended to be wealthy laymen, linked with the high priests and Temple authorities, but many of them were priests. They honored only the five books of Moses as Scripture. They did not believe in resurrection. Politically they cooperated with the Romans in private, discreet ways; yet they preserved Temple worship and sabbath, circumcision, and tithes. They were in continual tension with Pharisees, called "Hasidim" or "pious ones."

The *Pharisees* were laymen who were experts in the oral law and wanted to live strictly according to the law. Pharisees were offended by Greek culture and angered by those who cooperated with foreign powers. The Pharisees really wanted to be holy; they were faithful even in the minute details of the law.

The *Essenes* were one of the strictest groups. They thought everything in the Temple was wrong and corrupt. They lived in the desert at Qumran, where they left the Dead Sea Scrolls.

The *Zealots* were violently opposed to the Roman rule. They prayed for a political messiah to lead the revolt.

MARKS OF DISCIPLESHIP

The God of the universe is one God. God reveals the divine nature in Old and New Testaments, finally showing the very nature of God in Jesus Christ. Our sense of the

NOTES, REFLECTIONS, AND QUESTIONS

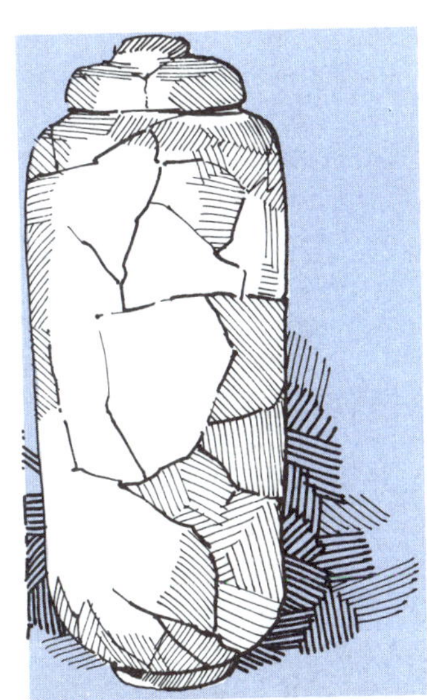

Jar with a lid, from Qumran, the type of container in which the Dead Sea Scrolls were stored

unity of the Bible and our unity with the historic people of God prepare us to hear the gospel of Jesus Christ.

The disciple waits for God's response to his or her desire for something more and trusts that God will respond.

Describe a period of time when you were waiting for something more to happen.

How does it feel to wait?

What connection with God do you feel during your times of waiting?

IF YOU WANT TO KNOW MORE

If you have time, read Haggai and Zechariah. Both books provide glimpses into the time between the testaments.

Chart of Biblical History

2000 B.C.	**Patriarchal period** **Abraham, Isaac, Jacob, Joseph**
1700 B.C.	**Joseph's family enters Egypt**
1260 B.C.	**Moses leads the escape from Egypt**
1220 B.C.	**Joshua leads the people into Canaan**
1210 B.C.	**Beginning of the period of the judges**
1020 B.C.	**Beginning of the monarchy** **Saul, David, Solomon**
935 B.C.	**Division into Northern and Southern Kingdoms after the death of Solomon** **North—Israel (capital: Samaria)** **South—Judah (capital: Jerusalem)**
722 B.C.	**Fall of Samaria to Assyria (capital: Nineveh)**
587 B.C.	**Fall of Jerusalem to Babylonia (capital: Babylon)** **Temple destroyed** **Exile into Babylon**
539 B.C.	**Persian period** **Jews return to Jerusalem**
515 B.C.	**Temple rebuilt**
333 B.C.	**Greek period** **Alexander the Great**
167 B.C.	**Jews revolt (Hasmonean period)**
63 B.C.	**Romans capture Jerusalem**
37 B.C.	**Herod the Great appointed king over Palestine**
4 B.C.	**Birth of Jesus**

NOTES, REFLECTIONS, AND QUESTIONS

THE NEW TESTAMENT

"Jesus left that place, and as he walked along, he saw a tax collector, named Matthew, sitting in his office. He said to him, 'Follow me.'

"Matthew got up and followed him."

—Matthew 9:9

18 Radical Discipleship

OUR HUMAN PROBLEM

We are anxious, concerned about keeping up with everyone around us. We conform to our culture, knowing all the while that it is sick and filled with brokenness and confusion. We fail to see what God requires of us.

ASSIGNMENT

We will study Matthew for two weeks. This week we read Matthew 1:1–13:52, listening for the call to radical discipleship, for descriptions of the Kingdom, and for God's requirements for living in the Kingdom.

Day 1 Matthew 1–2 (birth of Jesus)
Day 2 Matthew 3–4 (radical discipleship)
Day 3 Matthew 5–7 (Sermon on the Mount)
Day 4 Matthew 8–10 (healings, mission of the apostles)
Day 5 Matthew 11:1–13:52 (Jesus' authority)
Day 6 Read and respond to "The Bible Teaching" and "Marks of Discipleship."
Day 7 Rest.

PRAYER

Pray daily before study:
"Give me the desire to obey your laws
rather than to get rich.
Keep me from paying attention to what is worthless;
be good to me, as you have promised.
Keep your promise to me, your servant—
the promise you make to those who obey you" (Psalm 119:36-38).

Prayer concerns for this week:

Day 1 Birth of Jesus

Day 2 Radical discipleship

Day 3 Sermon on the Mount

Day 4 Healings, mission of the apostles

Day 5 Jesus' authority

Day 6 "The Bible Teaching"

DISCIPLE

THE BIBLE TEACHING

Matthew arranged the ancestors of Jesus into three groups of fourteen names each (Matthew 1:17). He omitted a few kings in order to achieve this neatness. The family line is Joseph's, since the usual legal way to trace a person's lineage was through the father's side.

Of extreme interest are the four women named: Tamar, Rahab, Ruth, and Bathsheba. Naming women in a Jewish genealogy was itself unusual, but these women were eyebrow raisers. They were either Gentiles, or their lives were scandalous, or both. Matthew wanted to make the point clear: Jesus Christ came into the sinful world, born of a sin-filled humanity, to save sinners. His name was Jesus, which is the Greek form of *Joshua,* meaning literally, "God is salvation."

Matthew wanted his Jewish readers to understand that Jesus came first of all to his own people, the Jews. However, the wise men, who are thought to have been non-Jews "from the East," show that Jesus came to save Gentiles also.

The Call to Radical Discipleship

Jesus made an absolute demand. When he said, "Follow me," he meant leaving something or someone or some place behind. To obey meant to walk into the unknown without looking back, ready to listen, to learn, to witness, to serve. The word *disciple* means "learner."

Simon and Andrew, James and John left their fishing nets and relatives. Matthew, also called Levi, left his tax office.

Jesus offered other persons radical discipleship, but they would not break loose from the things that held them. Jesus warned a teacher of the law, a prospective disciple, that he would often be sleeping on the ground. We hear no more of the man (Matthew 8:19-20). Another wanted to wait until his elderly father died. "Follow *now,*" said Jesus, and that man also faded (8:21-22). Still later a rich man considered discipleship. "Go and sell all you have . . . ; then come and follow me." But the man "went away sad, because he was very rich" (19:16-22). Even family members cannot stand in the way of discipleship (10:34-39). The Christian must have a single eye, seeking first God's kingdom and God's requirements (6:33; read again 13:44-46).

The Sermon on the Mount (5–7) distills some of Jesus' most demanding statements:

Speak only the truth.
Do not even lust in your hearts.
Get rid of rage from your emotions.
Forgive without measure.
Love your enemies.
Pray in secret.
Wash your face when you fast.
Give without getting credit.
Avoid being judgmental.
Work for peace.

NOTES, REFLECTIONS, AND QUESTIONS

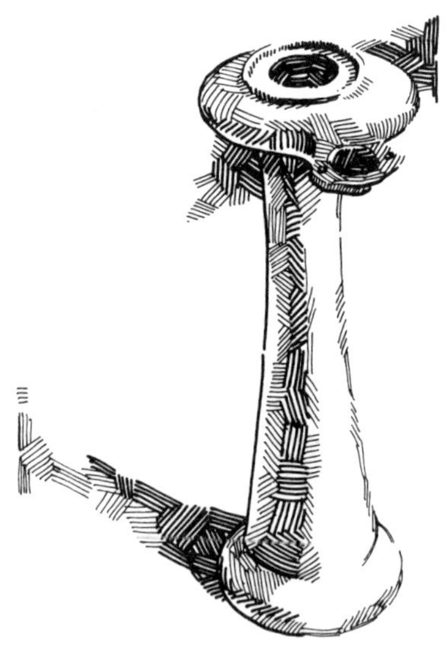

"No one lights a lamp and puts it under a bowl; instead he puts it on the lampstand, where it gives light for everyone in the house. In the same way your light must shine before people, so that they will see the good things you do and praise your Father in heaven" (Matthew 5:15-16).

Jesus' concern for righteousness is evident all through the Sermon on the Mount. This "new Israel" will be a peculiar people. They will live lives of quiet gratitude, simply asking for daily bread, just like the Hebrews receiving manna in the desert. If persecution comes, they should be grateful. Without doubt, these new disciples are expected to be "more faithful than the teachers of the Law and the Pharisees in doing what God requires" (5:20).

The first word in Jesus' ministry was *repent*: "Turn away from your sins" (4:17). Repent means not only to confess and be sorry for your sins but also, and more importantly, to turn around. Repentance means to change directions, have a new way of thinking and living, lead a new life.

What is the new righteousness? It is a life characterized by repentance, a life turned away from the world, now pointed in a fresh Kingdom direction.

Receiving forgiveness and new direction, disciples then extend forgiveness to others daily (as in the Lord's Prayer) and forever (as in seventy times seven). So repentance speaks of new beginnings and of continually fresh commitments to the ways of God.

Mission of the Disciples

The disciples are not just "to be." They are called "to do." The community of faith is sent into mission. A man with a skin disease cried out and was healed (Matthew 8:2-4). A Roman officer asked help for a paralyzed servant. Amazed at the faith of the Gentile soldier, Jesus remarked, "Many will come from the east and the west and sit down with Abraham, Isaac, and Jacob at the feast in the Kingdom of heaven" (8:5-13). In other words, Jesus came for people all over the world. The servant was healed.

After telling that Jesus healed Peter's mother-in-law and others, Matthew recalls the suffering servant passage from Isaiah 53:4: "He himself took our sickness and carried away our diseases" (Matthew 8:17). The prophet Isaiah wanted a reclaimed and recommitted Israel to be in mission. Jesus Christ activates that mission. Keep in mind that Jesus not only heals, cleanses, forgives, but guides and trains the disciples to follow his lead.

Notice that the two men with demons whom Jesus healed knew who Jesus was and called him "Son of God" (8:28-34).

Next Jesus did what only God can do—forgive sins. The paralyzed man was healed. Then he called Matthew the tax collector to be a disciple. At Matthew's dinner party, amid criticism for eating with the tax collectors who were ceremonially unclean and were hated because they collected Roman taxes, Jesus was still claiming people: "I have not come to call respectable people, but outcasts" (9:13).

What is happening? Jesus the Anointed One has come to bring the mission of God into the people's experience. The Kingdom is breaking in.

Now watch: The work of the Kingdom is designed to explode in magnitude. Jesus said to the disciples, "The

NOTES, REFLECTIONS, AND QUESTIONS

harvest is large, but there are few workers to gather it in. Pray to the owner of the harvest that he will send out workers to gather in his harvest" (9:37-38). Jesus actually expected the disciples to do the same things he had been doing! At first they are to go only to the Jews. Later they will go to the whole world. "Go and preach, 'The Kingdom of heaven is near!' Heal the sick, bring the dead back to life, heal those who suffer from dreaded skin diseases, and drive out demons" (10:7-8).

Imagine yourself one of the twelve disciples receiving those orders. Describe how you might have felt.

Secrets of the Kingdom

Now Jesus is ready to take the Twelve deeper into spiritual understanding. So much is hidden from their eyes. They must be taught.

John the Baptist sent messengers from his prison to ask, "Are you the one John said was going to come?" Jesus answered, "Go back and tell John what you are hearing and seeing: the blind can see, the lame can walk, those who suffer from dreaded skin diseases are made clean, the deaf hear, the dead are brought back to life, and the Good News is preached to the poor. How happy are those who have no doubts about me!" (Matthew 11:2-6). Most people expected a different kind of messiah. Jesus is interpreting the kind of messiah he is.

The Kingdom parables are mysterious yet life-changing. Generally a parable has one and only one point. When Jesus told a parable, it was a teaching device, a story to be told over and over by the community of faith. When you read a parable, try to understand the one essential meaning.

What is the point of the parable of the sower (13:3-9)?

The kingdom of God, like Israel, is not a place of isolation. Bible religion is not solitary, between you and God only. Bible salvation is corporate. We live out our faith in community, not all by ourselves.

Jesus wanted his disciples to be more concerned about moral law than ceremonial law. Recall that Jesus said he did not come to get rid of the law but to make its teaching come true (5:17). "This means, then, that every teacher of the Law who becomes a disciple in the Kingdom of heaven is like a homeowner who takes new and old things out of his storage room" (13:52).

The people of the Kingdom will draw upon old and new, the law of Moses and the teachings of Jesus. The old is not thrown away.

NOTES, REFLECTIONS, AND QUESTIONS

Why do you think it was important that Jesus explained his connection to the Law?

Some Jewish teachers, building on oral tradition, were "majoring in minors." Jesus focused on spiritual matters.

Jesus also was establishing community with all kinds of people whom the food ceremonies cut off. He ate with Jews who didn't wash their hands properly. He drank water from the hands of a Samaritan woman. Relationships are more important than rituals. The holiness of the new community would be a kind of holiness that would break down barriers rather than build up barriers between people.

MARKS OF DISCIPLESHIP

Can you see how often the church makes discipleship seem too easy? "Accept Jesus Christ as your Lord and Savior" is so true but often superficial, lacking the radical demands, the total commitment of discipleship: Give up everything and follow Jesus.

Have you responded to Christ's call, "Follow me"? In your own words, describe where you are in your discipleship.

Sometimes things or people or attitudes that we are unwilling to turn away from hold us back. Part of being a radical disciple is repentance. What in your life do you need to turn away from forever?

Why does the church often settle for making church members instead of making disciples?

IF YOU WANT TO KNOW MORE

Chart of Biblical History

4 B.C. **Birth of Jesus**

The Sermon on the Mount (5–7) contains some of the highest ethical insights ever proclaimed. Study it carefully. The Beatitudes (5:3-12) are the "essence of the essence." Paraphrase the eight Beatitudes in your own words.

NOTES, REFLECTIONS, AND QUESTIONS

THREAT

"If anyone wants to come with me, he must forget himself, carry his cross, and follow me. For whoever wants to save his own life will lose it; but whoever loses his life for my sake will find it."

—Matthew 16:24-25

19 Mounting Controversy

OUR HUMAN PROBLEM

We want the power to decide what is right and wrong. Jesus is a constant threat to our ways. His lifestyle conflicts with our values, and his word contradicts our life patterns. We hope he will go away; but when he does not, we reject, make fun of, and finally crucify him.

ASSIGNMENT

This week as we study, we look especially for value clashes, religious controversy, and political conflicts. We will read slowly and ponder what is classically called the Passion (entry into Jerusalem, Last Supper, garden of Gethsemane, trial, Crucifixion, and Resurrection).

Day 1 Matthew 13:53–18:35 (conflicts and miracles, Jesus' example to his followers)
Day 2 Matthew 19–23 (religious and political conflicts, entry into Jerusalem)
Day 3 Matthew 24–25 (the coming judgment)
Day 4 Matthew 26 (Last Supper, betrayal, trial before Caiaphas)
Day 5 Matthew 27–28 (trial before Pilate, the Crucifixion, the Resurrection, the Great Commission)
Day 6 Read and respond to "The Bible Teaching" and "Marks of Discipleship."
Day 7 Rest.

PRAYER

Pray daily before study:
"Be good to me, your servant,
so that I may live and obey your teachings.
Open my eyes, so that I may see
the wonderful truths in your law.
I am here on earth for just a little while;
do not hide your commands from me"
(Psalm 119:17-19).

Prayer concerns for this week:

THREAT

Day 1 Conflicts and miracles, Jesus' example to his followers

Day 4 Last Supper, betrayal, trial before Caiaphas

Day 2 Religious and political conflicts, entry into Jerusalem

Day 5 Trial before Pilate, Crucifixion, Resurrection, Great Commission

Day 3 The coming judgment

Day 6 "The Bible Teaching"

THE BIBLE TEACHING

NOTES, REFLECTIONS, AND QUESTIONS

The tension began with the birth. When the wise men from the East (Gentiles) asked, "Where is the baby born to be the king of the Jews?" (Matthew 2:2), a political crisis arose. This was because Herod the Great carried precisely that title, and he feared anyone who might claim the throne.

Matthew contrasts the two kings who command allegiance, Herod (and his successors) and Jesus. Herod the Great, extremely paranoid, was ruler of Judea at the time of Jesus' birth. He murdered his wife, his three sons, his mother-in-law, his brother-in-law, his uncle, plus all the boy babies in Bethlehem to protect that title. He began the restoration of Zerubbabel's Temple and rebuilt the seaport of Caesarea. He was one of the most important rulers in the Roman Empire, and his purpose was always to protect that status.

Herod Antipas, son of Herod the Great, became ruler of Galilee and Perea at his father's death. He is the Herod who executed John the Baptist. The Herods used all their resources to hold on to their earthly power.

Jesus, by contrast, was born in a tiny village of Jewish peasant stock, a refugee in Egypt (like the Hebrew slaves), a carpenter in the poorest section of the country. He had no wealth or political power and rejected the title of king (the common notion of messiah was that of a political leader). Peter called him Messiah (Christ, Anointed One). The Romans nailed the title "King of the Jews" to the cross (27:37).

Matthew contrasts the Herods, powerful rulers and representatives of the Roman Empire, and Jesus, who filled the dual role of successor to King David and Son of God, the only true ruler of the Jews. The contrast and the conflict between the Herods and Jesus go through the Gospel from beginning to end.

Herod's slaughter of the boy babies in Bethlehem reminds us that Pharaoh was drowning Hebrew boy babies in Egypt at the time Moses was born. The "slaughter of the innocents" is not to be passed over lightly. Jesus' coming caused evil forces to rage. Also, lest we reduce the birth of God's Son to candles and carols, this account reminds us that Jesus was born into the real world of political arrogance, warfare, bloodletting.

Controversy

Jesus' preaching immediately became controversial, "The word of God is alive and active, sharper than any double-edged sword. It cuts all the way through, to where soul and spirit meet" (Hebrews 4:12). Jesus said he did not come to do away with the law of Moses and the teachings of the prophets, but to make their teachings come true (Matthew 5:17-20). But look how he interpreted the law: "You have heard that people were told in the past, 'Do not commit murder [the law of Moses].' . . . But now I tell you: whoever is angry with his brother will be brought to trial" (5:21-22). No wonder the leaders of the Jews began to ask, Who does Jesus think he is to redefine the law of Moses? Where does he get his authority?

"You have heard that it was said, 'An eye for an eye, and a tooth for a tooth' [Exodus 21:24]. But now I tell you: . . . . If anyone slaps you on the right cheek, let him slap your left cheek too" (Matthew 5:38-39). Remember when we studied the law of Moses we learned that the law of a tooth for a tooth created justice and stopped terrible retributions (a life for a tooth). Now Jesus asked what seemed impossible—returning kindness, love, generosity in the face of shame, offense, injury. His words reversed the common understanding of justice.

Jesus' attack on superficiality was devastating, particularly in regard to religious pomp and hypocrisy. Why do we wear masks, pretend, show off? Are we like Adam and Eve covering themselves (Genesis 3:7)?

As you read Matthew, notice Jesus' strong condemnation of people who crave titles, places of honor, outward recognition (Matthew 6:1-7). Such people make a show of being religious. We ought to tithe, Jesus said, but we dare not neglect such important teachings of the law as justice and mercy and honesty (Matthew 23:23).

Jesus challenges us economically too. Everyone worries about what clothes to wear, whether they will have enough food to eat. He said, "These are the things the pagans [non-Jews] are always concerned about" (6:32). We are too. And to say God will clothe us and feed us if we are "concerned above everything else with the Kingdom of God and with what he requires" (6:33) threatens our two-car, two-job, money-hungry society.

Tension With Religious Leaders

To understand the New Testament, we must know something about four influential religious groups of the period.

Pharisees. Laymen, not priests, forerunners of rabbis, teachers in local synagogues. Serious about keeping and interpreting the religious laws, including all the oral interpretations. Pharisees had authority to interpret Scripture in the synagogue. They recognized Jesus as a teacher, so they had long discussions with him. They were conservative keepers of the law yet made room for mystery, freedom, resurrection. Great influence with the people.

Essenes. Second largest group, scattered in all the towns, later isolated in Judean wilderness preserving the "Dead Sea Scrolls." Thought everything in the Temple was wrong; believed the priests were illegitimate, the Temple corrupt. Conscientious, legalistic, conservative. Celibate, no marriage, no children (except those adopted by the community). Prayed for messiah, believed in "end times."

Sadducees. Priestly families, mostly living in Jerusalem and Jericho, descendants of Zadok who anointed Solomon.

NOTES, REFLECTIONS, AND QUESTIONS

Wealthy, "old-line families" who took Greek and Roman ways into their lives. Believed God rewarded the good with health and wealth, punished the evil with sickness and poverty. No heaven or hell, no resurrection. Cooperated with Romans to preserve Temple worship and their position. Controlled the ruling Sanhedrin during Jesus' ministry. Their concern: Temple worship.

Zealots. Violently opposed the Roman occupation. Eager for revolt, praying for a messiah-king to lead the uprising. Consisted of ex-slaves, superpatriots, and some outlaws. Four beliefs: (a) served no one but God; (b) opposed slavery; (c) violently opposed Rome (don't pay taxes or cooperate; hide a sword in your bed, ready for messiah); (d) preferred death, even by suicide, to slavery; willing to die for the cause.

Now let us see why Jesus came into conflict with these religious groups. Remember what we learned in the Old Testament. Abraham was blessed to be a blessing (Genesis 12:2-3). Israel is to be a light to the nations (Isaiah 42:6). Instead, however, close fellowship became exclusion, sabbath observance became a set of rules, and food laws made fellowship with others impossible.

When Jesus said about the Roman officer, "I tell you, I have never found anyone in Israel with faith like this" (Matthew 8:10), his statement offended the Zealots. When he ate with ceremonially unclean people at Matthew's dinner, his action offended the Pharisees in particular, because they were meticulous in keeping food laws and avoiding sinners as a form of righteousness (9:10-13). Jesus, like Hosea, argued that love was more important than ceremony. "I want your constant love, not your animal sacrifices. I would rather have my people know me than burn offerings to me" (Hosea 6:6).

But Jesus went further than the prophet: He came *precisely* to bring sinners, outcasts, and alienated people back into fellowship.

Jesus' inclusiveness offended. Jewish men of the times offered a daily prayer thanking God that they had not been born a slave, a Gentile, or a woman. Matthew stresses Jesus' attention to the poor, the outcast, the untouchable, and the foreigner. Remember the Canaanite woman (Matthew 15:21-28), the man with the skin disease (8:2-3), the Roman officer and his servant (8:5-10), as well as Matthew's outcast sinner friends (9:9-10).

A Different Messiah

The tension mounted when Jesus confronted the disciples in Caesarea Philippi, asking, "Who do you say I am?" (Matthew 16:15). He was doing two things: establishing their faith in him as Messiah, and equally important, clarifying what kind of Messiah he was to be. "Jesus began to say plainly to his disciples, 'I must go to Jerusalem and suffer much from the elders, the chief priests, and the

NOTES, REFLECTIONS, AND QUESTIONS

teachers of the Law. I will be put to death, but three days later I will be raised to life' " (16:21).

The Messiah was going to suffer. The Christian community would suffer as well. But look at what happened. When Jesus said that he must go to Jerusalem to suffer, Peter protested. Jesus rebuked him severely (16:22-23). Why? Because Jesus was walking the way of the cross. We will walk it too. The cross of Jesus will be the standard for the Christian community. We will be saved by that cross. We will live by that cross. "If anyone wants to come with me, he must forget himself, carry his cross, and follow me" (16:24). We are beginning to see what membership in the Kingdom means and what leadership in the church means.

The people thought messiah would come in power, a conquering hero on a white horse. They forgot the words of the prophet Isaiah:

"We despised him and rejected him;
he endured suffering and pain" (Isaiah 53:3).

Instead, they remembered the psalms of political victory and the prophetic promise of a free and independent nation.

Jesus carefully planned the entry into Jerusalem. He must try to present the Messiah not as a political King David but as God's compassionate and holy, yet vulnerable, Son-Messenger.

So he fulfilled the words of the prophet Zechariah:

"Look, your king is coming to you!
He comes triumphant and victorious,
but humble and riding on a donkey. . . .
Your king will make peace among the nations"
(Zechariah 9:9-10).

But if you read the entire chapter (Zechariah 9), you will understand that people saw Jesus' entry into Jerusalem in the context of a political messiah.

Nowhere is the coming Anointed One more vividly portrayed than when Jesus looked out over the holy city and said, "Jerusalem, Jerusalem! You kill the prophets and stone the messengers God has sent you! How many times I wanted to put my arms around all your people, just as a hen gathers her chicks under her wings, but you would not let me!" (Matthew 23:37). In Luke, our Lord saw the city and "wept over it, saying, 'If you only knew today what is needed for peace! But now you cannot see it!' " (Luke 19:41-42).

Picture in your mind Jesus standing looking over your town or city or country. What would he weep about?

____

____

____

NOTES, REFLECTIONS, AND QUESTIONS

Gathering Storm

Why were the religious leaders afraid of Jesus? Because if Jesus stirred up trouble, the Romans would come down hard on them. When the high priest said that it was better for one man to die for the people rather than for the nation to be destroyed (John 11:50), he meant it. A rebellion could destroy everyone, especially the Temple.

When the Pharisees asked Jesus to quiet the crowd on Palm Sunday (Luke 19:39-40), they were afraid the Roman soldiers would see them as an unruly mob disturbing the peace and kill hundreds.

Who killed Jesus? No one wanted to take the blame. The Sanhedrin, though offended by Jesus' teachings, though certain of his blasphemy, wanted him executed by Rome. So they charged him not with breaking the Jewish law but with resisting Roman authority. Pilate tried to pass the buck to Herod Antipas, who had killed John the Baptist. But Herod had to go back to Galilee. Pilate had Jesus whipped, which meant almost certain death through loss of blood, infection, or tetanus. No wonder Jesus could not carry his cross.

When Sanhedrin leaders demanded Jesus' death as an enemy of Rome, Pilate did the deed yet put the blame on the religious leaders once again. The title "King of the Jews" meant another rebel had been stamped out. (Notice that Pilate and Herod became friends over this incident; Luke 23:12.)

Perhaps Jesus was saddest of all over being crucified as a common Zealot, his messiahship misunderstood.

Who killed Jesus? Every hand lifted in anger, every lie, every act of self-interest. You and I and all the sinners of the world drove the nails.

MARKS OF DISCIPLESHIP

God came into the world in Christ Jesus, upsetting the world's systems, not by force but by a voluntary, vulnerable love that lays claim upon us. In experiencing that love and that claim, the disciple gives up show and pretense and becomes vulnerable, entering into a ministry of making disciples, teaching, baptizing, witnessing, healing, even if this lifestyle leads to conflict and tension as it did for our Lord.

As you look at your experience so far in the DISCIPLE study, what areas of your life have changed because of the freedom Jesus brings?

____

____

____

NOTES, REFLECTIONS, AND QUESTIONS

In what areas of your life does Jesus continue to threaten your values, your lifestyle?

As a participant in the Kingdom community, what tension, if any, are you experiencing in our society, our economic or political system? with your neighbors and friends? in your church? in your school?

Special Assignment

Because the commands are clear in Matthew 25, make one visit during the week to one of the following places or persons: a drug rehabilitation center or rescue mission, a hospital, a cancer patient, a nursing home, a jail or penitentiary, a shut-in, a person with a handicapping condition, a teenager who does not go to church, a person on social welfare, a person of another race. If appropriate, take a small gift (toothpaste to jail, cookies to shut-ins, reading material, flowers). Don't do all the talking; be there to listen.

Especially try to go into a situation where you have never been before. Be ready to tell the group members next week about your experience and what you learned about yourself.

IF YOU WANT TO KNOW MORE

Chart of Biblical History

A.D. **29–30** **Crucifixion of Jesus**

In a Bible dictionary, look up the following people who were involved in the Crucifixion and jot down a descriptive note or two about each one: Judas Iscariot, Caiaphas, Pilate, Barabbas, Simon of Cyrene, Mary Magdalene, Joseph of Arimathea, Herod Antipas (see Luke 23:6-12).

NOTES, REFLECTIONS, AND QUESTIONS

GOOD NEWS

" 'The right time has come,' he said, 'and the Kingdom of God is near! Turn away from your sins and believe the Good News!' "

—Mark 1:15

20 The Hidden Messiah

OUR HUMAN PROBLEM

Like the disciples, we do not understand who Jesus is. Sometimes we half understand, or misunderstand, or refuse to understand. We especially close our eyes and ears to his call for *self-denial* and *suffering*. This "good news" sounds like bad news to us. We know that bombs and dollars and headlines are powerful. We have difficulty trusting that Jesus is more powerful.

ASSIGNMENT

As you read Mark's Gospel, notice the urgency, the sense of intensity and movement. Observe Mark's emphasis on Jesus' actions.

Day 1 Mark 1–4 (Jesus chooses the Twelve, parables of the Kingdom)
Day 2 Mark 5–8 (preaching and healing)
Day 3 Mark 9–11 (Transfiguration, entry into Jerusalem)
Day 4 Mark 12–14 (Great Commandment, Passover meal)
Day 5 Mark 15–16 (Crucifixion, Resurrection)
Day 6 Read and respond to "The Bible Teaching" and "Marks of Discipleship."
Day 7 Rest.

PRAYER

Pray daily before study:

"Everything you do, O God, is holy.
No god is as great as you.
You are the God who works miracles;
you showed your might among the nations"
(Psalm 77:13-14).

Prayer concerns for this week:

GOOD NEWS

Day 1 Jesus chooses the Twelve, parables of the Kingdom

Day 2 Preaching and healing

Day 3 Transfiguration, entry into Jerusalem

Day 4 Great Commandment, Passover meal

Day 5 Crucifixion, Resurrection

Day 6 "The Bible Teaching"

THE BIBLE TEACHING

NOTES, REFLECTIONS, AND QUESTIONS

As you read Mark's Gospel, you may think, Haven't I read this before? You have, in Matthew. The Synoptic Gospels—Matthew, Mark, and Luke—have much common material. Both Matthew and Luke may have had the Gospel of Mark in front of them as they wrote. Many scholars think Mark was the first Gospel written. *Synoptic* means "seen alongside."

Mark has a special thrust. The Son of God proclaims the Kingdom and demands repentance, turning away from sins—now! Mark is the urgent evangelist. His Gospel is filled with action. The pace is rapid. Mark also shows that people did not understand until *after* the Crucifixion and Resurrection that Jesus was the Messiah. Mark does not record the birth stories, the Sermon on the Mount, or many of the parables. Instead he starts with the baptism and ends with the Resurrection, giving a short, powerful account of the ministry of Jesus.

The opening verse sets the stage: "This is the Good News about Jesus Christ, the Son of God" (Mark 1:1). Mark will write about the gospel, which means "good news," of Jesus the promised Messiah, strong Son of God, sent to save. He will show how the disciples were slow to understand, especially when the idea of suffering entered the picture.

In our study of Mark we will emphasize the power of Jesus Christ, the mystery of who he was and what his ministry was to be before the Crucifixion and Resurrection events, and the good news we now can receive.

The ministry begins with the baptism of Jesus by his relative John. All followers of Jesus are baptized as he commanded in Matthew 28:19 for purification, cleansing, initiation, and commitment. The Holy Spirit came upon Jesus, and his powerful ministry was ready to begin.

Jesus went into the desert, alone with the desolation, the animals, Satan (in Hebrew, "the Opposition"), and God. He stayed for forty days, symbolic of the Israelites' forty years in the Sinai, working out the nature of his ministry through prayer and fasting.

Jesus emerged from the desert preaching his first, and essential, sermon: " 'The right time has come,' he said, 'and the Kingdom of God is near! Turn away from your sins and believe the Good News!' " (Mark 1:15).

The people believed that someday God's kingdom would come when nations would "hammer their swords into plows" (Isaiah 2:4), when the blind would see and the hungry would be given food (Psalm 146). What happened? Jesus brought signs of the Kingdom. He healed a blind man, fed the multitude. The prophecies were being fulfilled!

The Jews were expecting God to act in such a way that God's rule would be acknowledged by Israel and the world.

Instead, a carpenter came out of Nazareth, announcing, "the Kingdom of God is near! Turn away from your sins" (Mark 1:15). Men and women were called to participate in the Kingdom—to change or to be changed radically into citizens of a new society, a new reign, a new way of living.

Jesus announced the Kingdom; even more, he ushered in the Kingdom. But the Jews were praying for a political messiah; the Romans feared a revolt. Jesus continually tried to interpret his Kingdom, but people could not understand.

When Jesus preached or taught or healed, he announced the reign of God. When he prayed, broke bread, took a child in his arms, touched a person with a skin disease, he activated the rule of God. God's power and kingdom were present in the words and acts of Jesus. Mark emphasizes mysterious power that would not be understood until after the Resurrection. Even the signs of the Kingdom were misinterpreted as signs of a hoped-for political messiah. That Jesus had power there was no doubt.

Power Over Evil Spirits

The most dramatic story of our Lord's power over evil spirits is in Mark 5:1-20. The man hurt himself, screamed, lived among the dead. He said his name was Mob. Jesus drove evil spirits out of the man. The evil spirits understood that they were confronting the power of God, but the people did not understand.

Power Over Disease and Physical Problems

Jesus "healed many who were sick with all kinds of diseases" (Mark 1:34). In Mark 1:40-42, Jesus healed a man who was sick with a dreaded skin disease. The healings were signs of the Kingdom, because where God's rule is acknowledged, disease is brought under God's power and control.

Some physical problems are caused by accident rather than disease. Others are present from birth. The deaf man (7:32-35) was not sick, had not sinned, was not ceremonially unclean. He could not hear and did not speak clearly. Jesus made him whole.

The Son of God is working to restore God's original harmonious creation. In Romans 8:21-22, Paul declared that "creation itself would one day be set free from its slavery to decay. . . . all of creation groans with pain, like the pain of childbirth."

Power Over Sin

Jesus dismissed the popular notion that *all* illness was caused by sin (John 9:1-3). But in Mark 2:1-12, the man's problem *was* sin and his need was forgiveness. His friends lowered their helpless companion through an opening in the roof. Mark's Gospel wants us to know that forgiveness and God's kingdom go together and that Jesus has the power to forgive sins.

NOTES, REFLECTIONS, AND QUESTIONS

NOTES, REFLECTIONS, AND QUESTIONS

Power Over Sabbath

Recall that the first Creation story (Genesis 1:1–2:4) was given to us to teach us to trust God and rest one day in seven. A saying of the Jews was, "We keep the sabbath; God keeps us." Nothing was more precious, nothing had become more complicated with protective laws and teachings, than sabbath. The day of rest (Friday sundown until Saturday sundown) had become a legal confusion. Sabbath keeping was difficult for some, tedious for others.

The issue is drawn sharply in Mark 3:1-6. Jewish law permitted medical attention on sabbath to save a person's life. A paralyzed hand could wait. Jesus deliberately asked if he could "help" on sabbath but got no answer.

So Jesus' view was that "The Sabbath was made for the good of man; man was not made for the Sabbath. So the Son of Man is Lord even of the Sabbath" (2:27-28). It is all right to do good, to heal, to extend mercy. Sabbath is to restore, not to restrict.

The early Christians rested on sabbath, the seventh day, and also worshiped on Resurrection Day, the first day of the week. By the early second century A.D., the first day of the week, Sunday, had become sabbath to them. Sunday became "the Lord's day" for most Gentile Christians.

Power Over Nature

There is disharmony. Mark records several times when Jesus exercised power over nature.

He stilled the storm (Mark 4:35-41).

He walked on the water (6:45-52).

Jesus' word was the word of power: "Courage! . . . Don't be afraid!" (6:50). Mark declares that the disciples did not understand with whom they were dealing. They were awestruck and confused.

Feeding the five thousand (6:30-44) was also an evidence of power over nature. What a Kingdom sign!

Power Over Death

The account of Jesus' raising Jairus's daughter from the dead (Mark 5:22-24, 35-43) has two problems. First, did Jesus have power to raise the dead? Second, was Jairus's daughter really dead? Mark gives us the story the way he received it. The early church had no doubt that Jesus had the power.

More important for Mark was Jesus' teaching about resurrection. He clearly told the Sadducees that their disbelief in resurrection was wrong (12:18-27).

Most important, Mark was leading up to our Lord's resurrection. When Jesus was raised from the dead, it made the matter of Jairus's daughter an irrelevant point. Whether she was in a coma or whether Jesus referred to death as "sleep" became insignificant. Her raising was another sign of the Kingdom.

The Hidden Messiah

Did you wonder, as you read Mark, why Jesus kept telling people to be quiet, not to tell others? For example, when the people with the evil spirits screamed, "You are the Son of God!" he ordered the evil spirits "not to tell anyone who he was" (Mark 3:11-12). After raising the twelve-year-old daughter of Jairus, he ordered the people not to tell anyone (5:43). He entered a house in the territory of the city of Tyre "and did not want anyone to know he was there, but he could not stay hidden" (7:24). When Peter said, "You are the Messiah," Jesus "ordered the disciples, 'Do not tell anyone about me' " (8:29-30). When Peter, James, and John came down the mountain after the Transfiguration, Jesus "ordered them, 'Don't tell anyone what you have seen, until the Son of Man has risen from death' " (9:9).

Why the mystery? Why the secrecy? With all the spiritual power being shown, why the request to keep it quiet?

Mark even suggests that Jesus used parables so people would not understand. At least he says that Jesus did not speak to the people "without using parables, but when he was alone with his disciples, he would explain everything to them" (4:34).

Didn't Jesus want people to know? Yes, but to know what? That is the point. They must have a right understanding of messiah. Jesus was not using reverse psychology, as some have suggested, telling people to be quiet, knowing that would make them even more talkative.

The efforts toward secrecy were neither reverse psychology nor false modesty. Jesus knew they were not understanding who he was. They wanted his power to become political; Jesus knew his love power would be vulnerable. They would wave branches and try to make him king; he would ride humbly on a donkey. They would see the healings as magic or miracle; he wanted the healings to call people to repentance and faith. Jesus was not running a sideshow or building momentum for a power play. He was preparing to offer himself as a sacrifice for the sins of the whole world.

He tried to explain to the disciples, but even they could not understand the nature of his sonship, the character of the Kingdom, the power of his suffering servant role until he was crucified and raised from the dead.

Jesus offered the world his power. He was in control. After his experience in Gethsemane (Mark 14:36), Jesus did what love does: He placed himself in the hands of others. So when Judas kissed him, Peter denied him, men spat on him, messiah was being reinterpreted. When the soldiers stripped him naked for crucifixion, as was the custom, they took his garments, one each—his head turban, his sash, his sandals, and his outer robe—and gambled for the inner tunic. It was the symbol, like the body on the cross, of total helplessness, total vulnerability, love laid open.

NOTES, REFLECTIONS, AND QUESTIONS

Thus when Jesus said, "It is finished!" (John 19:30), he meant he had given the world the active power of God's love and the passive helplessness of God's love. He gave it all.

NOTES, REFLECTIONS, AND QUESTIONS

MARKS OF DISCIPLESHIP

The disciple understands the Messiah as suffering servant and the Kingdom as one ruled by vulnerable love. How, then, would you describe the ministry of the disciple of this Messiah, in this Kingdom?

Being a disciple sometimes calls for self-denial and suffering. When have you experienced self-denial or suffering in order to be a disciple?

Most people see power in huge business enterprises, great political organizations, or mighty military machines. Christ's power seems hidden, weak, vulnerable. Yet Christians see a mighty spiritual power in Jesus.

Where do you see the spiritual power of Jesus Christ being displayed in our world today?

Have you personally experienced the power of Jesus Christ? When and how?

Disciples are not only *proof* of the power of Jesus Christ to call, to forgive, to save; they are also supposed to be a community that displays new Kingdom signs. Is your faith community causing people to see hints of the breakthrough of God's rule? What Kingdom signs are you doing?

Special Assignment if You Are Meeting During Lent

Look up Lent. What is it? How long? What is the symbolism of forty days? (See Mark 1:13; Genesis 7:12; Exodus 16:35; 34:28.) Would your DISCIPLE group be willing to fast during Lent by missing one meal a week, using that hour for study and prayer, and giving the money you saved to the church's Lenten offering for hungry people? Please discuss, and, if possible, enter into a covenant together.

IF YOU WANT TO KNOW MORE

Matthew was a tax collector. So was Zacchaeus (Luke 19:2). So were some of Matthew's friends who may have become believers (Matthew 9:9-13). What was a tax collector? How were they looked upon and treated? See *tax collectors, clean,* and *unclean* in a Bible dictionary.

NOTES, REFLECTIONS, AND QUESTIONS

LEAST

"The Spirit of the Lord is upon me,
because he has chosen me to bring good news to the poor.
He has sent me to proclaim liberty to the captives
and recovery of sight to the blind,
to set free the oppressed
and announce that the time has come
when the Lord will save his people."

—Luke 4:18-19

21 God Seeks the Least, the Last, the Lost

OUR HUMAN PROBLEM

I don't really like the poor. They're not always clean. I stay away from sick people. They smell bad. I don't understand people whose customs, culture, and ways of thinking are different from mine. They make me feel uncomfortable. I don't want to go to church or school with them. Actually, I enjoy being with people who are just like me.

ASSIGNMENT

For the most part this week we will be reading the portions of Luke that are unique to Luke's Gospel.

Day 1 Luke 1–2; 4:1-13 (births of John the Baptist and Jesus, temptation)
Day 2 Luke 9:51–12:59 (mission of the seventy-two, parables of watchfulness and faithfulness)
Day 3 Luke 13–15 (teaching and healing, parables of the lost)
Day 4 Luke 16:1–19:27 (parables of stewardship and prayer, Zacchaeus)
Day 5 Luke 19:28–24:53 (entry into Jerusalem, Passion, walk to Emmaus)
Day 6 Read and respond to "The Bible Teaching" and "Marks of Discipleship."
Day 7 Rest.

PRAYER

Pray daily before study:
"I am weak and poor;
come to me quickly, O God.
You are my savior and my LORD—
hurry to my aid!" (Psalm 70:5).

Prayer concerns for this week:

Day 1 Births of John the Baptist and Jesus, temptation

Day 4 Parables of stewardship and prayer, Zacchaeus

Day 2 Mission of the seventy-two, parables of watchfulness and faithfulness

Day 5 Entry into Jerusalem, Passion, walk to Emmaus

Day 3 Teaching and healing, parables of the lost

Day 6 "The Bible Teaching"

THE BIBLE TEACHING

NOTES, REFLECTIONS, AND QUESTIONS

The Gospel of Luke is the first volume of the two-volume work Luke-Acts. The first verses of Luke and Acts help us understand why and how each book was written. Read again Luke 1:1-4. Who was Theophilus? Apparently a socially prominent Gentile Christian. The name means "lover of God." Look to see how the second volume (Acts) begins.

The Birth of Jesus

Uniquely in Luke we read about the birth of John the Baptist, Jesus' relative, who came before him:

"Someone is shouting in the desert:
'Get the road ready for the Lord' " (Luke 3:4; see Isaiah 40:3).

In Mary's song of praise, the powerful Magnificat (Luke 1:46-55), Mary set the tone for Luke's Gospel—the mighty action of God on behalf of the poor.

Luke records the visit of the shepherds. Taking care of sheep at night was a miserable job—a job for old men, crippled men, or boys too poor or too young for other work. They were the "least" who heard the angels and knelt first at the manger (2:8-20).

Mary and Joseph kept the Jewish law and tradition by having Jesus circumcised on the eighth day (2:21). (Remember Abraham and the covenant people; Genesis 17:9-14.) The ceremony for Mary's purification came thirty-three days after Jesus' circumcision. Joseph and Mary offered a poor woman's sacrifice, two doves instead of a lamb (Luke 2:22-24; see Leviticus 12). The mother of the Lamb of God could not afford a lamb to sacrifice.

When Simeon took Jesus in his arms (Luke 2:25-35), he offered a prayer of thanks, which also established Luke's theme of the *universality* of Christ's mission:

"A light to reveal your will to the Gentiles
and bring glory to your people Israel" (2:32).

Luke again emphasizes the universality of Jesus' ministry in his genealogy (3:23-38), which traces Jesus' ancestors back to Adam rather than only to Abraham.

The devotion of Joseph and Mary to the law and tradition is shown not only by the circumcision and purification ceremonies but by their annual Passover trip to Jerusalem (2:41). Going to Jerusalem every year was expensive for poor people because of oppressive taxes, especially Roman "travel" taxes.

Temptation

As we have seen in Matthew and Mark, Jesus fasted and prayed for forty days in the desert. Luke gives more details on the temptation than Mark. It was a soul-shattering trial.

Break your fast. Turn stones to bread (Luke 4:1-4). Daily bread is necessary, but Jesus remembered Torah and rebuked the Devil: "Man cannot live on bread alone" (Luke 4:4; see Deuteronomy 8:3). Jesus' ministry was for a deep hunger, a hunger of the soul for God.

"All this [all the kingdoms of the world] will be yours, then, if you worship me," said the Devil (Luke 4:5-7). A new government might help the poor. But the price? Become Eve and Adam in the garden. Disobey as King Saul did. Fall into the passion of David. Rebel in arrogance as Solomon did. Then you can rule mighty empires. But Jesus said no: "The scripture says, 'Worship the Lord your God and serve only him!' " (Luke 4:8; see Deuteronomy 6:13).

Jesus must have remembered that nonpolitical vow later when he mounted a donkey for his humble entry into Jerusalem and when he said to Pilate, "My kingdom does not belong to this world" (John 18:36). The Jews wanted a political leader; Jesus gave the world a Savior.

Next the Devil himself quoted Scripture. Do a mighty sign! Jump off the Temple! Draw a crowd! For as the psalmist said, "God will order his angels to take good care of you" (Luke 4:10; see Psalm 91:11). What an opportunity to preach the gospel, suggested the Devil. Maybe the common people would believe.

No. Jesus again reached into Torah: "Do not put the Lord your God to the test" (Luke 4:12; see Deuteronomy 6:16). Then the Bible says that the Devil "left him for a while" (Luke 4:13).

Christians have always been grateful to know about the terrible, agonizing temptation of Jesus. His experience helps us when we are struggling. The writer of the Letter to the Hebrews put it dramatically: "Our High Priest is not one who cannot feel sympathy for our weaknesses. On the contrary, we have a High Priest who was tempted in every way that we are, but did not sin. Let us have confidence, then, and approach God's throne, where there is grace. There we will receive mercy and find grace to help us just when we need it" (Hebrews 4:15-16).

At Home in Nazareth

The Judaism of Jesus' day took two forms: worship through sacrifices in the Temple and the synagogue for study of Scriptures in Jewish congregations all over the world.

Jesus went to his home-town synagogue "as usual" (Luke 4:16). He read the great, familiar messianic passage from Isaiah:

"The Spirit of the Lord is upon me,
because he has chosen me to bring good news to
the poor.
He has sent me to proclaim liberty to the captives
and recovery of sight to the blind,
to set free the oppressed
and announce that the time has come
when the Lord will save his people" (Luke 4:18-19).

NOTES, REFLECTIONS, AND QUESTIONS

This stone was found at the foot of the wall at the southwest corner of the Temple Mount, where it had fallen from the highest point (pinnacle) of the Temple. The inscription, "To the place of trumpeting," probably refers to the place from which a priest blew a trumpet to signal the beginning and ending of the sabbath or a holy day. Recall that when the Devil was tempting Jesus, he challenged him to jump from the highest point of the Temple to prove that he was God's Son and that God would take care of him.

No problem—until Jesus claimed the role and announced the time. To show that the Messiah would be rejected by his own people and that his ministry would extend to the whole world (4:24-27), Jesus reminded the people of a foreign widow who received Elijah and of the Syrian general healed by Elisha. The people were furious and tried to kill him (4:28-30). So began his ministry.

Samaritans

You will remember that the Samaritans were Jewish people who across the centuries had intermarried with their non-Jewish neighbors. They lived in the Northern Kingdom and had been destroyed by invading armies and often cut off from Jerusalem. There was also a North-South prejudice, because for centuries the Samaritans had worshiped at Mount Gerizim near the old Canaanite city of Shechem; the Southerners, the Judeans and their pure Jewish descendants, had worshiped in Jerusalem.

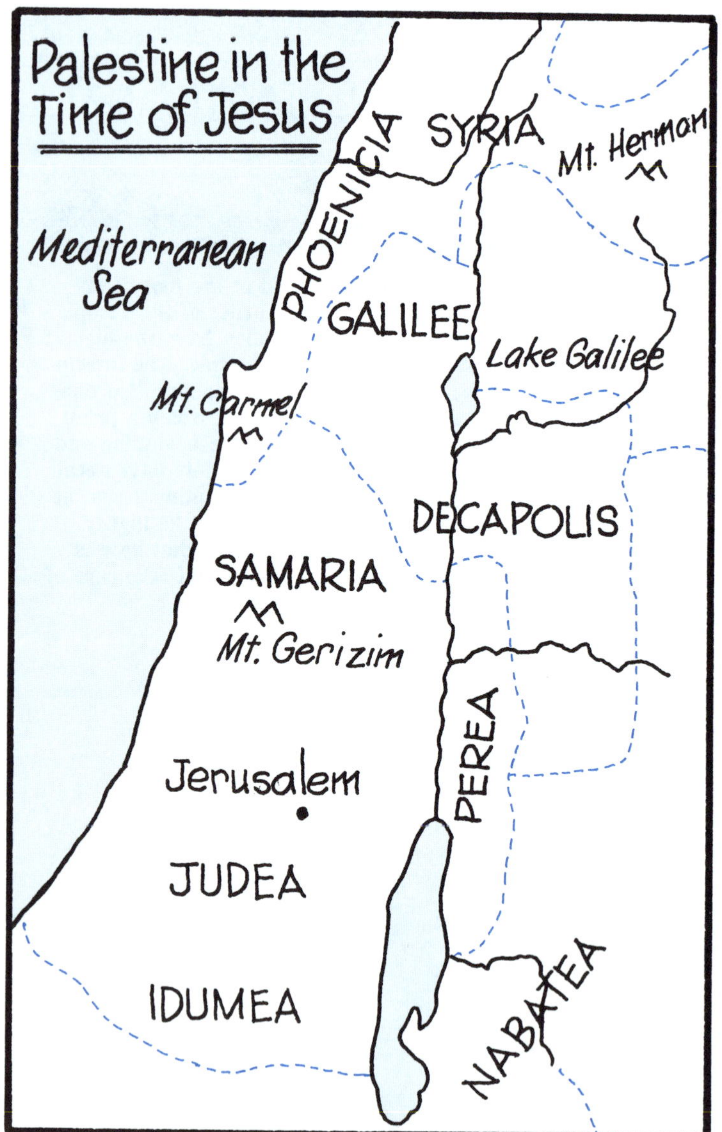

NOTES, REFLECTIONS, AND QUESTIONS

At the time of Jesus the bitterness was intense. Jews traveling from the north would normally cross over the Jordan to the east so they would not have to walk through Samaria. The Jews and the Samaritans hated each other.

Jesus, when he left Galilee, "made up his mind and set out on his way to Jerusalem" and went directly through Samaria. But the Samaritan people would not receive him (the prejudice was two-sided) because he was on his way to Jerusalem. The disciples wanted to call fire down from heaven to destroy them. But Jesus rebuked the disciples (Luke 9:51-56).

When Jesus answered the lawyer's question, "Who is my neighbor?" (10:29), he told a story of a man who was attacked by robbers on the road between Jerusalem and Jericho. Was the man dead? If so, a Jew who touched him would become ceremonially unclean. Did the priest help him? Did the Levite? Who helped? A Samaritan—a hated halfbreed, a foreigner (10:29-37). Jesus deliberately chose a Samaritan to be the hero of his story.

Later Jesus healed ten men suffering from a dreaded skin disease. They stood beside the road, separated from others, calling "Unclean, unclean." Only one of them stopped to say thanks, and he "was a Samaritan" (17:16). When people experience pain, tragedy, and terrible disease, social barriers break down, as they had for the ten sick men. Later we will see that the blood of Jesus also breaks down barriers.

In John 4, we will read of the great breakthrough when Jesus received many believers among the Samaritans.

Women

In all the Gospels, Jesus reached out to women with tenderness and compassion. He treated women with dignity. Luke's Gospel emphasizes Jesus' attitudes toward women. The birth stories show Elizabeth, Mary, and Anna with great personal strength and spiritual maturity.

In the town of Nain, Jesus raised from the dead the only son of a widow. Luke records, "His heart was filled with pity for her, and he said to her, 'Don't cry' " (Luke 7:13). Another woman, who "lived a sinful life" but who wept at Jesus' feet, not only received forgiveness but became an example for the Pharisees of the deep meaning of love (7:36-50).

Apparently several women traveled with Jesus and the disciples, providing money and food and encouragement: Mary Magdalene, "from whom seven demons had been driven out"; Joanna, the wife of Chuza, an officer in Herod's court (a rather prominent woman); Susanna; and many others, "who used their own resources to help Jesus and his disciples" (8:1-3).

Perhaps Mary, the sister of Martha, best revealed what was happening in this social revolution that now included women. Normally, men talked about the law and the

NOTES, REFLECTIONS, AND QUESTIONS

prophets. Remember Job said he used to sit at the gate of the city and talk with the men about deep matters (Job 29:7-12).

But Mary "sat down at the feet of the Lord and listened to his teaching" (Luke 10:39). In response to Martha's criticism, Jesus replied, "Mary has chosen the right thing, and it will not be taken away from her" (10:42).

The Lost

The parables of the lost are found in Luke 15: the lost sheep, the lost coin, and the lost son or lost sons. No one was more "lost" in the eyes of the Jews than the tax collectors who contracted with the Romans to collect taxes. They were seen as contributing to Roman domination and were ostracized. Luke's Gospel carefully records Jesus' contact with Zacchaeus and Levi (Matthew), both tax collectors.

MARKS OF DISCIPLESHIP

We can look at the least, the last, and the lost two ways. One way is to think of people who fall into those categories. Who are the poor today?

____

____

Who are the social outcasts?

____

____

What are you or your church doing to include them in the grace and fellowship of your community of faith?

____

____

The other way to look at the least, the last, and the lost is to include ourselves in that group. Some of us are women. Most of us are Gentiles. Some of us are poor. All of us have been sick. A few have been or are alcoholics or drug users. Some of us have been publicly shamed. Some have been in jail. For some, divorce or death of a family member cuts us off from others. Paul wrote to the Corinthians (and to us), "Few of you were wise or powerful or of high social standing. God purposely chose what the world considers nonsense in order to shame the wise, and he chose what the world considers weak in order to shame the powerful. He chose what the world looks down on and despises and thinks is nothing, in order to destroy what the

NOTES, REFLECTIONS, AND QUESTIONS

world thinks is important. This means that no one can boast in God's presence" (1 Corinthians 1:26-29).

In your experience, have you ever felt on the outside, ashamed, cut off, "unclean," or outcast? If so, how did you feel?

____

____

What helped you overcome that feeling?

____

____

Deep down, the disciple knows that his or her wealth, power, and prestige are worthless. Deep down, the disciple knows he or she is desperately in need of Jesus Christ's grace. Deep down, each disciple understands that God has a special concern to include the outcast, the oppressed, the widow, and the orphan. The disciple puts his or her energy into God's mission to the least, the last, and the lost.

IF YOU WANT TO KNOW MORE

Read the sections of Luke not assigned for daily reading, Luke 3; 4:14–9:50. These sections report John the Baptist's preaching and Jesus' public ministry in Galilee.

Memorize Luke 4:18-19, the Scripture Jesus chose to describe his mission.

NOTES, REFLECTIONS, AND QUESTIONS

LIFE

"I have come in order that you might have life—life in all its fullness."

—John 10:10

22 Lifegiver

OUR HUMAN PROBLEM

Most of the time I'm bored. What is the point of living? I try to get close to others, but often I feel left out. How can my living make a difference? How can I be happy and at peace with myself and others?

ASSIGNMENT

We will divide John's Gospel into two parts, 1–12 and 13–21. In the first we study life, abundant and eternal. The theme of the second part will be the Holy Spirit promised by Jesus Christ.

Look for these symbols: bread, water, light, life, shepherd, door. Also look for vivid contrasts: light and darkness, truth and lies, life and death, love and hate.

Day 1 John 1–2 (the Word became a human being, miracle at Cana)
Day 2 John 3–4 (the new birth, Samaritan woman)
Day 3 John 5–7 (healing the sick, the bread of life, life-giving water)
Day 4 John 8–10 (light of the world, healing the blind man, the good shepherd)
Day 5 John 11–12 (Lazarus, entry into Jerusalem, "believe in the light")
Day 6 Read and respond to "The Bible Teaching" and "Marks of Discipleship."
Day 7 Rest.

PRAYER

Pray daily before study:

"How precious, O God, is your constant love!
We find protection under the shadow of your wings.
We feast on the abundant food you provide;
you let us drink from the river of your goodness.
You are the source of all life,
and because of your light we see the light" (Psalm 36:7-9).

Prayer concerns for this week:

LIFE

Day 1 The Word became a human being, miracle at Cana

Day 4 Light of the world, healing the blind man, the good shepherd

Day 2 New birth, Samaritan woman

Day 5 Lazarus, entry into Jerusalem, "believe in the light"

Day 3 Healing the sick, the bread of life, life-giving water

Day 6 "The Bible Teaching"

THE BIBLE TEACHING

NOTES, REFLECTIONS, AND QUESTIONS

The Gospel writers were not biographers. Rather, they were evangelists, trying to help their readers know and follow the Son of God. John is especially so. Even time sequences of events were not significant to John. John was trying to get to the meaning behind the story.

Think now of the issue of life and death.

Most people think only of physical death and physical life. Recall that the snake in Genesis thought like that. But when Adam and Eve "died," they "died inside." Guilt, shame, fear, loneliness, alienation, pretense became signs of their deterioration. They were driven out of the garden of Eden into a world of spiritual darkness described in this lesson as "Our Human Problem."

So when the Lifegiver comes, he brings life into the here and now, into the "inside" of a person where meaninglessness resides. Life is not a gift after death; life is a gift to the believer now.

As Martha stood beside her brother Lazarus's grave and confessed, "I do believe that you are the Messiah, the Son of God, who was to come into the world" (John 11:27), death died within her. Life was born. Fear was changed to trust, loneliness to companionship, pretense to openness. What God had wanted for Adam and Eve was happening in Martha.

Notice that the raising of Lazarus was a dramatic confrontation. Jesus used the event to teach the disciples that he was Lord of death. But others were offended. The Sadducees were angry because they did not believe in resurrection. They also feared a revolt, with Roman retaliation. The Pharisees were upset because people were flocking to listen to Jesus and to see Lazarus. The chief priests planned to put Lazarus to death, because on his account many Jews were believing in Jesus (12:9-11, 17-19).

If you read John 11 carefully, you will see that Martha's gift of spiritual life was more important than Lazarus's gift of physical life. Lazarus would experience physical death again. Martha experienced the gift of eternal life, which, said Jesus, "will never die" (11:26).

John wanted people to find God's life, abundant life, eternal life in the Son of God.

Consider Nicodemus. He was a better Jew than most of us are Christians. He kept the law. He was a double tither, a man who fasted and prayed, spoke the truth, served his people and his country. But he was empty inside. He was hungry, not for religion but for God. Jesus said he needed to be "born again" (3:3).

The Woman at the Well

If you go to Jacob's well today, you can still drink water from it. The well is 105 feet deep, located on the site of ancient Shechem near modern Nablus. Nearly two thousand years before Jesus, Abraham, Isaac, and Jacob grazed their flocks there. Jacob bought a field near Shechem, dug a well, and gave it to his son Joseph. Later Joseph's bones were buried at Shechem (Joshua 24:32). It was in the heart of Samaria.

Jesus left Jerusalem before sunup and walked briskly north toward Galilee, arriving at Jacob's well at high noon.

As we have learned, Jews would not speak to Samaritans. They would walk across the road to avoid social contact. If a Samaritan's shadow fell across the path of a law-abiding Jew, the Jew would go to the Temple for cleansing. When Jews spoke the word *Samaritan,* they would utter a curse and spit on the ground. Samaritans sometimes would follow a Jew, put bits of straw in his tracks, and set fire to the straw. Good riddance, they would think.

Jesus sat down, in hostile territory, looking at Mount Gerizim, where the Samaritans had worshiped in their own temple for centuries, on one side and Mount Ebal, where Joshua had built an altar, on the other. Then a Samaritan woman walked up, ready to draw water for herself.

In a world of mutual prejudice, Jesus asked for a drink of water. The woman replied defensively, "You are a Jew, and I am a Samaritan—so how can you ask me for a drink?" (John 4:9).

Jesus said, "If you only knew what God gives [life] and who it is that is asking you for a drink, you would ask him, and he would give you life-giving water" (4:10). Her answer was totally beside the point. She was dying in a material world; she had no understanding of the spiritual. She said, in effect, "Mister, I walk from the village two miles here and two miles back every day. If you have a better way so I don't have to carry water, I'd like to know about it."

Jesus pushed toward life issues: "Go and call your husband" (4:16). She answered that she had no husband. Jesus complimented her, saying, in effect, "You have told the truth."

Did you ever wonder why this woman came to the well at noon? All the other women of the village came in the cool of the morning, earthenware pots on their heads, to visit, to laugh, to exchange village gossip, to get water for the day. This woman came to the well at noon in the heat of the day after the other women had left. She was isolated, cut off, even in her own village. She was dying of loneliness.

Now she ducked the life issue again, preferring to talk about religion. Many people are eager to talk about religion so they do not have to deal with God. The woman was unacceptable in polite society, would not have been welcome in the church, and she wanted to argue about the proper place to worship.

The woman spoke with longing: "I know that the Messiah will come" (4:25). Jesus said simply, "I am he, I

NOTES, REFLECTIONS, AND QUESTIONS

who am talking with you" (4:26). The miracle of life came to her, for she dropped her jar and ran into town, crying out with joy, "Come and see the man who told me everything I have ever done" (4:29).

It had been a long time since she had run like a happy child. It had been a long time since she had talked openly and unashamedly with the villagers. Suddenly she was drinking of the life-giving water. John records that this "dying" person shouted her witness, and "Many of the Samaritans in that town believed in Jesus because the woman had said, 'He told me everything I have ever done' " (4:39).

Now the witness of John's Gospel bubbles with excitement. "The Son gives life to those he wants to" (5:21). "Whoever hears my words and believes in him who sent me has eternal life" (5:24).

John 3:16 has been called the gospel in miniature: "For God loved the world so much that he gave his only Son, so that everyone who believes in him may not die but have eternal life." Right here and now, a foreigner, a female, and a failure can drink the water of eternal life. The life-giving water is for everyone.

Conflict With Unbelievers

We have emphasized new life, light (sight), and healing action. But John's Gospel also shows Jesus encountering spiritual blindness and death. Just as mounting tension is recorded in the other Gospels, particularly in Matthew, conflict is recorded in John. A conflict between life and death. Be clear as you read John's Gospel that "the Jewish authorities" (John 7:1) or "the Pharisees" (8:13) represent the world that rejects the claims of its Creator.

Jesus compared himself to the manna that God had given the Hebrews in the desert. "I am the bread of life," he said. "He who comes to me will never be hungry" (6:35). Jesus Christ will be the daily bread for believers. Those who ate manna eventually died (a physical death), but those who feed on Jesus Christ will never die (a spiritual death) (6:49-51).

Then came the question of the covenant people. The Jews were descendants of Abraham, the chosen ones, circumcised, given the law of Moses, made to be a set-apart people. Yet Jesus said they, like all people, were enslaved to sin. "I know you are Abraham's descendants. Yet you are trying to kill me, because you will not accept my teaching" (8:37).

The blindness was everywhere. Physical circumcision was not enough. As the prophets had said, salvation would require a circumcised heart. "This is how the judgment works: the light has come into the world, but people love the darkness rather than the light, because their deeds are evil" (3:19).

NOTES, REFLECTIONS, AND QUESTIONS

The Prologue

Now we are ready to understand the Prologue of John (John 1:1-18). Jesus is the Word, spoken by the Father. Just as God spoke the Word in Creation, so God speaks now in the Son. The same creative energy and love that formed the universe now has become a human being. God is, in Jesus Christ, restoring the entire creation.

Jesus interprets God for us: "The only Son, who is the same as God and is at the Father's side, he has made him known" (1:18).

MARKS OF DISCIPLESHIP

For John, a disciple is one who has found light in a blind and darkened world, spiritual food and drink in a hungry and thirsty world, meaning in a confusing and seemingly meaningless world, one who has found a shepherd in a lost and lonely world.

Try, in your own words, to describe the "life" you have found in Jesus Christ.

____

____

____

____

What meaning, what purpose does your life have in Christ?

____

____

____

Describe how your life is more abundant with Christ than it would be without Christ.

____

____

IF YOU WANT TO KNOW MORE

Memorize "the gospel in miniature," John 3:16.

NOTES, REFLECTIONS, AND QUESTIONS

ASSURANCE

"Whoever remains in me, and I in him, will bear much fruit; for you can do nothing without me."

—John 15:5

23 Holy Spirit

OUR HUMAN PROBLEM

We want more than religion. We want to experience God as a living presence in our lives. Going through religious ceremonies or trying to be good isn't enough. We desperately want assurance that we are God's children and that our future is secure.

ASSIGNMENT

Nowhere in the Gospels are the demands of discipleship stated more forcefully than in the Scripture you will be reading this week. Watch for the promises of the presence and power of the Holy Spirit for meeting those demands.

Day 1 John 13–14 (washing the disciples' feet, the coming of the Helper)
Day 2 John 15–16 (the real vine, the Spirit who reveals the truth about God)
Day 3 John 17–18 (Jesus prays for his disciples, arrest and trials)
Day 4 John 19–20 (Crucifixion, Resurrection, Resurrection appearances)
Day 5 John 21 (appearance by the lake, instruction to Peter); 1 John 1:5-10 (God is light)
Day 6 Read and respond to "The Bible Teaching" and "Marks of Discipleship."
Day 7 Rest.

PRAYER

Pray daily before study:

"LORD, I have given up my pride
and turned away from my arrogance.
I am not concerned with great matters
or with subjects too difficult for me.
Instead, I am content and at peace.
As a child lies quietly in its mother's arms,
so my heart is quiet within me" (Psalm 131:1-2).

Prayer concerns for this week:

ASSURANCE

Day 1 Washing the disciples' feet, coming of the Helper

Day 2 Real vine, the Spirit who reveals the truth about God

Day 3 Jesus prays for his disciples, arrest and trials

Day 4 Crucifixion, Resurrection, Resurrection appearances

Day 5 Appearance by the lake, instruction to Peter, God is light

Day 6 "The Bible Teaching"

THE BIBLE TEACHING

NOTES, REFLECTIONS, AND QUESTIONS

Only John records the washing of the disciples' feet. This powerful symbolic act is set amid controversy, strife, and tension. Outside the room, forces are at work to destroy Jesus. Inside the room, Judas in his heart has already betrayed him. And the disciples are arguing over who will be greatest in the Kingdom (Luke 22:24-27).

Common courtesy called for the host or servants to wash the dusty feet of the guests, as we today would open the door, hang up coats, offer a room to wash, give a cold drink. But the full significance of Jesus' act of love in this everyday courtesy, no doubt, did not become apparent to his disciples until after his crucifixion.

Jesus continually showed his disciples that the Son of Man came to serve and called his disciples to serve also (John 13:1-15). He made his actions clear with his words: Those greatest in the Kingdom are those who serve.

As disciples, you too will be asked to give humble service rather than to seek high honor.

The Promise of the Holy Spirit

The Gospels often refer to the Spirit. John the Baptist said, "I baptize you with water, but he will baptize you with the Holy Spirit" (Mark 1:8). The Holy Spirit came down on Jesus at baptism "like a dove" (1:10). Luke recorded, "As bad as you are, you know how to give good things to your children. How much more, then, will the Father in heaven give the Holy Spirit to those who ask him!" (Luke 11:13).

Now in John's Gospel, Jesus offers the Holy Spirit, who is the Helper—comforter, counselor, advocate. This is the same Spirit "who reveals the truth about God" (later in Paul's writings, the Spirit of Jesus Christ). The Spirit will help disciples walk the way, for Jesus now proclaims himself as "the way, the truth, and the life" (John 14:6).

Disciples will do even greater things than Jesus did in his earthly ministry (14:12). Why? Because Jesus will go to the Father and because the Father will send the Holy Spirit, "who will stay with you forever" (14:16).

Do you recall in Mark's Gospel how hard it was for the disciples to understand? So much that Jesus had taught became clear after the Crucifixion and Resurrection and after the Holy Spirit came upon the disciples at Pentecost. When Jesus said, "Tear down this Temple, and in three days I will build it again" (John 2:19-21), he was speaking about his body. By the counsel of the Holy Spirit, Old Testament prophecy took on new meanings: The suffering servant took upon himself "the punishment all of us deserved" (Isaiah 53:4-6).

In John 15, the disciples are moving into a new level of intimacy with Jesus; but now fresh spiritual uniting takes place. "I am the vine, and you are the branches" (John 15:5).

Recall that in Matthew, Mark, and Luke Jesus was training disciples to do the very works of compassion and conversion that he did. With the Holy Spirit, they and we will be empowered to do those works. The fruit will grow on the vine if the branches flow with the Word and Spirit.

Last-Minute Instructions

"I did not tell you these things at the beginning, for I was with you. But now . . . it is better for you that I go away. . . . But if I do go away, then I will send him [the Holy Spirit] to you. And when he comes, he will prove to the people of the world that they are wrong about sin and about what is right and about God's judgment" (John 16:4-8). We know and understand Jesus Christ now, enlightened by the Spirit. Even the apostles did not understand until the Holy Spirit opened their eyes. Times will be tough. You will be driven from the synagogues, scattered, killed. But the promise matches the times. "The world will make you suffer. But be brave! I have defeated the world!" (16:33). What does that mean? That you will have no trouble? No. It means rejoice even in suffering because the final victory belongs to God (see Romans 8:31-39).

Jesus Prays

Jesus' prayer in John 17 is called the "high priestly prayer" because in it Jesus dedicated himself as the one perfect sacrifice for the sins of the world and then dedicated his disciples for service to win the world for God.

In 17:1-5, Jesus prays for himself, that he may return to the glory he left in order to come into the world. It is nearly time to say on the cross, "It is finished!" (19:30). The Messiah's role of obedient Son of Man (the person Adam and Eve should have been) exemplified peace and healing and forgiveness and justice so we would know what life in the Kingdom will be like. He performed his ministry as suffering servant (the servant Israel was meant to be). He accomplished the work God gave him to do. He was obedient, a "first" in the history of the world.

The second part of the prayer (17:6-19) is for the disciples "that they may be one just as you and I are one" (17:11). Jesus knew that without unity of heart and purpose their mission would fail. Christ's mission still depends on Christians everywhere being in harmony and unity with one another.

Christian believers are set apart to serve. But they are not to be isolated, spiritual saints. "I do not ask you to take them out of the world, but I do ask you to keep them safe from the Evil One. . . . I sent them into the world, just as you sent me into the world" (17:15-18). And so Jesus prays that they may be equipped for the work to which they are sent.

The final portion of the prayer (17:20-26) is for the worldwide church, that they may be one, may be filled with

NOTES, REFLECTIONS, AND QUESTIONS

the Spirit of the Father who created the universe and the Son who was Word made human being "so that the world will believe" (17:21) and "in order that the world may know" (17:23). Before the world was made, before, as God said to Job, "the stars sang together" (Job 38:7), God's love for his creation was manifested in his Word. Now, Jesus prays that God will express that love through all believers to the whole world. His prayer is that all of his disciples will be unified so that the world will be confronted by a single loving witness. What a disgrace denominational pride makes of Jesus' great prayer. What a hindrance to witness is our lack of unity!

The Passion in John

In John, the experience in Gethsemane focuses on the betrayal and arrest. Notice that Peter was not prepared to meet the crisis. He was confused by the foot-washing, angry enough to cut off a slave's ear during the arrest, and full of denials when asked if he was one of the disciples. Amid the Crucifixion turmoil Peter fled Jerusalem and went back to his old ways, fishing in Galilee.

In John 21, Jesus appeared to Peter and to the others in Galilee. Jesus, in resurrected form, offered them breakfast of bread and fish. Again he was made known to them in the breaking of bread. Watch now, in 21:15-23, what happened to Peter. Three times he had denied Jesus before the rooster crowed. Now Jesus carefully questioned him, using his given name *Simon* (not the name Jesus had given him, *Peter,* which means rock, for he was no longer a rock, stable and secure in his faith). He had reverted to predisciple behavior, so Jesus used his predisciple name to reclaim him.

"Simon son of John, do you love me more than these others do?" "Yes, Lord." Then "Take care of my lambs." "Simon son of John, do you love me?" "Yes, Lord." "Take care of my sheep." Then Jesus asked a third time, "Simon son of John, do you love me?" The denial had been threefold; so was the demand. The betrayal had been three times; so was the forgiveness. After Jesus told Peter about his future martyrdom, Jesus repeated the words he had used to call him into radical discipleship three years earlier, also by Lake Galilee: "Follow me!" (21:19).

Peter, still very much the "old" Peter, wanted to know what would happen to "that other disciple, whom Jesus loved" (probably John). People are always looking out of the corner of their eye to see what will happen to someone else. God's providence is mysterious. One person's discipleship may take him or her into danger; another person's may not. One goes to Africa as a missionary; another stays home and teaches Sunday school.

Tradition, which says Jesus gave Mary into John's care from the cross (19:26-27), says that John cared for Mary until her death and then was exiled on the island of Patmos. Tradition says Peter was crucified upside down in Rome.

NOTES, REFLECTIONS, AND QUESTIONS

Two more thoughts on the Resurrection: Mary did not recognize Jesus at first. His was not a revived body but a resurrected body. "Do not hold on to me, . . . because I have not yet gone back up to the Father" (20:17). But notice this powerful point: Mary Magdalene recognized Jesus when he called her by name. God always calls his people by name, for we are his children; "we are his flock" (Psalm 100:3). We know he is alive when he calls us by name.

Also, just as Matthew records the Great Commission, "Go . . . to all peoples everywhere and make them my disciples" (Matthew 28:19), John records a similar sending forth: " 'As the Father sent me, so I send you.' Then he breathed on them and said, 'Receive the Holy Spirit. If you forgive people's sins, they are forgiven; if you do not forgive them, they are not forgiven' " (John 20:21-23). We know God is alive when the Almighty breathes the spirit of mission into us.

MARKS OF DISCIPLESHIP

The Christian doctrine of assurance means that the Christian can know in his or her heart that he or she has life, abundant and eternal.

We have three witnesses that disciples are the children of God: the Holy Spirit, the water of baptism, and the blood of Christ. All three agree and give us our assurance.

In a world of falseness where most religion is a going through the motions, as a disciple, are you able to say with Paul, "I know whom I have trusted, and I am sure that he is able to keep safe until that Day what he has entrusted to me" (2 Timothy 1:12)? Do you have a sense of assurance? How would you describe your feelings?

____

____

Try to identify some evidence of spiritual power:

in the life of an individual

____

in the life of a congregation

____

in your own life

____

IF YOU WANT TO KNOW MORE

Read 1 John 1–5. Christ's love is both our model and our motivation.

NOTES, REFLECTIONS, AND QUESTIONS

POWER

"When the Holy Spirit comes upon you, you will be filled with power, and you will be witnesses for me in Jerusalem, in all of Judea and Samaria, and to the ends of the earth."

—Acts 1:8

24 The Explosive Power of the Spirit

OUR HUMAN PROBLEM

We believe in God. We want to witness, to heal, to convert, to serve, to change society; but we seem like ordinary people. We have so little spiritual power.

ASSIGNMENT

In some ways, it is too bad Acts does not follow Luke, for Luke and Acts were written as two volumes of one work. Luke recorded the ministry of Jesus Christ, and Acts witnessed to the work of the early church. Still, there were powerful reasons for putting the three Synoptic Gospels together with John as the fourth Gospel. Matthew, Mark, and Luke take a similar approach to telling the story of the life and mission of Jesus and have much of the same material. But John concentrates on presenting Jesus as the Messiah and contains material that the other three Gospels do not have.

Day 1 Acts 1–2 (Judas's successor, Pentecost)
Day 2 Acts 3–6 (bold Peter and John, Barnabas, Stephen)
Day 3 Acts 7:54–11:30 (Stephen's martyrdom, Saul's conversion)
Day 4 Acts 12–13 (James killed, Peter imprisoned and freed)
Day 5 Acts 14:1–15:35 (Paul and Barnabas as missionaries)
Day 6 Read and respond to "The Bible Teaching" and "Marks of Discipleship."
Day 7 Rest.

PRAYER

Pray daily before study:

"God, be merciful to us and bless us;
look on us with kindness,
so that the whole world may know your will;
so that all nations may know your salvation" (Psalm 67:1-2).

Prayer concerns for this week:

POWER

Day 1 Judas's successor, Pentecost

Day 4 James killed, Peter imprisoned and freed

Day 2 Bold Peter and John, Barnabas, Stephen

Day 5 Paul and Barnabas as missionaries

Day 3 Stephen's martyrdom, Saul's conversion

Day 6 "The Bible Teaching"

THE BIBLE TEACHING

NOTES, REFLECTIONS, AND QUESTIONS

Acts falls naturally into two parts: The first part concentrates on the early church in and near Jerusalem and the second part on Paul and his mission journeys. Acts traces the spread of the church from Jerusalem to Rome.

Acts could be titled the Acts of the Holy Spirit in the Early Church. As we read, we sense the wonder that there was a church at all, but believers knew they existed because of the activity of God.

The author of Acts is generally thought to be a Gentile physician named Luke who was often a companion of Paul. Paul mentions Luke's being with him in Colossians 4:14 and in 2 Timothy 4:11.

Pentecost

Every community needs to remember its beginning, for that in part defines what the community becomes. So we sometimes say that Pentecost is the birthday of the church. But the birthday figure is only partly true. Certainly there was a new, powerful burst of faith and zeal, but the community of faith reached backward into Israel, back to Abraham and Sarah themselves.

Jesus taught clearly that the Holy Spirit would come to all believers, not just to the Twelve. "When the Holy Spirit comes upon you, you will be filled with power [*dunamis*—the root word of *dynamic, dynamite*]" (Acts 1:8).

So they waited patiently in the upper room. "They [the eleven disciples] gathered frequently to pray as a group, together with the women and with Mary the mother of Jesus and with his brothers" (1:14). Notice the sense of unity and harmony among men and women, family and friends, apostles and other believers. Unity is reemphasized in 2:1: "When the day of Pentecost came, all the believers were gathered together in one place."

Pentecost, the festival of first fruits fifty days after Passover, was a Jewish holy day. Now Christians celebrate Pentecost fifty days after Easter to recall the explosive power of the Spirit that launched the Christian community into mission.

How do you describe a dramatic religious experience? Luke used imagery: a sound "like a strong wind blowing" and "what looked like tongues of fire" (2:2-3). Then people began to speak in various languages, seemingly in the languages of the nations of the world. The tower of Babylon was reversed. Sin destroyed communication; the Holy Spirit restored communication. The experience was not primarily the speaking in unknown tongues. Rather, it was a driving missionary force, thrusting the believers into a worldwide ministry.

Peter, who had sworn he had never heard of Jesus during the trial, now stood up in the main street of Jerusalem and preached. The power had come.

Then Peter proclaimed that Jesus was crucified and raised from the dead. The listeners "were deeply troubled" and asked, "What shall we do?" (2:37). Peter's answer, and our answer to people who are open to God, is "Each one of you must turn away from his sins and be baptized in the name of Jesus Christ, so that your sins will be forgiven; and you will receive God's gift, the Holy Spirit" (2:38). Three thousand people were baptized.

But watch! They were immediately gathered into house groups. Since they had no churches, they met in one another's homes, almost daily. Look carefully at what they did. "They spent their time in learning from the apostles, taking part in the fellowship, and sharing in the fellowship meals and the prayers" (2:42).

Miracles and wonders of the Kingdom occurred. Instead of being selfish, the believers shared with one another and gave to the needy. They went to the Temple, kept the sabbath, and day after day went in and out of one another's homes praising God. Then this glorious verse: "And every day the Lord added to their group those who were being saved" (2:47).

Now what Jesus had promised was happening: Disciples would perform miracles and wonders of the Kingdom as he had. Peter and John healed a man lame from birth (3:1-10). The healing became an opportunity for witnessing and a call to repentance (3:11-21). Peter and the others showed boldness again, for they "were teaching the people that Jesus had risen from death" (4:2). Peter and John were in trouble because the Sadducees did not teach belief in resurrection. But powered now by the Holy Spirit, Peter and John continued to act and speak boldly: "We cannot stop speaking of what we ourselves have seen and heard" (4:20). When the church rejoiced over their release, they sang or chanted Psalm 2, interpreting it now as their own (4:24-26).

The people were no longer merely tithers. Now they were free from anxiety over food and drink or clothes (Matthew 6:25). They gave to one another and to the common treasury. Then Barnabas, one of the greatest servants of the church, appeared. He sold his field and gave all the money to the apostles (Acts 4:36-37).

Now, in deliberate contrast, Ananias and Sapphira sold their land and gave only a part of the money to the apostles (5:1-11). Was the issue money? No. They did not need to give anything. Then why were they confronted so dramatically by Peter and the Holy Spirit? Because they lied! The church could not tolerate deception. A lie will bring down a family, a church, a business, even a government. The newly formed Christian community was so transparent, so open with one another, so filled with giving and joy, so honest with one another that all kinds of healings and forgiveness and conversions were taking place. Now came "Adam and Eve" wanting to have their apple and eat it too. Peter rightly said, "Carry them out"; for either they died, or the church died.

NOTES, REFLECTIONS, AND QUESTIONS

NOTES, REFLECTIONS, AND QUESTIONS

Stephen

Members of the early community of faith shared with one another and took care of widows. But some members were native Jews who spoke Aramaic and had traditionally resisted Greek language and culture. Others were Hellenists, Jews who had lived in different parts of the world and who spoke Greek. Barnabas and Saul were Hellenist Jews. So was Stephen.

Whoever was providing food for the widows seemed to be favoring the native Jews. The "daily manna" was not evenly distributed. The twelve apostles (Judas had been replaced by Matthias in Acts 1:15-26) called the body together and acted to reduce the tension.

The apostles needed to be giving their time and energy to prayer, preaching, and teaching the word. So they selected seven helpers to serve tables, men who were filled with the Spirit and had good reputations. Notice that all seven were Hellenists. That is, they were from the group doing the complaining. Do you remember Jethro's advice to Moses about spreading the labor (Exodus 18:13-27)?

When these helpers were chosen and harmony restored, "the word of God continued to spread. The number of disciples in Jerusalem grew larger and larger" (Acts 6:7).

Stephen was the first of the Christian martyrs. He was so filled with the Spirit that he began to witness as well as wait tables. His speech in Acts 7:2-53 retraced Hebrew history, seeing it through "Resurrection glasses." Like the prophets, he accused the Jews of being stubborn and deaf to God's message. When he looked to heaven and declared that he saw "the Son of Man [Jesus] standing at the right side of God" (7:56), the Jews were furious. They violated Roman law, which did not allow the religious council to carry out a death sentence on its own authority, and stoned Stephen to death (7:58-60). Stephen's prayer echoed the prayers of Jesus: "Lord Jesus, receive my spirit!" (Acts 7:59; see Luke 23:46). "Lord! Do not remember this sin against them!" (Acts 7:60; see Luke 23:34).

Saul (Paul)

As you now meet Saul (Paul), answer the following questions. Acts 8:1-3; 9:1-31; 22:3-16; and Galatians 1:13-17 will help you.

What was Saul's background?

____

____

Why might Saul seem to be the *least likely* candidate for missionary?

____

____

Gentiles

If Christianity was to become more than a Jewish sect, it had to break loose among the Gentiles.

Why did Luke, the writer of Acts, record Philip's conversion of the Ethiopian eunuch (Acts 8:26-39)?

What did Peter's vision at Joppa mean (10:1-35)?

MARKS OF DISCIPLESHIP

Being a disciple calls for active response and passive response. Sometimes Jesus requires us to get up and do something: "Come and follow me" (Mark 10:21). Sometimes Jesus requires us to wait and pray: "You must wait in the city until the power from above comes down upon you" (Luke 24:49). Remember that Jesus began his ministry by receiving the Holy Spirit in baptism and by "waiting" forty days in fasting and prayer. Too often we do not wait and pray together to receive the power.

Does your DISCIPLE group feel strongly the power of the Holy Spirit? Do any bad feelings among group members stand in the way?

How is the power of the Holy Spirit affecting your own life?

What about your church? Are healing, witnessing, serving, and new birth occurring in the congregation? Where?

IF YOU WANT TO KNOW MORE

Chart of Biblical History

A.D. **30–31**	**Stoning of Stephen**
A.D. **10**	**Paul's birth**
A.D. **30–31**	**Paul's conversion**
A.D. **44–49**	**The Jerusalem Council**

Memorize the names of the books of the New Testament.

NOTES, REFLECTIONS, AND QUESTIONS

Eunuchs were males who were castrated, either accidentally or intentionally. Often they held important and influential positions in the royal households, particularly as guards or managers of the king's harem. Sometimes the term is used in the New Testament to refer to persons who remain celibate to give themselves completely to God's service.

CONVERSION

"To Jews and Gentiles alike I gave solemn warning that they should turn from their sins to God and believe in our Lord Jesus."

—Acts 20:21

25 The Gospel Penetrates the World

OUR HUMAN PROBLEM

We are uncomfortable witnessing about our faith to people we don't know and people of different religions. Even with our families and next-door neighbors we hesitate to talk about God. We are afraid that people will make fun of us and reject us. Besides, what gives us the right to tell others what to believe?

ASSIGNMENT

The church with its gospel of Jesus Christ continues to expand across the Mediterranean world and to Rome. Locate on the maps on page 175 the cities or areas about which you are reading. Observe the adaptability of the gospel in the many settings in which it is proclaimed.

Day 1 Acts 15:36–18:28 (Paul goes to Macedonia, preaches in Athens and Corinth)
Day 2 Acts 19–20 (Paul in Ephesus)
Day 3 Acts 21–23 (return to Jerusalem, arrest, Paul's defense before the council)
Day 4 Acts 24–26 (Paul's appeal to the emperor, defense before Agrippa)
Day 5 Acts 27–28 (storm and shipwreck, in Rome)
Day 6 Read and respond to "The Bible Teaching" and "Marks of Discipleship."
Day 7 Rest.

PRAYER

Pray daily before study:

"I will sing about your strength;
every morning I will sing aloud of your constant love.
You have been a refuge for me,
a shelter in my time of trouble.
I will praise you, my defender.
My refuge is God,
the God who loves me" (Psalm 59:16-17).

Prayer concerns for this week:

CONVERSION

Day 1 Paul goes to Macedonia, preaches in Athens and Corinth

Day 2 Paul in Ephesus

Day 3 Return to Jerusalem, arrest, defense before the council

Day 4 Appeal to the emperor, defense before Agrippa

Day 5 Storm and shipwreck, in Rome

Day 6 "The Bible Teaching"

THE BIBLE TEACHING

The powerful personality of Paul, driven by the Holy Spirit, dominates the remainder of Acts. Through Paul's missionary activity and the work of countless others, the gospel moved by foot, by horseback, by ship all over the known world. The Greek language was spoken nearly everywhere, and Roman roads and Roman peace made travel easier than it had ever been.

Jewish communities and synagogues existed almost everywhere; so wandering Jews, even if they were Jewish Christians, were, at least at first, given Jewish hospitality.

As a result of an inner drive to witness and increasing communication and access, the gospel went worldwide. Paul led the way. Hosts of others, including the apostles, scattered out. Persecution, at first in Jerusalem and later elsewhere, caused believers to hurry from one place to another.

Early on, the team was Barnabas and Paul, as Barnabas nurtured the young Pharisee Christian. Soon, however, it became Paul and Barnabas, as Paul's driving leadership took over. Then a disagreement occurred that served the cause well (Acts 15:36-41). Barnabas wanted to take John Mark, his nephew. Paul refused, for the lad had been homesick and left them on an earlier trip. The solution was for Paul and Barnabas to separate. Barnabas and John Mark went to Cyprus, Paul and Silas to Asia Minor.

Usually Paul and his companions would enter a city as they did Philippi: "We spent several days there. On the Sabbath we went out of the city to the riverside, where we thought there would be a place where Jews gathered for prayer. We sat down and talked to the women who gathered there" (16:12-13). For centuries now, Jews in various towns and cities had gathered in sabbath groupings, often at the riverside. Such a gathering was an informal synagogue without a building, a place to sing psalms, offer prayers, study and discuss the Scriptures, and remember who they were. Some God-fearers attended and some Gentiles who were proselytes or who were attracted to worship of the one true God.

Lydia, a traveling merchant and a Gentile God-fearer, was converted and baptized along with her household. She insisted that Paul and Silas stay in her home.

In Thessalonica there was a regular synagogue. According to his usual custom, Paul went to the synagogue. (Had not Jesus said the gospel came first to the Jews?) "There during three Sabbaths he held discussions with the people, quoting and explaining the Scriptures, and proving from them that the Messiah had to suffer and rise from death" (17:2-3). Remember, "scriptures" at this time meant the Old Testament. None of the New Testament had yet been written. Again people were converted—a few Jews and "many of the leading women and a large group of Greeks who worshiped God" (17:4).

NOTES, REFLECTIONS, AND QUESTIONS

At the time of Paul, Roman merchant ships such as this sailed the Mediterranean. The Book of Acts vividly details Paul's voyage to Rome.

God-fearers were Gentiles who accepted the Jewish teaching on God, the sacred books, laws of cleanliness, and the observance of sabbath. They did not accept circumcision or full observance of the law. Proselytes were Gentile converts to Judaism. They accepted Judaism in its entirety, including circumcision and total adherence to the law.

Maps of Paul's Journeys

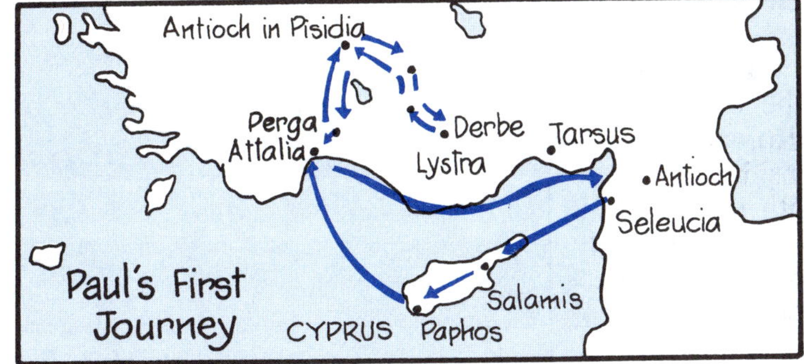

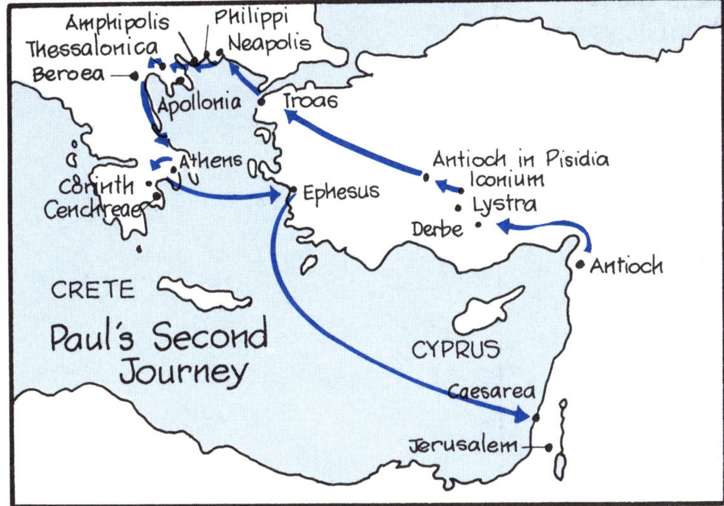

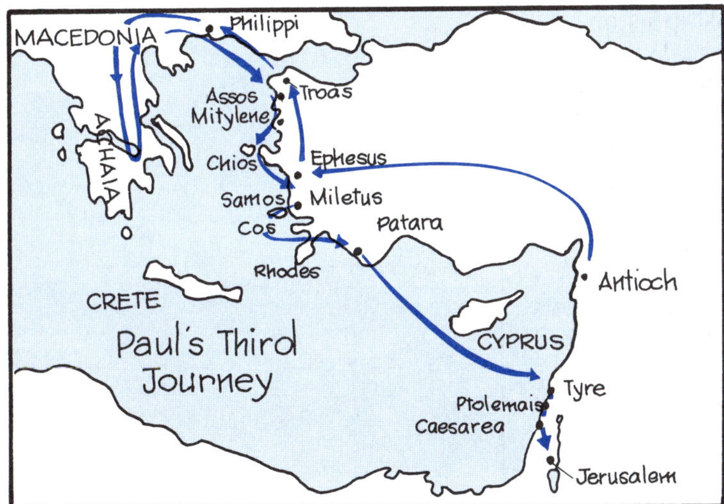

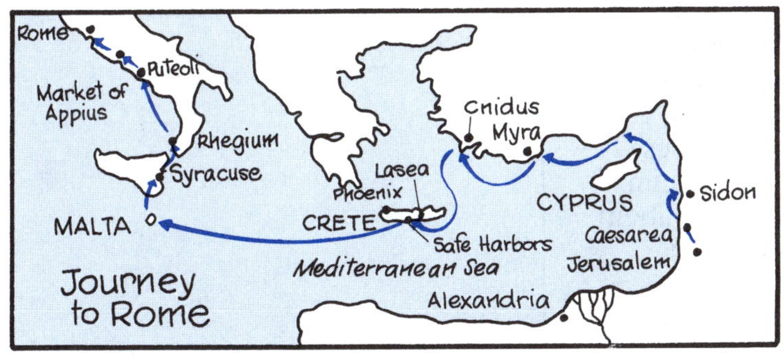

NOTES, REFLECTIONS, AND QUESTIONS

In Athens Paul spoke in the city council where philosophers loved to gather and talk (17:22-31). Paul had little effect, but a few believed.

In Corinth Paul had great success. Corinth was a busy seaport city filled with people from all over the world—sailors, shippers, merchants, slaves, prostitutes, Romans, Greeks, Jews. It was a melting pot; many considered it a sewer. The temple of Aphrodite was there with its one thousand sacred prostitutes. What a place to start a church!

At Corinth Paul stayed with Aquila and his wife Priscilla. Aquila was a tentmaker by trade; so was Paul. So he used both his occupation and his relationship with a Jewish family to begin his work. "He held discussions in the synagogue every Sabbath, trying to convince both Jews and Greeks" (18:4).

As you read Acts, you discover that Paul and his associates continually ran into conflict. But Paul used everything to make converts: his Jewish race, his Greek language, his tentmaking skills, his training in Torah, and even his Roman citizenship. He wrote to the Corinthian church, "I become all things to all men, that I may save some of them" (1 Corinthians 9:22; read 9:19-23).

When you read Paul's defenses in trials, you learn a lot about him, but you also learn a lot about Jesus. Paul used the court proceedings as a chance to convert. King Agrippa, distinguished and experienced, protested, "In this short time do you think you will make me a Christian?" (Acts 26:28).

Paul was a Roman citizen. To have the prized Roman citizenship, one must have been born a free Roman citizen, bought Roman citizenship, or received citizenship as an honor for military or civil service to the empire. We do not know how Paul's (Saul's) father became a Roman citizen, but we know Paul was proud to have been born a citizen.

Why did he finally claim his rights as a Roman citizen? And when he did, did he make a mistake? Agrippa said to Festus in Caesarea, "This man could have been released if he had not appealed to the Emperor" (26:32). Was he weary of two years of harrassment and jail? Or did he want to carry the gospel to Spain by way of Rome? One suspects that the symbolism of going to the heart of the empire and to the end of the world (Spain) was a powerful motive. Paul did not make it to Spain; but his witness in and to Rome, his letters to the churches while in prison in Rome, and his eventual martyrdom in Rome made the Christian movement international.

The closing verses of Acts make a point about how God works. Paul, sent to Rome by the anger of a dozen cities, enjoyed the greatest opportunity of his career to offer to others abundant and eternal life. "For two years Paul lived [in Rome] in a place he rented for himself [under house arrest], and there he welcomed all who came to see him. He preached about the Kingdom of God and taught about the Lord Jesus Christ, speaking with all boldness and freedom" (28:30-31).

NOTES, REFLECTIONS, AND QUESTIONS

MARKS OF DISCIPLESHIP

Disciples are to be witnesses. Paul used everything he had to bring men and women to God, every relationship, every aspect of background or culture. What do you have to offer that could relate you to other people in witness and converting power? Are you Hispanic? white? Black? Asian? Native American? What languages do you speak? Are you rural? urban? poor? rich? Are you a former alcoholic or drug user? Have you ever been fired from a job? Are you athletic? artistic? musical? a good reader or talker?

Think of ways you could use who you are and your experience to help lead people to Christ Jesus.

____

____

Where are some places that you can witness?

____

____

Who are some people unfamiliar or unknown to you to whom you can witness?

____

____

Who are some people well-known to you to whom you can witness?

____

____

IF YOU WANT TO KNOW MORE

Chart of Biblical History

A.D. **46–47**	**Paul's first journey**
A.D. **50–52**	**Paul's second journey**
A.D. **52–56**	**Paul's third journey**
A.D. **60–61**	**Paul's journey to Rome**
A.D. **62–68**	**Paul martyred**
A.D. **62–68**	**Peter martyred**

Read Ephesians 1–4.

Ephesians is a letter to all the churches, not just to the church at Ephesus. Converts are not won to be individual, solitary saved souls. No, God is forming the new humanity. In the midst of a world speaking countless languages (and hating one another), Christ is breaking down barriers and building oneness. The blood of Christ will bring us all together. To that mission, Paul gave his life.

NOTES, REFLECTIONS, AND QUESTIONS

JUSTIFIED

"Now that we have been put right with God through faith,
we have peace with God through our Lord Jesus Christ."
—Romans 5:1

26 Put Right With God Through Faith

OUR HUMAN PROBLEM

Part of the time we rebel on purpose. We do what we please. We go directly against God. But part of the time we "religious people" work hard to win God's approval, only to fail. We lack peace with ourselves and others.

ASSIGNMENT

The importance of Romans to the early church is indicated by its position in the New Testament. It is placed first among Paul's letters, even though Paul had written other letters earlier. Content rather than age, no doubt, influenced its location in the Bible.

Day 1 Romans 1–4 (Jews and Gentiles, no one righteous)
Day 2 Romans 5–7 (right with God, alive in Christ, purpose of the law)
Day 3 Romans 8–10 (life in the Spirit, salvation for all)
Day 4 Romans 11–13 (the wild olive joined, life in God's service, love one another)
Day 5 Romans 14–16 (do not judge, plans to visit Rome)
Day 6 Read and respond to "The Bible Teaching" and "Marks of Discipleship."
Day 7 Rest.

PRAYER

Pray daily before study:

"LORD, your constant love reaches the heavens;
your faithfulness extends to the skies.
Your righteousness is towering like the mountains;
your justice is like the depths of the sea"
(Psalm 36:5-6).

Prayer concerns for this week:

JUSTIFIED

Day 1 Jews and Gentiles, no one righteous

Day 2 Right with God, alive in Christ, purpose of the law

Day 3 Life in the Spirit, salvation for all

Day 4 The wild olive joined, life in God's service, love one another

Day 5 Do not judge, plans to visit Rome

Day 6 "The Bible Teaching"

THE BIBLE TEACHING

When Paul wrote Romans, he was not a new convert, no longer a young, struggling missionary. Paul was at the height of his powers, disciplined by torture, sharpened by prayer and preaching, able to state the Christian faith with clarity and persuasive power. Paul wrote to the Romans from Corinth, where he was teaching in the Corinthian church, collecting money for the poor in Jerusalem, and dreaming of going to Rome and to Spain to encourage the church everywhere.

Sin and Justification

To understand Paul's Letter to the Romans, we first must remember Genesis 1–11. To comprehend the height of our salvation, we must know the depth of our sin.

Paul recalls that we do not merely do bad things; we are out of harmony with God. As Adam and Eve and King Saul were disobedient, so we are disobedient. As Cain and King David were passionately rebellious, so we are passionately rebellious. As King Solomon and those who built the tower of Babylon were arrogant and proud, so we are arrogant and proud.

The Gentiles have no excuse, because just looking at the universe should have revealed the true nature of the great and glorious Creator. All of us, even the Gentiles, have a conscience, know right from wrong, and know there is God. We all stand condemned.

The Jews were given the law of Moses, but they did not keep it. The law in fact showed up their sin the way a plumb line shows up a crooked wall. Further, many Jews indulged in the very things they condemned in the Gentiles. Their hearts were proud and stubborn; they were self-centered, wrote Paul.

The net result is that all women and all men, the Gentile with the law of conscience, the Jew with the law of Moses, are sinners. Paul insists, "The Gentiles do not have the Law of Moses; they sin and are lost apart from the Law. The Jews have the Law; they sin and are judged by the Law" (Romans 2:12). He therefore quotes the psalmist:

> "There is no one who is righteous. . . .
> All have turned away from God;
> they have all gone wrong;
> no one does what is right, not even one"
> (Romans 3:10-12; see Psalm 14:1-3).

Sin turns us in a downward spiral. First we exchange the truth about God for a lie and worship and serve what God has created rather than the Creator (Romans 1:25). Then when we live in twisted relationships, God gives us over to the passions of our hearts. Out of a polluted well comes polluted water. Paul lists the terrible weakness of mind and body that we use to destroy one another. Our lives deteriorate until finally we not only do evil deeds but applaud others who do evil (1:32).

NOTES, REFLECTIONS, AND QUESTIONS

God had to act. We could not free ourselves from self-centeredness. The disease was too widespread, the separation too severe, the spiritual relationship too strained. We were helpless. God had to act.

Jesus has made a breakthrough for us. Paul explains it this way: "All are put right with him [God] through Christ Jesus, who sets them free" (3:24). Paul was comparing us to slaves who could be bought and set free. "He [God] bought you for a price," wrote Paul (1 Corinthians 6:20).

When the Hebrews were slaves in Egypt, God freed his people from slavery. Hosea redeemed his wife by paying the price of a slave and setting her free to be his wife again (Hosea 3). Jesus Christ frees sinners.

To whom or what were we enslaved? To our own self-interest? Yes, and more, to that passionate disobedience we call sin. The result of that enslavement is doom. But we have been bought and set free.

Paul uses the phrase *by his sacrificial death* (Romans 3:25). Just as the blood of the sacrificed lamb was wiped on the doorposts of the Hebrews in Egypt in order that death would not destroy the first-born of God's people, so the blood of Christ has been wiped on the doorposts of our hearts so that evil would not destroy us. God's wrath will pass over God's people.

Another phrase Paul uses is *the one righteous act* (5:18). Paul understood that Jesus did something no one else in all history had ever done: He lived his life in right relationship with the Father. Amid a broken humanity Jesus said, "The Father and I are one" (John 10:30). Jesus did something the whole of humankind had been waiting for: He lived out the obedient life, right to his final words on the cross, "It is finished!" (John 19:30). With Christ's act of obedience, he broke a hole in the enemy's lines so that his followers can walk through.

Perhaps the most helpful word Paul uses is *justify* (Romans 5:1, RSV), or *put right with God* (TEV). God justifies us, puts us right through faith in Jesus Christ. To be righteous (put right) does not mean to be "pure" or "good" but rather to be in harmony, in right relationship.

When a person accepts this action of God in faith, a kind of death occurs, the death of self-centeredness. Burial by baptism symbolizes that death. A resurrection occurs as we stand up from baptism with a new master, bought for a price, passed over because of his blood, imitating the breakthrough of his obedience, and put into right relationship with the Creator of the universe.

Abraham trusted in God even before he was circumcised. "Abraham believed God, and because of his faith God accepted him as righteous" (4:3). The circumcision was *sign* of the covenant, not source. So we Gentiles in Jesus Christ are joined to God's true people by faith. We now, with Abraham, walk into the future unafraid, as children of the covenant. We are blessed, ready to be used as a blessing to the world.

NOTES, REFLECTIONS, AND QUESTIONS

Grace, accepted by faith, makes us sons and daughters of God. That is what God wanted all along, not robots, but not rebels either. Since we are children of God, then we are able now to possess the blessing God intended his children to have (8:14-17). Now we know some things we never knew before.

We know we have a new status.

We understand that suffering can be a creative and positive force.

We participate in a new humanity.

No power in the universe can prevent us from obtaining ultimate victory in Jesus Christ.

Restoration of Israel

Today people wonder, Should we dismiss the Old Testament and Judaism as irrelevant? No. We in the DISCIPLE study know that we cannot understand the gospel without its Old Testament roots.

How are we to think about the relationship of Jews to Jesus? Paul says their rejection of Jesus as the Messiah made the good news available to the Gentiles. God who works for good in all things, used the crucifixion of Jesus to atone for sin and used rejection by the Jews to open the door of salvation to the whole world.

Should we try to win them through our witness to grace? Yes, as we would try to win all people by our witness. But remember the Jews are our spiritual ancestors. Paul uses the metaphor of the olive tree to help us here. The branches of believing Gentiles (you and I) are joined to the olive tree (Israel). Nonbelieving Jews are branches broken off. Those joined to the tree have no basis for pride; in fact, if we show arrogance, God must prune us off too.

Will Israel be restored? Will God save the chosen people? Yes. Paul says that when they see Gentiles becoming possessors of the promises made to Abraham, they will turn to Christ in faith. Thus God's plan for both Jews and Gentiles will be accomplished (Romans 11:11-32). Now in the new covenant we are blessed to be a blessing.

Grace and Peace

Paul usually began his letters by offering grace and peace to his readers. Peace is that vibrant *shalom* that hints at harmony—being at one with God, with neighbor, and with self. The entire universe is yearning for the peace that characterized creation on the seventh day but was destroyed by the disobedience of humankind. Peace through Christ and his indwelling Spirit gives assurance to every Christian that all is well. Love drives out fear and brings peace.

In that peace we know we are never alone, never defeated. We have the assurance that God will care for us and guide our ways. (Theologians call it providence.) "We know that in all things God works for good with those who love him" (Romans 8:28). What a sense of inner peace to trust

NOTES, REFLECTIONS, AND QUESTIONS

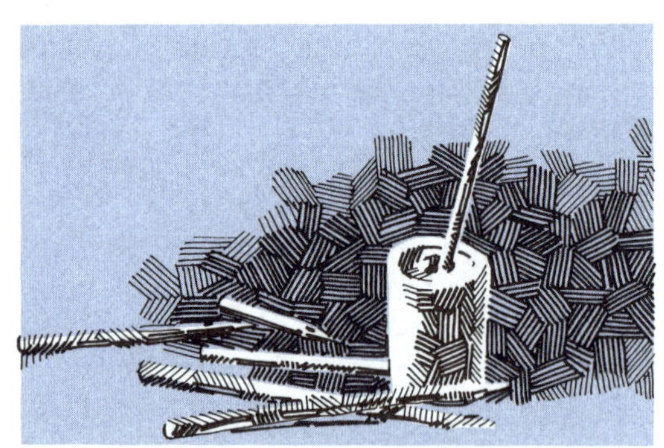

Pens cut from reeds and black ink made from soot mixed with gum or oil were the writing tools common to Paul's time. Most inkwells were made of clay.

that nothing "will ever be able to separate us from the love of God which is ours through Christ Jesus our Lord" (8:39).

Grace is the sacrificial, accepting, forgiving love of God expressed and revealed in Jesus. Paul always mentions it first, for grace is the source of our peace. Grace is love with no strings attached, poured forth in the life, death, and resurrection of Jesus Christ. To be saved means to fling one's soul on that grace. Christians sing the hymn,

"Amazing grace! how sweet the sound
That saved a wretch like me!"

It was written by John Newton, a slave trader, after his conversion. It expresses the joy of a person found by God's seeking love.

"I once was lost, but now am found,
Was blind, but now I see."

MARKS OF DISCIPLESHIP

We are saved by grace through faith. A claim is laid upon our lives; our acceptance must be accepted. The forgiving love must be received. The work of God must be claimed by an act of trust. Disciples accept and trust the forgiving love of God in Jesus Christ.

Think of times you have chosen to go against God.

____

____

Think of times you have specifically tried to please God but failed to feel at peace.

____

____

Write in your own words what you think it means to be put right with God through faith.

____

____

When is it hard for you to accept the forgiving love of God without doing anything to deserve it? Why?

____

____

IF YOU WANT TO KNOW MORE

Read Colossians, one of Paul's letters that we will not have a chance to read during the daily assignments.

NOTES, REFLECTIONS, AND QUESTIONS

LOVE

"It is love, then, that you should strive for. Set your hearts on spiritual gifts."

—1 Corinthians 14:1

27 A Congregation in Ferment

OUR HUMAN PROBLEM

We hate to leave the lifestyles of the world. We are so used to them. But when we convert to the faith and fellowship of Christ, we discover that people, including ourselves, still argue, still cause division, and are still self-centered. The church is not as perfect as we thought it would be.

ASSIGNMENT

Paul's Corinthian letters are not so much concerned with theology and doctrine as with the affairs of the church. Watch for insights into the life of the early church and for Paul's suggestions for solving its problems, many of which continue to trouble the church today.

Day 1 1 Corinthians 1–4 (divisions in the church)
Day 2 1 Corinthians 5–7 (sexual morality, directions about marriage)
Day 3 1 Corinthians 8–11 (Christians and pagans, the Lord's Supper)
Day 4 1 Corinthians 12–14 (different gifts but one Spirit; love is the greatest gift)
Day 5 1 Corinthians 15–16 (the resurrection, final words)
Day 6 Read and respond to "The Bible Teaching" and "Marks of Discipleship."
Day 7 Rest.

PRAYER

Pray daily before study:

"Examine me and test me, LORD;
judge my desires and thoughts.
Your constant love is my guide;
your faithfulness always leads me"
(Psalm 26:2-3).

Prayer concerns for this week:

LOVE

Day 1 Divisions in the church

Day 2 Sexual morality, directions about marriage

Day 3 Christians and pagans, the Lord's Supper

Day 4 Different gifts but one Spirit, the greatest gift

Day 5 Resurrection, final words

Day 6 "The Bible Teaching"

THE BIBLE TEACHING

NOTES, REFLECTIONS, AND QUESTIONS

Scholars say Paul wrote several letters to the Corinthian church, letters that have been combined into First and Second Corinthians. The Corinthians also wrote to Paul (1 Corinthians 7:1). Paul loved this church. He was its spiritual father. He visited it, sent messengers to it, asked its congregation for offerings for the poor in Jerusalem. He wrote these letters to scold and encourage, and because he could not go himself. The letters contain guidance a father wanted to give his spiritual children.

Keep in mind what Corinth was like. We have said it was a sea town. Rather than sail all the way around the coast, many shipowners preferred to move their small sailing ships on rollers across the narrow isthmus. Other ships stopped for trade and supplies. Not a sophisticated city like Athens, not a power city like Rome, not a holy city like Jerusalem, Corinth was a trade and commerce center for the eastern Mediterranean.

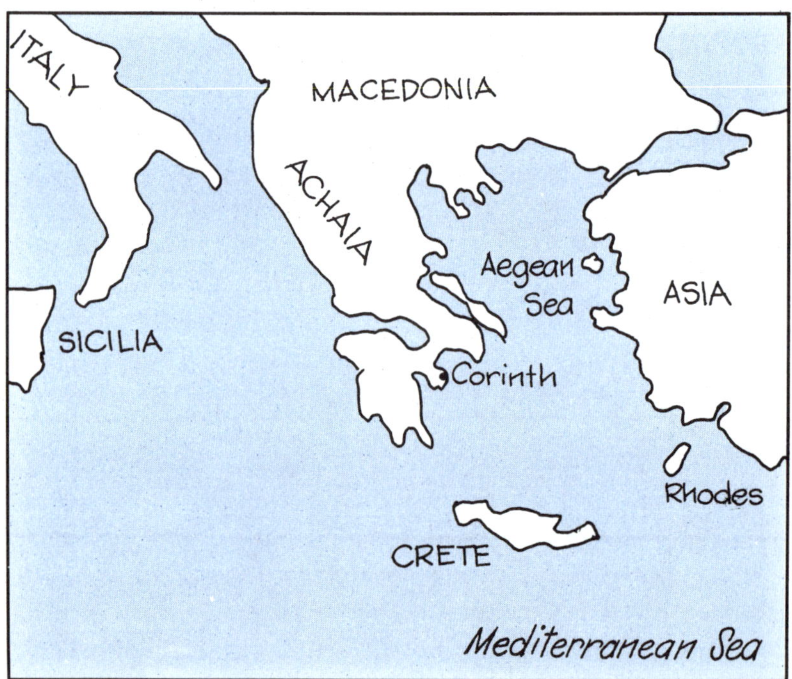

Everybody passed through—slaves from all over the empire, Roman soldiers, Greeks, Persians, Syrians. In Corinth people practiced every conceivable sin. Corinth was no Jewish colony; Jews there were definitely strangers in a strange land. The markets sold meat that had been offered to idols in pagan temples. Prostitutes walked the streets and served in the temples. Every day, including sabbath, meant big business in the marketplace.

The congregation contained a few converted Jews, a few God-fearers (persons who believed in the Jewish God without becoming Jews), but mostly Gentiles who had been converted. These Gentile converts had not been trained in the law of Moses concerning sexual morality, sabbath worship, tithing, food laws, hospitality, marriage within the religion, sobriety, devotion to the Torah, or respect for the authority of the elders.

Into this world the gospel came. The resulting congregation was a miracle, but they had a lot to learn.

Unity

Given a dog-eat-dog economy, a culturally mixed social scene with constant competition, it is no wonder there was quarreling. Paul pleaded "that there will be no divisions among you" (1 Corinthians 1:10), but there were. Some persons were boasting that they had been converted by Paul. Others were proud they had been converted under Apollos. Some claimed that they stuck strictly to Peter's teachings. A few boasted with pride that they were above all that: *They* belonged to *Jesus*. Paul was angry. Was Paul crucified for you? or Apollos? No, Christ cannot be divided (1:13).

Some claimed that they were wise in the ways of Christianity, perhaps because they were early converts, or because they knew the Jewish Scriptures, or because they had more education.

Paul was quite upset. Where is the wise man, the scholar, the debater? Truth is, God uses the simple to show faith and love. "Few of you were wise or powerful or of high social standing. God purposely chose what the world considers nonsense in order to shame the wise, and he chose what the world considers weak in order to shame the powerful. He chose what the world looks down on and despises and thinks is nothing, in order to destroy what the world thinks is important. This means that no one can boast in God's presence" (1:26-29). Why, said Paul, you are acting like people of the world, with jealousy and quarreling among you (3:3). He says, in effect, You are a common lot, which gives credit to the power of God.

Paul used many images of unity—the human body in 1 Corinthians 12, a building in 1 Corinthians 3. The task is to fit together, complement one another, be humble, and build up the body.

A powerful message explodes in 3:21-23: You have no need to boast like an insecure person. Everything belongs to you! Every apostle is yours; the Bible is yours; the universe is yours; life, the kind John wrote about, belongs to you. You do not belong to death; death belongs to you. The future belongs to you; for you belong to Christ, and Christ belongs to God.

Sex

You can imagine the problems this group would have had with sexual conduct. Paul had promised the apostles in the Jerusalem Council (Acts 15) that he would not allow

NOTES, REFLECTIONS, AND QUESTIONS

immorality among the Gentile converts. In 1 Corinthians 5–7 Paul commented on the following problems:

- a man sleeping with his stepmother
- sexual activity with prostitutes
- adultery and sexual perversion
- marriage
- sexual relations within marriage
- marriage with an unbeliever
- the single life like Paul's
- if a man were already circumcised
- if a man were not circumcised
- marriage after the death of a spouse

Remember that in these matters Paul wanted nothing to stand in the way of intensity and zeal for the gospel. He also was influenced by his belief that Christ was coming soon. Notice too that Paul was unsure of his ground when offering pastoral advice on whether or not to marry: "I do not have a command from the Lord, but I give my opinion as one who . . . is worthy of trust" (1 Corinthians 7:25). He concludes by saying, "I *think* that I too have God's Spirit" on this matter (7:40, italics added).

Some people have thought Paul was putting down sex as unchristian or unspiritual. Not at all. He shared the high regard of the Jews for God's good gift of sexuality.

For the Jews, it was normal and wholesome for a husband and wife to enjoy sexual relations. "Enjoy life with the woman you love, as long as you live" (Ecclesiastes 9:9).

Even a tough, independent bachelor like Paul understood the sexuality of marriage. Paul wrote that husbands and wives ought to satisfy each other's sexual needs. Do not refuse one another except by common agreement—for a period of prayer. He even suggested that the prayer time ought not be too long (1 Corinthians 7:3-5)!

Why his emphasis on singleness? Because of his zeal for the gospel. Family life takes time and energy, and Paul had turned his total energy toward winning men and women to Christ. He wanted others to do the same.

Women

People misread Paul because they fail to understand his society. In Near Eastern society women were either quiet in the back rooms while the men talked or were loose women of the streets. Suddenly, in the church, a revolution was occurring. Men and women were together, in prayer, in testimony, in witness and work. Priscilla instructed Apollos in the ways of the Holy Spirit. Some women went wild with their newly found freedom. They let their hair down like women of the streets. Some, uninformed in the Scriptures, were like dry sponges, eager to soak it all up. They were continually asking questions, shattering social customs of good conduct, and aggravating the congregations. To the women who got carried away speaking in tongues, asking too many questions, violating accepted customs, Paul wrote, Be quiet; ask your husband those questions when you get

NOTES, REFLECTIONS, AND QUESTIONS

home. At that moment in history the women were overstepping their bounds.

Picture the Corinthian church: People got drunk at Holy Communion. They grabbed food in front of one another at the church suppers. (The Lord's Supper and church supper were not yet separated.) They experienced religious excitement and spoke in unknown tongues. Women were careless in dress and talked too much in their new world of acceptance and freedom. Order, wrote Paul; have order, good conduct, decency, and mutual respect between wives and husbands.

Paul wrote to the Galatians, "There is no difference between Jews and Gentiles, between slaves and free men, between men and women; you are all one in union with Christ Jesus" (Galatians 3:28). Love and respect for the other person were the key.

Food

Those to whom Paul wrote were freed from Jewish food laws (except they did not drink blood), but a religious problem existed regarding animals offered in pagan sacrifice. These new Christians did not offer sacrifices in the temples of Aphrodite or Zeus, of course. Nor did they go to celebrations where the meat was eaten as an act of worship. But much of the meat that had been sacrificed to idols was sold in meat markets. Should they eat *that* meat? Paul quotes the newly free people who said "an idol stands for something that does not really exist" (1 Corinthians 8:4). True, so meat is meat—except to some who had only recently been idol worshipers and who had a tender conscience on this matter. If they ate the meat that had been sacrificed to idols, they were afraid it would mean they were still worshiping Zeus or Aphrodite. What to do?

Paul said the issue is love. If you destroy someone else by your new freedom, you are not building up the church. "If food makes my brother sin, I will never eat meat [that has once been dedicated in idol worship] again, so as not to make my brother fall into sin" (8:13).

An analogy might be made to alcohol. We "have knowledge" that Jesus drank the wine at Jewish meals and worship. Paul knew that young Timothy, in his zeal to be totally dedicated, drank only water (which was not pure). So Paul advised, Timothy, you are having continual stomach problems. "Take a little wine to help your digestion" (1 Timothy 5:23). But today in our fast-moving society, where many people are alcoholics and problem drinkers, where people are fighting to live sober Christian lives, many people choose not to drink because they might wound a weaker conscience and cause a brother or sister to stumble. " 'We are allowed to do anything'—but not everything is helpful. No one should be looking out for his own interests, but for the interests of others" (1 Corinthians 10:23-24). Love for Christ and one's neighbor governs our freedom.

NOTES, REFLECTIONS, AND QUESTIONS

NOTES, REFLECTIONS, AND QUESTIONS

Tongues

In every great revival of Christian faith, the Holy Spirit has poured forth. People have spoken in prayer language, unknown tongues. This experience is not mentioned in Matthew, Luke, or John, but it occurred in the Corinthian church. Without doubt, Paul spoke in tongues. But the issue is love. The overriding concern is what builds up the church. First Corinthians 12–14 is a unit; for the love chapter, 1 Corinthians 13, is set in the middle specifically to deal with speaking in tongues.

Read again 12:1-8, 27-30. Now watch. Paul says, "I will show you a still more excellent way" (12:31, RSV). More excellent than preaching? More excellent than healing? More excellent than performing miracles or speaking in prayer language? Yes! "I may be able to speak the languages of men and even of angels. . . . I may have the gift of inspired preaching; I may have all knowledge and understand all secrets; I may have all the faith needed to move mountains—but if I have no love, I am nothing" (13:1-2). The climax is really 14:1: "It is love, then, that you should strive for."

Paul spoke in tongues, but he did not want his doing so to bring confusion in the church or to keep people from understanding the gospel.

But will it benefit the church? "In church worship I would rather speak five words that can be understood, in order to teach others, than speak thousands of words in strange tongues" (14:19). So no one is put down, order and love in the church are restored, and the priority is rightly placed on helping newcomers find the truth of Christ.

Life After Death

In 1 Corinthians 15 Paul emphasizes that resurrection is central to the Christian gospel. Some people were saying there is no resurrection. Others were wondering how it would happen, what kind of bodies they would have. Paul's point is this: Without the resurrection there is no gospel. If there is no gospel, we are still dead in our sins, still Adam and Eve wandering in disobedience somewhere east of Eden (1 Corinthians 15:12-19).

The power of resurrection faith is much more than belief that we will live after the grave. As John's Gospel proclaimed, eternal life begins here and now. We are already born anew. Resurrection is within us; we can never be destroyed. No matter what happens, God has other options for us.

"We are often troubled, but not crushed; sometimes in doubt, but never in despair; there are many enemies, but we are never without a friend; and though badly hurt at times, we are not destroyed" (2 Corinthians 4:8-9).

We live in a culture where death rules like a lord. Ever since Adam, death has claimed to have the last word. But a victory has been won. For those who accept the gospel, Christ has death behind him. He will never die again. Death does not lord it over him anymore. In the gospel we share that victory. When we die with Christ, we are raised in him and live with him. Now death has no power to hurt. Death is not lord; Jesus is Lord.

MARKS OF DISCIPLESHIP

The mark of discipleship is love. What signs do you see in yourself that you are growing in love?

____

____

What people or kinds of people do you find easy to love?

____

____

What people or kinds of people do you find difficult to love?

____

____

____

Some sinful things in our world we have got used to and take for granted as accepted common practice. What are some harmful attitudes or practices you have come to accept in the areas of sex and alcohol use?

____

____

____

To believe in resurrection means in part that God always has new options, fresh possibilities. Describe a time in your life when you thought you had run out of options.

____

____

IF YOU WANT TO KNOW MORE

Read Second Corinthians. If your time is limited, at least read 2 Corinthians 3–5. Memorize 4:8-9.

NOTES, REFLECTIONS, AND QUESTIONS

FREEDOM

"Freedom is what we have—Christ has set us free! Stand, then, as free people, and do not allow yourselves to become slaves again."

—Galatians 5:1

28 The Son Shall Set Us Free

OUR HUMAN PROBLEM

I don't know whether I'm free or not. There are so many rules. Sometimes I do my own thing, acting as if there were no moral restraints. But other times I try to be "religious" and follow the rules taught me by my family or my church. When I try to follow all the rules, I fail and feel guilty. When I have some success, I feel real religious. But I'm not very happy.

ASSIGNMENT

As you read, sense the emotion that fills Galatians. Paul is defending his message and ministry. Look particularly for his defense of his apostleship in 1:6–2:21, his defense of his gospel in 3:1–4:31, and his defense of his moral standards in 5:1–6:10.

Keep in mind that the basic question of Galatians for modern readers is the question of relationship—How do persons relate to God?

Day 1 Galatians 1 (the one gospel)
Day 2 Galatians 2 (Paul's rebuke of Peter)
Day 3 Galatians 3 (time for faith)
Day 4 Galatians 4 (children of God's promise)
Day 5 Galatians 5–6 (free in Christ, do good to everyone)
Day 6 Read and respond to "The Bible Teaching" and "Marks of Discipleship."
Day 7 Rest and prayer.

PRAYER

Pray daily before study:

"Be merciful to me, O God,
because of your constant love.
Because of your great mercy
wipe away my sins!
Wash away all my evil
and make me clean from my sin!" (Psalm 51:1-2).

Prayer concerns for this week:

Freedom

Day 1 The one gospel

Day 4 Children of God's promise

Day 2 Paul's rebuke of Peter

Day 5 Free in Christ, do good to everyone

Day 3 Time for faith

Day 6 "The Bible Teaching"

THE BIBLE TEACHING

NOTES, REFLECTIONS, AND QUESTIONS

Galatians explains the basic difference between living by the law and living by the Spirit. The question is this: Since Jesus was a Jew and honored and quoted the Old Testament, and since Jesus was the Messiah, must Gentiles become Jews?

Galatians has two powerful meanings for us. First, without Paul's teachings in Galatians the Christian church either might have remained a Jewish sect, holding on to Christ and Jewish law and customs at the same time, or might have spun off into a new religion without Old Testament and Jewish roots. It did neither.

Second, there is a tendency in Christianity to become "moralistic" or "legalistic." To become "free" from a religion of rules without becoming a person with no standards is our task. Galatians will help us.

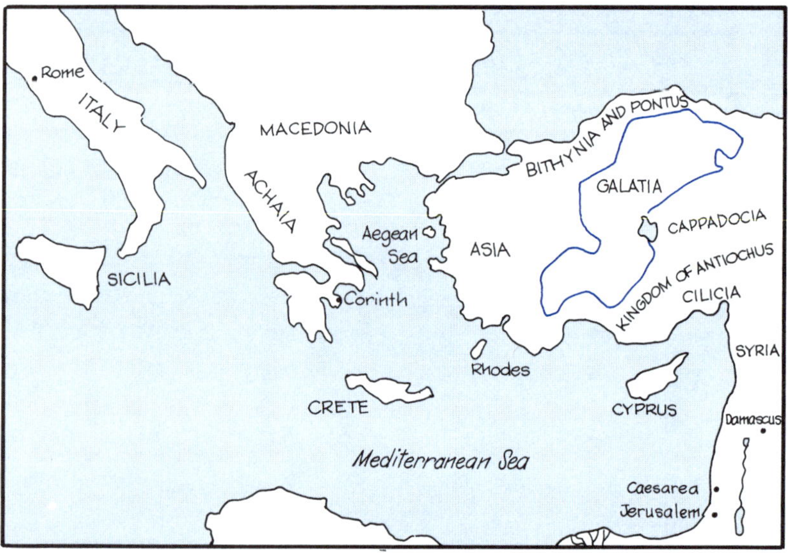

Galatia was a region in Asia Minor, not a city. Several congregations were scattered there. Paul had founded some of them. Now he learned that some Jewish and Gentile Christians had come into these churches and were spreading false and dangerous teachings. They questioned Paul's authority, accusing him of not being Jewish enough or not being a true apostle. Besides that, they were present and Paul was absent. The issues were so crucial that Paul wrote in frustration and anger, "If anyone preaches to you a gospel that is different from the one you accepted [and some were], may he be condemned to hell!" (Galatians 1:9). Again, "I wish that the people who are upsetting you would go all the way; let them go on and castrate themselves!" (5:12). We are dealing with spiritual life-and-death matters.

These people kept suggesting that, yes, faith in Christ was important, but other things were also important: circumcision; certain Jewish food laws; special Jewish holy days; perhaps separation into groupings of slave and free, men and women.

These Gentile, Jewish Christians may have been influenced by those who believed there were higher forms of knowledge, higher forms of righteousness. If such belief were combined with Jewish ritual and practice, persons could gain salvation by their achievements.

Paul blasted these ideas because they taught the idea of an earned redemption. He, better than they, knew the full meaning of the law. They were playing with it; he had taken it absolutely seriously. He had been Pharisee of the Pharisees, trying with total life commitment to keep every aspect of the law. Why? Because if you are going to be saved by the law, you have to keep it all, not just selected parts.

Circumcision for Paul was not just a ritual. It was a sign of placing oneself under Jewish law. Are you going to observe every one of the Jewish holy days as prescribed in Leviticus? Are you going to eat certain foods, not eat others? Or are you going to heal the sick on the sabbath? Are you going to eat with non-Jews in their homes? Will you work side by side with women? with Gentiles?

You who want to say that belonging to Christ Jesus is not enough, that there are other things you must do, where will you stop? Is God's saving work in Jesus Christ not enough? Is his sacrifice only partial so that you must sacrifice a few animals besides? Is the righteousness Christ Jesus gives only ninety percent of your needs?

Either you are saved by God through the cross of Jesus Christ or you are not, declared Paul. You can't have it half way or both ways.

Paul reminded his readers that even Peter and Barnabas had wavered. They had seen with their own eyes uncircumcised Gentiles converted, forgiven, filled with the Holy Spirit, motivated by love of Jesus and neighbor. Yet, when criticized by conservative Jews for eating with Gentiles, they drew back. Paul confronted Peter face to face. Either they (Peter and Barnabas) were saved by grace or not. Either they were one in Christ or not. Paul understood clearly. They could not have it both ways (2:1-21).

Now Paul had to deal with related issues. Why then did we have the law of Moses in the first place? To show what wrongdoing is and to restrain us from sin. The law, he wrote, took care of us in the way a legal guardian takes care of a minor who is not yet ready to assume full responsibilities as son or daughter. But now, in Jesus Christ, we've come of age; we're full children of God. We live not by rules but in relationship (3:21–4:7).

Historical Observations

Most people play with the law, and then only parts of it, obeying it when it pleases them. When someone comes along who takes the law seriously, it leads to imprisonment of the soul. Martin Luther and John Wesley are examples of people who become spiritually imprisoned by their law-filled understanding of Christianity.

NOTES, REFLECTIONS, AND QUESTIONS

NOTES, REFLECTIONS, AND QUESTIONS

Luther, trying to please God, became a Roman Catholic priest, then a monk, then a disciplined scholar—studying the Bible, confessing daily, fasting, whipping himself to the point of exhaustion, finally going to Rome and kissing the steps of Saint Peter's Church. Were not these acts works of righteousness? Did they not bring saving grace? No, they were imprisoning. Luther, when his salvation came, knew that he was saved by the grace of God alone.

John Wesley walked a similar path. Child of a preacher, honor student, thrifty, sexually pure, he honored mother and father. He visited the prisons, fasted, prayed, studied Scripture in Greek and Hebrew, became an Anglican priest and then a missionary to the Indians in Georgia.

But at Aldersgate he felt the burden of keeping the law fall away. He said that he felt his heart strangely warmed. He felt he did trust in Christ alone for salvation. He felt the personal assurance that Christ had taken away his sins and had saved him from the law of sin and death.

The Freedom Lifestyle

Now the issue becomes this: What does the believer do with his or her newfound freedom? "You were called to be free. But do not let this freedom become an excuse for letting your physical desires control you. Instead, let love make you serve one another" (Galatians 5:13).

The believer is not only saved *by* Christ; he or she is called to live *in* Christ. The new life is the life of love, for "the whole Law is summed up in one commandment: 'Love your neighbor as you love yourself ' " (5:14). The whole purpose of the law was to cause the people of God to love God and neighbor. Now in Christ, people not only fulfill the law but rejoice in doing so.

The Spirit-led person lives *above* the law; that is, as Jesus suggested, a life more righteous than that of those who lived *by* the law. When believers are living in the Holy Spirit, they want to please God. Not as a burden, but because they love God. They live in God. They want to live lives better than the law.

A son or a daughter can live grudgingly according to household rules. But a loving son or daughter can move beyond that into an acceptance, a fellowship, a spiritual unity. For those who live in Christ's Spirit, "the Spirit produces love, joy, peace, patience, kindness, goodness, faithfulness, humility, and self-control. There is no law against such things as these" (5:22-23).

An old legend reads that people came wanting to buy what the Spirit produces. They were told, "We don't sell the fruit; we sell the seeds." These traits of the holy life are not forced, not strived for, certainly not bought. Rather, they grow out of the believer's heart. They grow out of the indwelling presence of Jesus, the promised Holy Spirit.

Paul wants us to be free, free to love, free to embrace the very intent of the law in joyous obedience, free to live in the harmony God intended from the beginning of Creation. "If we live by the Spirit, let us also walk by the Spirit" (5:25, RSV). That means we will "Help carry one another's burdens" (6:2). That means "as often as we have the chance, we should do good to everyone, and especially to those who belong to our family in the faith" (6:10).

Luther and Wesley, like Paul, freed from the law's imprisonment, were able to serve with a joyous heart. They were so full of freedom and love that the old rules could hold them no longer. Faith itself became for them the way to true holiness.

MARKS OF DISCIPLESHIP

Disciples are persons whose faith is nourished by hope, whose life is powered by love. Disciples are set free by Christ to love. Their newfound freedom does not cause them to do whatever they wish, but, rather, to live in the spirit of love and self-giving a lifestyle higher than any set of rules.

How do you feel you are imprisoned by religious rules?

People often say, "Go ahead; be a Christian. You can still do whatever you want, because God forgives you." How does Paul's message of freedom differ from this idea?

How are you using your freedom in Christ?

IF YOU WANT TO KNOW MORE

A book we will not have time to read is Paul's letter to the Philippians. Written from prison, it bubbles with joy and confidence. You'll enjoy reading it, especially such familiar passages as 2:5-11; 3:12-14; 4:8.

NOTES, REFLECTIONS, AND QUESTIONS

TRAINING

"Take the teachings that you heard me proclaim in the presence of many witnesses, and entrust them to reliable people, who will be able to teach others also."

—2 Timothy 2:2

29 A Pastor Gives Guidance

OUR HUMAN PROBLEM

I am bored by old-fashioned advice. People say they did it this way or that way. Old-timers sound pious, strict, "preachy." What do they know? These are new days, and I want to find out things for myself.

ASSIGNMENT

Watch for the phrase "this is a true saying," which is repeated throughout the letters to Timothy. The phrase points to the letters' emphasis on the importance of sound doctrine.

Day 1 1 Timothy 1–2 (keep faith and pray)
Day 2 1 Timothy 3–4 (duties of church leaders and helpers)
Day 3 1 Timothy 5–6 (duties of widows and elders)
Day 4 2 Timothy 1–2 (an approved worker)
Day 5 2 Timothy 3–4 (counsel and instructions)
Day 6 Titus 3:1-8 (Christian conduct); read and respond to "The Bible Teaching" and "Marks of Discipleship."
Day 7 Rest and prayer.

PRAYER

Pray daily before study:

"Teach me your ways, O LORD;
make them known to me.
Teach me to live according to your truth,
for you are my God, who saves me.
I always trust in you" (Psalm 25:4-5).

Prayer concerns for this week:

TRAINING

Day 1 Keep faith and pray

Day 4 An approved worker

Day 2 Duties of church leaders and helpers

Day 5 Counsel and instructions

Day 3 Duties of widows and elders

Day 6 Christian conduct, "The Bible Teaching"

THE BIBLE TEACHING

NOTES, REFLECTIONS, AND QUESTIONS

Three short books, First and Second Timothy and Titus, are called the Pastoral Letters. They are more like manuals for Christian conduct and church administration than they are like personal letters. Most ordination services for ministers today contain quotations from First or Second Timothy. Priests and pastors, bishops, elders, and deacons listen carefully to Paul's instructions to Timothy.

Readers of these letters will quickly recognize that they are encountering some of Paul's most intimate thoughts and feelings, yet are dealing with a more mature church at a later time in history. Many scholars think that in these letters Paul's personal correspondence to Timothy has been organized and designed by fellow missionaries to meet some of the needs of a later period of church life. That is helpful for us, because many issues dealt with under these more "settled" conditions still face us today.

Timothy's father was Greek (Acts 16:1), and his mother was a Jewish Christian. Timothy was like a son to bachelor Paul, a faithful and trusted young colleague. His character was beyond question; he was extremely conscientious. Paul sent Timothy to struggling churches in Thessalonica and Corinth. The two men traveled together to Jerusalem and finally to Rome. At some point, Timothy was in prison (Hebrews 13:23).

Paul's Pastoral Counsel to Timothy

• Help people stick to the central doctrines of the faith; concentrate on the essentials. Always in religious circles, some people want to argue. They end up in conflict and waste valuable time. Serious searching for sound teachings is quite different from irresponsible debating of ideas without any intention of personal commitment. In one case the Word becomes flesh; in the other case the Word becomes words.

• Teach carefully. Teaching sound doctrine to growing Christians is a difficult and awesome responsibility. The Letter of James declares, "Not many of you should become teachers. As you know, we teachers will be judged with greater strictness than others" (James 3:1).

That is true, of course, because the teacher teaches and shapes the minds and the lives of the learners. Yet Paul urged Timothy to teach with diligence. "Hold firmly to the true words that I taught you. . . . Through the power of the Holy Spirit, who lives in us, keep the good things that have been entrusted to you" (2 Timothy 1:13-14).

To Paul and Timothy, teaching was more than "head knowledge." Teaching means making disciples, training people in the Christian walk. Biblical knowledge and the understanding of the scriptural meaning are essential. Today with the New Testament added to the Old Testament, the words of Paul are even more true: "All Scripture is inspired by God and is useful for teaching the truth, rebuking error, correcting faults, and giving instruction for right living, so that the person who serves God may be fully qualified and equipped to do every kind of good deed" (3:16-17).

While it is true that not everyone should be a teacher, it is also true that the need for teachers is overwhelming. Already in the early church, the task was too great for the apostles. Just as Moses needed help in supervising the Hebrews in the desert, so pastors and priests in a crowded world cannot carry on the teaching ministry without help from disciplined, trained lay teachers.

Listen to Paul: "Take the teachings that you heard me proclaim in the presence of many witnesses, and entrust them to reliable people, who will be able to teach others also" (2:2).

But you say, teaching is tough. Absolutely! Look again at the expectations laid on Timothy. He was expected to have the discipline of a soldier, the dedication of an athlete, the willingness of a farmer to work hard (2:1-7).

• Spiritual authority and leadership. We are to learn and to teach respect for certain kinds of authority. We give respect and authority to church leaders (bishops, literally overseers, sometimes translated "presbyter" or "elder"). We expect spiritual leaders to care for their families, be sober, not hungry for money, apt teachers, and not new converts so they will not "swell up with pride" (1 Timothy 3:1-7). Church helpers (deacons) have similar requirements.

• Care for the family. With normal sickness and death increased by persecution and martyrdom, many widows existed with little hope of livelihood.

The task was heavy for the early church. First, every family should take care of its own, for "If anyone does not take care of his relatives, especially the members of his own family, he has denied the faith and is worse than an unbeliever" (1 Timothy 5:8).

Second, young widows should remarry if possible so they would not waste their time going from house to house as gossips and busybodies (5:13). Keep in mind that opportunities for employment were almost nonexistent. Prostitution and slavery were the most likely options. But widows who were women over sixty, without family, were the responsibility of the church. The miracle of love in the congregation was to care for these women as long as they lived. The Christian communities took seriously Paul's words to the Galatians, "We should do good to everyone, and especially to those who belong to our family in the faith" (Galatians 6:10).

• Money. Is money evil? Money can do so much good and so much harm. Jesus taught more about money than he did about prayer. He warned against anxiety over what we would eat and wear. "It is much harder," he said, "for a rich person to enter the Kingdom of God than for a camel to go through the eye of a needle" (Matthew 19:24).

NOTES, REFLECTIONS, AND QUESTIONS

Both First and Second Timothy warn that disciples will be led astray by concern for money. "For the *love of money* is a source of all kinds of evil. Some have been so eager to have it that they have wandered away from the faith and have broken their hearts with many sorrows" (1 Timothy 6:10, italics added).

Think carefully about what you read in the Bible. How can we avoid "love of money"? Consider the following:

Put God first. How can we do that with money?

We are to use our God-given talents. Some people have a talent for making money. Some people are so talented as entertainers, athletes, physicians, business and professional people that money comes to them. How can they be Christians? Read 1 Timothy 6:17-19. Can rich people be saved? How?

Conclusion: The wisdom of the older has been given to the younger. Youth is no handicap. "Do not let anyone look down on you because you are young, but be an example for the believers in your speech, your conduct, your love, faith, and purity" (1 Timothy 4:12). Old age must pass the responsibilities of leadership to the young. Paul, in a final burst of inspiration, passed the torch to his spiritual son and disciple: "You must keep control of yourself in all circumstances; endure suffering, do the work of a preacher of the Good News, and perform your whole duty as a servant of God.

"As for me, the hour has come for me to be sacrificed; the time is here for me to leave this life. I have done my best in the race, I have run the full distance, and I have kept the faith" (2 Timothy 4:5-7).

Wouldn't it be wonderful if every Christian believer could say those words at the close of life!

NOTES, REFLECTIONS, AND QUESTIONS

MARKS OF DISCIPLESHIP

A disciple respects authority and wants to learn from the wisdom of an older leader or helper.

What kind and amount of authority and respect should you give your Sunday school teachers, church leaders, pastors and priests, bishops, elders, deacons, and stewards?

Paul taught Timothy and then sent him out to continue the ministry. If you were sent out now, in what ways would you feel ready?

In what areas would you feel the need of more wisdom and guidance from older persons?

IF YOU WANT TO KNOW MORE

Titus is the third of the Pastoral Letters. Read Titus 1–2; 3:12-15. Look for ideas that sum up the gospel message.

NOTES, REFLECTIONS, AND QUESTIONS

SACRIFICE

"Let us, then, hold firmly to the faith we profess. For we have a great High Priest who has gone into the very presence of God—Jesus, the Son of God. Our High Priest is not one who cannot feel sympathy for our weaknesses. On the contrary, we have a High Priest who was tempted in every way that we are, but did not sin. Let us have confidence, then, and approach God's throne, where there is grace. There we will receive mercy and find grace to help us just when we need it."

—Hebrews 4:14-16

30 Our Great High Priest

OUR HUMAN PROBLEM

We cannot figure out a way to be cleansed of our sins. Our faith grows tired and powerless. So we live lives of quiet desperation or turn to punishing ourselves, worrying, deadening our spiritual pain with alcohol or drugs, or developing neurotic symptoms.

ASSIGNMENT

As you read Hebrews, you will discover many verses, phrases, and ideas familiar to you from their frequent use in the sermons, hymns, and rituals of the church. Scattered throughout the book you will find clues to its purpose: In the face of persecution and suffering, a kind of weariness in the faith was taking over. The writer calls readers to steadiness, patience, and endurance.

Day 1 Read and respond to "The Bible Teaching."
Day 2 Hebrews 1–2 (Christ greater than angels)
Day 3 Hebrews 3–4 (Christ greater than Moses)
Day 4 Hebrews 5–7 (priesthood of Christ)
Day 5 Hebrews 8–10 (earthly worship, arranger of a new covenant)
Day 6 Hebrews 11–13 (faith, discipline rewarded by righteousness, how to please God); read and respond to "Marks of Discipleship."
Day 7 Rest.

PRAYER

Pray daily before study:

"LORD God Almighty, none is as mighty as you;
in all things you are faithful, O LORD" (Psalm 89:8).

Prayer concerns for this week:

SACRIFICE

Day 1 "The Bible Teaching"

Day 2 Christ greater than angels

Day 3 Christ greater than Moses

Day 4 Priesthood of Christ

Day 5 Earthly worship, arranger of a new covenant

Day 6 Faith, discipline rewarded by righteousness, how to please God

THE BIBLE TEACHING

The majestic Letter to the Hebrews is a mystery book to those who do not know Leviticus. Today animal sacrifices and blood offerings seem obscure, offensive, ancient rituals.

But are we so wise, we moderns? Where will we go to get rid of our guilt? What is the cure for our anxious consciences? What will take away our sin?

Some Jewish Christians were giving up, falling away, going back to Judaism. Why? Persecution. Fading faith. Familiar practices of kosher food, sabbath rules, and Temple sacrifices. Pressure from the Jewish community. The Letter to the Hebrews was written to say that Jesus is greater than the prophets, greater than the angels, greater than Moses. Hebrews proclaims that the once-and-for-all sacrifice of Jesus Christ ushers Christians into a clean conscience and an eternal salvation. Christians must hold fast as did the faithful men and women of old.

We need to understand some conccpts:

Purification for sins: Purification by water, fire, blood, and sacrifice was necessary to the Jews to be clean from moral, physical, and ritualistic impurity.

Purify (Hebrews 2:11): to make holy or Godlike—a person freed from the evil desires of the heart now trying to be obedient to the will of God.

High Priest (4:14): the Temple official who entered the Most Holy Place on the annual Day of Atonement to sprinkle blood on the lid of the Covenant Box (Exodus 25:17-22).

Melchizedek, king of Salem and priest of the Most High God, came to be regarded as the ideal priest-king who foreshadowed the Son of God (Genesis 14:17-20).

Levitical priesthood (Hebrews 7:11): Tribe of Levi who performed the rituals in the Temple. The priesthood was inherited since the Levites did not receive land.

New covenant (8:8): Term originating with Jeremiah (Jeremiah 31:31), a new arrangement between God and God's people in which the law of holy love would be written on the people's hearts.

Most Holy Place (Hebrews 9:3): The Tent and later the Temple was divided into three parts: an open-air court; the Holy Place; and behind a curtain, the Most Holy Place or "the place where God speaks." The Most Holy Place contained the Covenant Box.

Atonement

Our needs are different from the needs of those Jewish Christians to which Hebrews was addressed, and yet they are the same. They needed to realize that animal sacrifices were no longer adequate. (In A.D. 70, when the Temple was destroyed by the Romans, Temple sacrifice ceased and never again was practiced among the Jews. Hebrews was probably written before A.D. 70.)

NOTES, REFLECTIONS, AND QUESTIONS

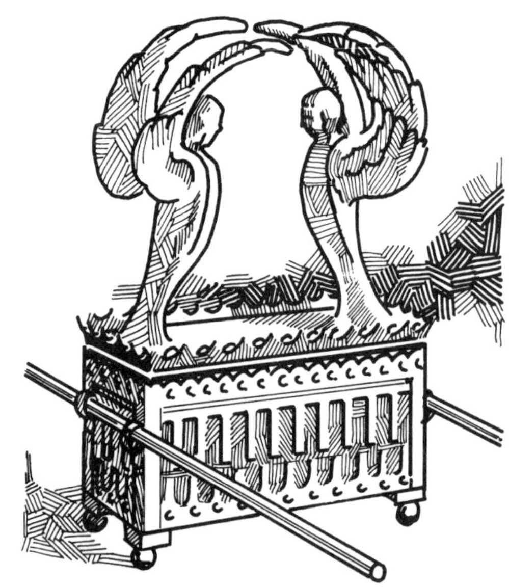

The ark of the covenant (called the Covenant Box in Today's English Version), a wooden chest overlaid with gold (Exodus 25:10-22), was a symbol of God's presence among the Hebrews. It was placed in the Most Holy Place of the Tent and later in the Temple.

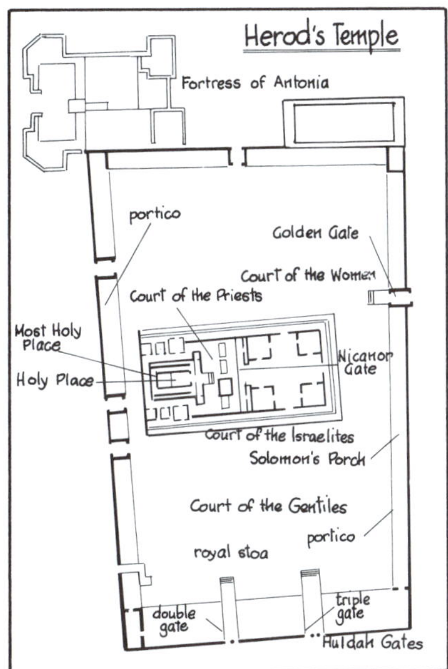

We too face the need for cleansing, for inner purification and peace. But we cannot grasp that a sacrifice is necessary, that a sacrifice is available to us, and that a sacrifice can be claimed for our spiritual lives.

Hebrews in deep, closely reasoned argument shows the way by reminding us who Jesus is. He is the Son of God; he "is the exact likeness of God's own being" (Hebrews 1:3). He is not an angel, a prophet, or a servant like Moses. He is fully God. He is also fully human. Hebrews proclaims that Jesus became like us and shared our human nature. He was human as we are human (2:14).

Anselm, a twelfth-century theologian, wrote that Jesus had to be fully man in order to reach us and had to be fully God in order to save us. He echoed Hebrews.

NOTES, REFLECTIONS, AND QUESTIONS

Herod's Temple incorporated and restored what was left of the Second Temple. It was still under construction in the time of Jesus, and the entire complex was not finished until A.D. 62–64. This is the Temple to which Jesus came.

Now comes the overwhelming comparison. The old covenant was confirmed by blood, the blood of animals sacrificed to God. The new covenant was also confirmed by blood, the blood of Jesus Christ. No more sacrifice will ever be needed.

Hebrews spotlights the blood sacrifice, which was at the heart of the old covenant. If a religion is going to have high moral expectations and important prescribed duties, that religion must have a way to remove guilt. For, as Paul wrote to the Romans, "everyone has sinned and is far away from God's saving presence" (Romans 3:23). Hebrews argues against going back to the old animal sacrifice when God has initiated a cleansing new covenant through the eternal Son and his sacrifice. Are you going to abandon or deny the atoning work of God? Study Hebrews to see the careful parallels between the old and new covenants. Notice that it is the same God who acted in both covenants.

What were the sacrifices offered for sin? Look again at Leviticus 16.

Who offered the sacrifices in the old covenant?

From whom did the priest receive his authority?

Why do you think the sacrifices continued *daily* in the Temple in Jesus' day?

What was the sacrifice Jesus offered?

Who was this Jesus who offered the sacrifice in the new covenant?

From whom did he receive his authority?

Notice that Jesus was not a levitical priest but was a descendant of the tribe of Judah. That is where the strange reference to Melchizedek comes in—no genealogy, no birth, no death, no reference to Aaron or the Levites. In fact, this strange, mysterious priest-king is greater than Abraham

NOTES, REFLECTIONS, AND QUESTIONS

or Levi. His order of priesthood is directly from God, not inherited or transmitted.

The former priests were many in number (Hebrews 7:23); Jesus stands alone. They died, so new ones had to be chosen. Jesus holds his priesthood permanently (7:24).

Although the animals were to be perfect, they had to be offered by imperfect men over and over. In Jesus, the offering was without sin, and the offerer was without sin. It was a perfect sacrifice, done once and for all (7:27).

Jesus was no martyr struck down by political intrigue. He was God in human person, offering a perfect gift of love and life's blood sacrifice for the sins of the whole world.

The word *atonement* means to break down the barrier of sin between people and God. The arranger of the new covenant brings people and God together. He brings peace between the two. Atonement means at-one-ment, the Holy God at one with us.

Hebrews points to the power of the divine sacrifice to cleanse our hearts. Remember that repentance was always necessary for the sacrifice to be effective. Repentance does not mean simply saying "I'm sorry"; it means a turning away from sin toward God, a turning over of life purpose to the loving will of God.

Atonement means becoming a new being, clean and at peace with God. To experience "the blood" is to experience the forgiveness or grace of God. The Letter to the Hebrews insists, "sins are forgiven only if blood is poured out" (9:22). Blood is the ultimate sacrifice. In the Bible "blood" and "life" were the same. The ancients thought that life was in the blood. As the blood drained out, the life drained out. To give one's blood is to give one's life.

"Hold on Firmly"

Because Hebrews is concerned about those who might fall away from this great salvation, the letter reminds us to "hold on firmly" and "be concerned for one another, to help one another to show love and to do good. Let us not give up the habit of meeting together, as some are doing. Instead, let us encourage one another all the more" (Hebrews 10:23-25).

Some people, as they drift away from fellowship, from Holy Communion, from scriptural remembrances, and from mutual encouragement, forget what Christ accomplished on the cross and forget his pleas on their behalf.

The Letter to the Hebrews now becomes stern. If after receiving this great sacrifice, we drift away and "purposely go on sinning," we "wait in fear for the coming Judgment" (10:26-27). "What, then, of the person who despises the Son of God? who treats as a cheap thing the blood of God's covenant which purified him from sin? who insults the Spirit of grace? Just think how much worse is the punishment he will deserve! . . . It is a terrifying thing to fall into the hands of the living God!" (10:29-31).

NOTES, REFLECTIONS, AND QUESTIONS

Few passages in Scripture are as powerful and as inspiring as Hebrews 11–13. In an effort to encourage Christians to hold firmly to their faith, the writer recalls witnesses recorded because of their faith—Abel, Enoch, Noah, Abraham, Sarah, Isaac, Jacob, Joseph, Moses, Rahab. Yet in spite of their great faith, they need *us* in order to be perfected.

We need them; they need us. "So then, let us rid ourselves of everything that gets in the way, and of the sin which holds on to us so tightly, and let us run with determination the race that lies before us. Let us keep our eyes fixed on Jesus, on whom our faith depends from beginning to end" (12:1-2).

MARKS OF DISCIPLESHIP

A sacrifice can be powerful. A mother scrubs floors so her daughter can go to college. An older brother offers a kidney transplant so his younger brother can live. A man or woman chooses a vocation like teaching or preaching or scientific research at considerable financial sacrifice. A pilot missionary is shot by a rebel soldier, making the final sacrifice of his faith.

A sacrifice is measured by who is giving it, by whether it is voluntary, by how much the sacrifice costs, and by the cause in which the sacrifice is given.

A pastor sometimes has a person come into his or her study acknowledging a serious sin. The pastor may speak of forgiveness, but the person responds, "I guess it is true that God forgives people. But I don't know if God can forgive me. Even if there was some sort of divine forgiveness, I don't think I could ever forgive myself."

If that person were willing to listen to you, what would you say?

___

___

___

Disciples accept God's forgiveness and their cleansing from sin.

Have you experienced a mercy, an amazing grace in which you felt that your sins were forgiven and that you were cleansed and made right with God? Comment.

___

___

___

NOTES, REFLECTIONS, AND QUESTIONS

Not only are we surrounded by a great crowd of biblical witnesses, but we also have some people in our lifetime cheering us on. List a few people across your life or right now who are pulling for you and encouraging you to be a faithful Christian.

____

____

If they are still alive, why not drop them a note, thanking them for their encouragement.

IF YOU WANT TO KNOW MORE

Read aloud Hebrews 11–13.

Covenant always means a compact entailing God's loving initiative and humankind's response in faithfulness. As you recall God's covenant with Abraham (Genesis 12:1-4), confirmed in the law of Moses, list some essential elements of the confirmation of the old covenant. Here are some references to help: Genesis 15; 17:9-14; Exodus 19:1-6; 24:1-8, 12, 15-18; 25:8, 10, 16-17, 21-22; 28:1-4; 29:1-9; 30:1-10; 31:12-18; Deuteronomy 14:22-23.

NOTES, REFLECTIONS, AND QUESTIONS

HOLY

"You are the chosen race, the King's priests, the holy nation, God's own people, chosen to proclaim the wonderful acts of God, who called you out of darkness into his own marvelous light."

—1 Peter 2:9

31 A People Set Apart

OUR HUMAN PROBLEM

I don't like to be "different"; do you? Even appearing to be different makes me uncomfortable. People make fun of others who seem strange and out of step with the crowd. And I surely don't want to be thought of as "holy." I don't even want to *be* holy—what a bore! Nothing turns folks off more than proud, self-righteous, holier-than-thou persons.

ASSIGNMENT

The letters of Peter certainly call into question the popular idea that "it pays to serve God," that we will be rewarded for our goodness. Clearly, holy living was resulting in suffering for the readers of these letters. Notice also that stressful times leave people open to false teachings, hence the call to remain faithful.

Day 1 1 Peter 1–2 (new life and living hope, God's own people)
Day 2 1 Peter 3–5 (changed lives, suffering, instruction and encouragement)
Day 3 2 Peter 1–3 (false teachers and teaching)
Day 4 Leviticus 11; 19 (clean and unclean, holiness and justice)
Day 5 Ephesians 5–6 (living in the light, armor of God)
Day 6 Read and respond to "The Bible Teaching" and "Marks of Discipleship."
Day 7 Rest and worship.

PRAYER

Pray daily before study:
"May my words and my thoughts be
acceptable to you,
O LORD, my refuge and my redeemer!"
(Psalm 19:14).

Prayer concerns for this week:

Day 1 New life and living hope, God's own people	Day 4 Clean and unclean, holiness and justice
Day 2 Changed lives, suffering, instruction and encouragement	Day 5 Living in the light, armor of God
Day 3 False teachers and teaching	Day 6 "The Bible Teaching"

THE BIBLE TEACHING

NOTES, REFLECTIONS, AND QUESTIONS

Holy means set apart for God. A chalice is set apart for Holy Communion, not used for orange juice at breakfast. A sanctuary is set apart for worship, not used for roller skating on Saturday night. In a secular world, some things are set apart as sacred. In an ordinary workaday world, some things are set apart to be special, dedicated, precious.

Holy has the same root as words like *whole, wholesome, holistic, heal, health,* and *hallow*. To be holy is to be whole, clean, healthy, harmonious.

We learned from the beginning that God called a special people to be set apart, to be different, to be peculiar. First Peter helps us understand how the Christian community has become the "set-apart people." We could not understand First Peter if we had not read Old Testament history.

If you wonder why we are rereading passages from Leviticus, it is to remind us of our powerful symbolic roots in Israel's experience.

Baptism

Some scholars think First Peter was a baptismal sermon before it became a general letter to the churches of Asia Minor. Baptismal images abound. The words "he gave us new life" (1 Peter 1:3) not only recall our Lord's appeal to Nicodemus (John 3:3) but also Paul's reference to the death of self and resurrection with Christ in baptism (Romans 6:4). In First Peter, we have a strong emphasis on the new creation in Christ rather than only on a washing away of sin's stain. A baptized Christian is born anew and lives in a new community. Baptism, like circumcision of old, signified initiation into the corporate life of God's people.

First Peter reminds us that in Noah's flood eight persons were "saved by the water," and compares the saving power of baptism. Water, "which was a symbol pointing to baptism, which now saves you. It is not the washing off of bodily dirt, but the promise made to God from a good conscience. It saves you through the resurrection of Jesus Christ" (1 Peter 3:21). Of course, Christian baptism also calls to memory the *deliverance* in the crossing of the water of the Red Sea and the *promise* in the walking through the water of the river Jordan.

In a desert country, minimal amounts of water were available. The early church used a three-cupped shell for baptism and ultimately ruled that three drops of water were minimal for baptism in the name of the Father, the Son, and the Holy Spirit.

We are not sure when infant baptism began. The Philippian jailer was baptized along with "all his family" (Acts 16:33). Were infants involved? No one knows. Without doubt, entire families were baptized before long.

In Rome, unwanted babies were discarded on open hillsides or in courtyards to die of exposure. Early Christians, at least by the beginning of the second century, slipped out into the night and rescued these tiny babies. They brought them into their homes and church meetings and baptized them into the protected community of faith. Thus, through baptism, the children were delivered, given new life, and received by the people of God.

When you see a baby baptized in the church, in what ways do you believe that child is "set apart"?

____

____

Blood

Just as the Hebrews in Egypt wiped their doorposts with the blood of the sacrificial lamb (Exodus 12:21-23; 12:5), the holy people (people and priests) were sprinkled with blood (24:8; 29:21), and so later Christians have symbolically been sprinkled with the blood of Christ. "You know what was paid to set you free . . . . it was the costly sacrifice of Christ, who was like a lamb without defect or flaw" (1 Peter 1:18-19). As Christians, we remember the divine sacrifice when we drink the cup of wine in Holy Communion and when we sing hymns of God's grace, atonement, and forgiveness. As you think about receiving Holy Communion, in what ways have you understood yourself and others to be "set apart"?

____

____

____

The Cornerstone of the New Temple

Without question, something world-changing happened in Jesus Christ. As predicted, the Temple in Jerusalem was destroyed, but a new holy temple was built. This temple is constructed of the faithful followers of Jesus Christ. The cornerstone, a dramatic Old Testament image, is Jesus Christ himself. People thought the cornerstone was unworthy, so they tossed it aside. But God claimed it.

> "The stone which the builders rejected as worthless
> turned out to be the most important of all"
> (1 Peter 2:7; Psalm 118:22).

Paul thought of that same stone as "a message that is offensive to the Jews and nonsense to the Gentiles" (1 Corinthians 1:23). The new holy, set-apart temple has been constructed to glorify God and to save people.

NOTES, REFLECTIONS, AND QUESTIONS

List three or four ways Jesus Christ is an offensive message or a worthless stone for many people today.

____

____

____

NOTES, REFLECTIONS, AND QUESTIONS

The Covenant People

In the Old Testament, elderly Abraham and Sarah were called to found a "chosen people," to walk out in faith, turning away from idols. They and their offspring formed a covenant community characterized by male circumcision, the tithe, rest on the sabbath, hospitality to strangers, family loyalty, and rejection of infant sacrifice. Later the covenant people were commanded to be unusually compassionate with the poor, especially careful with the weak, and never forgetful that they too were once helpless slaves in the land of Egypt (Leviticus 19). Because of the food laws given to Moses and Aaron (Leviticus 11), the covenant people became increasingly "peculiar." Then they were really set apart.

The Levites, you recall, were especially "set apart." Not only were they Hebrews, but they were the one tribe not given any land. They were to be the priests, descendants of Aaron, dedicated to the Lord, offering the continual sacrifices, eating the food of God, transmitting and administering divine law, working continually with holy things.

Now, First Peter tells us we are to be "the chosen race, the King's priests, the holy nation, God's own people"(1 Peter 2:9). What does that mean? We are called to be holy *as God is holy*. Notice the descriptions in First Peter of the new Christian community: "alert" (1 Peter 1:13); "obedient to God," not shaped by "those desires you had when you were still ignorant" (1:14); obedient "to the truth," showing "a sincere love for your fellow believers . . . with all your heart" (1:22). This new holy priesthood of all believers is supposed to "rid yourselves, then, of all evil; no more lying or hypocrisy or jealousy or insulting language" (2:1). As "priests" we are to "offer spiritual and acceptable sacrifices to God" (2:5), abstaining from "bodily passions" (2:11). We must show such good conduct "among the heathen" (for us that would be the world) that "they will have to recognize your good deeds and so praise God" (2:12).

"For the sake of the Lord submit yourselves to every human authority" (2:13). Apparently, unless state loyalty meant denial of God or God's work (Acts 4:19-20), Christians were to show respect and obedience to civil authority, pay their taxes, honor the emperor. Later, as we will see in Revelation, when Rome demanded worship of the emperor rather than honor, Christians refused and were martyred.

We are to be distinctively honest, humble, and caring.

NOTES, REFLECTIONS, AND QUESTIONS

Marriage

The husband-and-wife dynamics are fascinating. Keep in mind the heavy patriarchal (male-dominated) family life of the Near East. Read between the lines to see the spiritual revolution taking place. "You wives must submit yourselves to your husbands" (1 Peter 3:1). Why? "So that if any of them [husbands] do not believe God's word, your conduct will win them over to believe. . . . because they will see how pure and reverent your conduct is" (3:1-2).

Husbands, who had nearly life-and-death power over their families, are urged to treat their wives with respect (3:7). Why? Because they also will receive, along with their husbands, "God's gift of life" (3:7). This teaching about understanding and respect was a considerable advance over the idea that wives were property.

Suffering

Throughout the Bible we have studied and discussed suffering. Joseph suffered in an Egyptian prison, but God used it for good. The Israelites suffered in the desert, but God disciplined and tempered them. David suffered in his soul (and in his family) for his sins of passion. Israel suffered punishment that brought the nation shame and destruction because of their sins. Job experienced unrelieved tragedy and suffering that had no apparent meaning, except that God cared for him. God had reasons that were not revealed to Job.

Jesus Christ suffered and died in total obedience to the Father. We, through the eyes of faith, see in that cross the saving, sacrificial work of God. Paul suffered shipwreck and beatings, sharing in the sufferings of Christ. Paul's painful physical ailment was not removed; God's grace was enough. Paul wrote, "We also boast of our troubles, because we know that trouble produces endurance, endurance brings God's approval, and his approval creates hope. This hope does not disappoint us" (Romans 5:3-5).

Now in First Peter, we explore new dimensions of suffering. Christians are to avoid suffering that comes from evil. "If any of you suffers, it must not be because he is a murderer or a thief or a criminal or a meddler in other people's affairs" (1 Peter 4:15). Yet suffering may come to the Christian in spite of model behavior. Suffering may come precisely because a person is a Christian, a member of the body of Christ.

If you are insulted, you are blessed. Why? Because "the glorious Spirit, the Spirit of God, is resting on you" (4:14). "It is better to suffer for doing good, if this should be God's will, than for doing evil" (3:17). "If you endure suffering even when you have done right, God will bless you for it" (2:20).

"Christ himself suffered for you and left you an example" (2:21). Now the language reflects Isaiah 53. "When he was insulted, he did not answer back with an insult. . . . It is by his wounds that you have been healed" (1 Peter 2:23-24). Remember too not only the sufferings of Christ but the sufferings of other Christians. "Be firm in your faith . . . , because you know that your your fellow believers in all the world are going through the same kind of sufferings" (5:9). God will "give you firmness, strength, and a sure foundation" (5:10).

The Second Coming

Some people were giving up. They had been promised in the preaching that Christ would come soon, very soon. Some abandoned the faith; some stayed in the church rejoicing in their newfound freedom; some became bitter and cynical (2 Peter 2).

Remember, you who have lost hope, God is trying to save others. Remember too, "There is no difference in the Lord's sight between one day and a thousand years; to him the two are the same" (3:8). The new heaven and the new earth will come; but they will come as Jesus said, like a thief (3:10). Therefore, continue to be a set-apart, holy people. "Do your best to be pure and faultless in God's sight and to be at peace with him" (3:14).

MARKS OF DISCIPLESHIP

Disciples know themselves as a distinctive, peculiar people who are set apart. Some things are a no-saying: drunkenness, adultery, lying, and the like. Some things are a yes-saying: witnessing, practicing hospitality, striving for peace and justice, caring for the broken and the hard-pressed. Holiness, of an arrogant form, usually emphasizes a few "no" rules, ignores others, and entirely forgets sacrificial ministry in the world. When Mother Teresa of India says about her care for the dying, "I do it for Jesus' sake," she catches the spirit of Peter.

The disciple may wear the same kind of clothes others are wearing, speak the same language, live in the same city; but the disciple is different and knows this must be. Called out of worldly pursuits and careless living, the disciple, like Abraham, is called to be a part of a "set-apart" people blessed to be a blessing.

Think about your own life. Describe how Christ has helped you be "set apart." Give some specific examples.

NOTES, REFLECTIONS, AND QUESTIONS

Think about your own life. Describe some areas in which you need to be "set apart."

____

____

____

____

____

Recall times you have suffered because you did what was right or because you did something for your faith in Jesus Christ.

____

____

IF YOU WANT TO KNOW MORE

Study the words and phrases in Isaiah 52–53 and 55:1–56:8 and list as many as you can that have special meaning for "set-apart" people today. Add your interpretations as you prepare your list.

NOTES, REFLECTIONS, AND QUESTIONS

VICTORY

" 'These words are true and can be trusted. And the Lord God, who gives his Spirit to the prophets, has sent his angel to show his servants what must happen very soon.'

" 'Listen!' says Jesus. 'I am coming soon!' "

—Revelation 22:6-7

32 We Never Lose Hope

OUR HUMAN PROBLEM

Wars and rumors of wars continue. Prejudice, crime, disease, and drugs pervade the planet. Weeping and pain and death are constant. Justice escapes us. Where is the victory? Where is hope?

ASSIGNMENT

Do not get bogged down in detail. You are listening to an urgent sermon by an inspired preacher pleading for repentance. You are hearing a martyr urging the faithful to remain steadfast. You are reading a vision of end times that is more like poetry than prose. Don't be shocked: Christians were and are living and dying in a world of war, famine, and persecution. Those who suffer for their faith cling closely to John's Revelation.

Day 1 Preface to The Revelation, Revelation 1:1-3 (introduction); read "The Bible Teaching."
Day 2 Revelation 1:4–3:22 (letters to the seven churches)
Day 3 Revelation 4–7 (the Lamb, six seals)
Day 4 Revelation 8–12 (seventh seal, angels with trumpets, the woman and the dragon)
Day 5 Revelation 17–20 (fall of Babylon, bride of the Lamb, the final judgment)
Day 6 Revelation 21–22 (new Jerusalem); read and respond to "Marks of Discipleship."
Day 7 Rest.

PRAYER

Pray daily before study:

"Praise the LORD, all nations!
Praise him, all peoples!
His love for us is strong,
and his faithfulness is eternal.

Praise the LORD!" (Psalm 117).

Prayer concerns for this week:

VICTORY

Day 1 Preface to The Revelation, introduction, "The Bible Teaching"

Day 2 Letters to the seven churches

Day 3 Triumph of the Lamb, opening the first six seals

Day 4 Seventh seal, seven angels with trumpets, the woman and the dragon

Day 5 Fall of Babylon, bride of the Lamb, the final judgment

Day 6 New Jerusalem

THE BIBLE TEACHING

NOTES, REFLECTIONS, AND QUESTIONS

Nero lighted the streets of Rome by burning Christians on tar-soaked crosses in A.D. 64. Others were crucified or decapitated. Both Peter and Paul apparently were martyred at that time in Rome. Tradition says Peter was crucified upside down because he said he was not worthy to be crucified as Jesus was. Vespasian, Nero's successor, sent his son Titus to destroy Jerusalem in A.D. 70 in an effort to put down the Jews. When Domitian became Roman emperor in A.D. 81 and declared himself a god, the entire empire trembled. Domitian, a jealous, moody, unpredictable tyrant, cut down everyone he considered a threat. He executed his niece's husband on a charge of atheism, presumably for refusing to consider him a god. Coins found around the empire show his face and the words *Domitian Divine Caesar.* He demanded worship of himself as lord and god.

Later persecution of the Christians would be much worse. Domitian used selective terrorist tactics during his reign (A.D. 81–96). A letter from Clement of Rome to the church at Corinth about A.D. 95 refers to "the sudden and repeated misfortunes and calamities which have befallen us."

A new temple for the cult of the emperor was built in Ephesus, putting additional pressure on the Christians of Asia Minor. John, the author of Revelation, was exiled on Patmos, the penal island for political offenders, because of his loyalty to Christ (Revelation 1:9). A Christian named Antipas, a member of the church at Pergamum (a center of emperor worship) had been put to death for his fidelity to Jesus (2:13). John says that some Christians at Smyrna will face death (2:10). The souls under the altar are martyrs; others are to be killed as those had been (6:9-11). John prophesied that even more fierce persecution lay ahead for the church. Persecution did continue from time to time until the emperor Constantine saw a cross in the sky and became sympathetic to Christianity in A.D. 312. John wanted his revelation to give Christians encouragement to hold fast and remain faithful to the Lord.

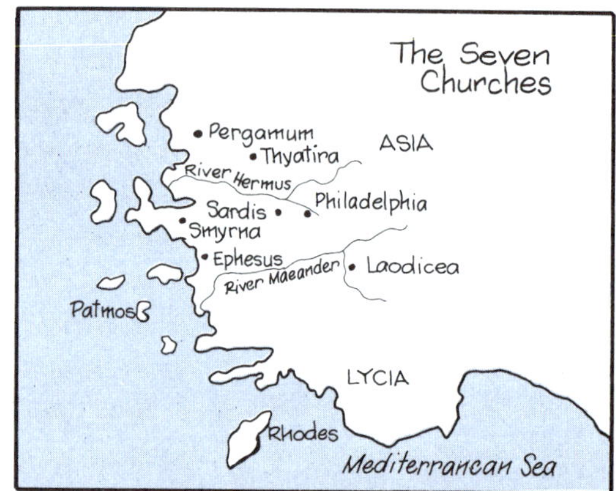

A Difficult Book

Most scholars believe that a great Christian leader, highly respected and very well known in Asia Minor, whose name was John, but not John the apostle, wrote his Revelation during this time of trouble, tension, and impending martyrdom (about A.D. 81–96).

The title of the book is "The Apocalypse," which means something hidden or unknown. It has been translated "The Revelation to John" and has come to mean the hidden revelation of end times. We were introduced to apocalyptic literature in Daniel. Prophecy in apocalyptic writings moves beyond preaching about soon-to-come events, as in Amos or Hosea, and enters into visions of last days or end times.

We know that we are going to have difficulty understanding the book. Everyone does, for several reasons.

First, apocalypses do not yield their messages easily to us because we are so far removed from the historical events, strange symbols, and ancient concepts. We must first ask what the book meant to its original readers. We are reading a spiritual vision of end times in antique terms. Like Daniel seeing visions of beasts (Daniel 7), like Ezekiel seeing the valley of the dry bones (Ezekiel 37), so John described his vision in the language of his day.

Second, as John said, he was caught up in the Spirit. An important gift of the Holy Spirit is the ability to prophesy, to proclaim the truths of God. John claimed to be standing in the role of prophet, caught up in the Spirit of God. "On the Lord's day the Spirit took control of me" (Revelation 1:10). In a vision he ate a scroll (God's Word). And he was told, "Once again you must proclaim God's message" (10:8-11).

A third reason the book is difficult is that it was intended to be. Revelation is a secret document, deliberately written "underground" to deceive the Roman authorities and all other enemies. John used mysterious symbols and perplexing numbers to cause the casual reader to think the material was written by a lunatic. Only insiders knew the secret symbols and strange names. Consider the following images:

- Babylon—really means Rome, the great city set on seven hills (18:2);
- the great beast like a leopard, bear, lion—the evil empires of Daniel, now rolled into one—Rome (13:1-2);
- the famous prostitute—again Rome (17:1);
- the Lamb—Jesus (14:1);
- the beast—the enemy of Christ (antichrist);
- Sodom—Jerusalem (11:8; see Isaiah 1:9-10);
- the woman (Israel), the child (Jesus), and the dragon (Satan) (Revelation 12);
- the red beast—the Roman Empire (17:3);
- "names insulting to God written all over it" (17:3; 13:1)—divine titles given to Roman emperors (17:9-11);
- Armageddon—hill of Megiddo in Palestine where Israel won important battles, symbolically the place of final victory (16:16).

In ancient numerology, numbers had meanings. Consider the numbers:

Number 1 stood for God, a holy number.

Number 3 stood for heaven and the Trinity.

Number 4 stood for earth, the four corners, four winds.

Number 6 is a human number, incomplete, evil.

Number 7 was considered perfect, holy, divine because it was the combination of 3 (heaven) and 4 (earth). Seven churches, seven lampstands, seven bowls (as in the Temple), seven trumpets.

Number 13 has been an "unlucky" number for hundreds of years because it is the sum of six and seven.

NOTES, REFLECTIONS, AND QUESTIONS

Number 12 is very important in Revelation. Twelve tribes of Israel in the Old Testament and twelve apostles in the New Testament refer to the people of God. The twelve tribes provided gates into the holy city.

Number 24 is two times twelve, the twelve sons of Jacob (tribes) and the twelve apostles. Together they comprise the faithful Jews and Christians of the full covenant.

The number 666: How would you mention the emperor Domitian without getting your head cut off? You could write 666, which means evil, evil, evil. Since Hebrew numbers serve also as letters, another way to write the evil Neron Caesar was 666, symbolizing Domitian (13:16-18).

Twelve thousand times twelve is 144,000, a complete number, not to be taken literally, but to describe a "perfected people of God," the complete household of faith (14:1-5). The language was complex but necessary to communicate a hidden message.

The Message to the Christians in Asia Minor

Briefly, remember these four points:

• The churches are called to burn again with the passionate fire of evangelism and faithfulness: Turn away from food offered to idols, turn away from immorality and from the teachings of the Nicolaitans who said "anything goes." Avoid the Jews who are harrassing the churches. Do not have an eye to money. Repent of lukewarm religion, and God will save you from falling away under stress.

• John warns that trouble is coming. Be sure which side you are on. The four horsemen—conquest, war, famine, and death—are coming. Be sure you are in the Lamb's victory. There is no middle ground. The earthquakes and the plagues (like in Egypt) are God's way of giving last-minute grace, but many will not repent. Notice in Revelation 11:1-2 that the outer courts of the Temple where the heathen gathered will be trampled. You are either in or out, washed in the blood of Christ or doomed, wearing either the mark of the Lamb or the mark of the beast.

• Rome will fall. "She has fallen! Great Babylon has fallen!" (18:2). Right then it appeared that Rome was all-powerful; but remember, as Isaiah said,

> "To the LORD the nations are nothing,
> no more than a drop of water" (Isaiah 40:15).

Before God all nations must bow.

Stand firm. The day will soon come when the Roman Empire, awful prostitute, slayer of God's people, will be gone from the face of the earth.

• Evil will be destroyed once and for all. Christ is married to his bride, his holy people (Revelation 19:7). Satan first will be chained (20:2) and then finally thrown into a lake of fire (20:10). Even death itself shall die (20:14), and God will bring a new heaven and a new earth (21:1).

NOTES, REFLECTIONS, AND QUESTIONS

The Message to Us

Read carefully Revelation 21–22. Notice that the God who will bring a new heaven and a new earth is the same God who created Adam and Eve, who called Abraham, and who gave his only Son. "I am the first and the last, the beginning and the end" (21:6). The one God of the universe will redeem the whole creation.

In one sense, it is all done. "It is done!" said the one who sits on the throne (21:6). But in another sense, God's mercy is still open, even in this last hour. To the repentant, God will still reach out. "To anyone who is thirsty I will [still] give the right to drink from the spring of the water of life" (21:6).

The faithful must hold on, living the Christlike life; for they are married to the Bridegroom, the Lamb of God. "Whoever wins the victory will receive this from me: I will be his God, and he will be my son" (21:7). Do not sell out or betray the Lamb!

The Holy City is symbolic in its size, its imagery, its gates, its light (21:10-27).

Watch carefully the closing of the book, beginning 22:6.

"Listen! . . . I am coming soon!" (22:7). There is still time to offer the gospel to others.

"Happy are those who obey the prophetic words in this book" (22:7). In Revelation 11, two witnesses prophesied, dressed in sackcloth. They appealed to people to repent. In the earthquake seven thousand were killed, but "the rest of the people were terrified and praised the greatness of the God of heaven" (11:13). A moment of possibility remains.

Where does it end? It ends in a garden, a garden of innocence like the garden of Eden before the Fall. No evil is permitted there, not even a snake, for the Tempter is dead. The spiritual death has been overcome by the blood of the Lamb. Death has been slain. We stand beside a tree, in the intimacy of God. It is the tree of life, the "other" tree in the garden of Eden (Genesis 2:9). We are "naked" and not afraid. Whereas Adam and Eve hid, lonely, guilt-ridden, afraid, hoping God would not find them, we will then live with God in the full light of day. The Bible begins with people hiding from God; it ends with people praying, "Come, Lord Jesus!" (Revelation 22:20).

We pray now for the coming, the soon coming, of the kingdom of God, which Jesus the Christ introduced and which he will one day complete. Meanwhile, we never lose hope, because the final victory belongs to Christ Jesus, our Savior and our Lord.

MARKS OF DISCIPLESHIP

The disciple must remain faithful even in the midst of persecution and suffering. No matter how bad the times, we hold on to our loyalty to Jesus Christ, knowing that the victory rests ultimately with God.

NOTES, REFLECTIONS, AND QUESTIONS

If you were to describe a "Babylon" today, what would it look like?

Do you feel like one of the seven churches sometimes? Which one? Why?

How is the vision of God's final victory helpful to you?

If times are short, and they certainly are for some people, who are some people you should be praying for, witnessing to right now? Name them.

IF YOU WANT TO KNOW MORE

Compare Daniel 7 with Revelation 11–13. Describe similarities and differences.

Read and write down your thoughts and questions on Revelation 13–16.

Chart of Biblical History

4 B.C.	**Jesus' birth**
A.D. 29–30	**Crucifixion of Jesus**
A.D. 30–31	**Stoning of Stephen**
A.D. 10	**Paul's birth**
A.D. 30–31	**Paul's conversion**
A.D. 44–49	**The Jerusalem Council**
A.D. 46–47	**Paul's first journey**
A.D. 50–52	**Paul's second journey**
A.D. 52–56	**Paul's third journey**
A.D. 60–61	**Paul's journey to Rome**
A.D. 62–68	**Paul martyred**
A.D. 62–68	**Peter martyred**
A.D. 70	**Destruction of Jerusalem**

NOTES, REFLECTIONS, AND QUESTIONS

Look Back on Your Journey and Remember

Record here the high points (and perhaps the low points) of your journey into and through the Bible—the insights, truths, and experiences you now treasure; the distances you traveled in time and faith; the friends you made and the companions you had along the way; and the view you now have of discipleship.

If you make my word your home you will indeed be my disciples.
—John 8:31
The Jerusalem Bible

MINISTRY

"We have many parts in the one body, and all these parts have different functions. In the same way, though we are many, we are one body in union with Christ, and we are all joined to each other as different parts of one body. So we are to use our different gifts in accordance with the grace that God has given us."

—Romans 12:4-6

33 Gifts and Graces of Each Disciple

OUR HUMAN PROBLEM

Others can do so many things better than I can. I don't have any real talent or gifts that I can use in God's work. Besides, if I did something, it might not be any good. Let somebody else do it.

ASSIGNMENT

The key to this week's task will be personal preparation for the group discussion.

Day 1 Read "The Bible Teaching." Writing related to the seven gifts will be assigned on later days.

Day 2 Read Romans 12. What are some gifts disciples should exhibit?

____

____

Read 1 Corinthians 12. What does the comparison to the human body tell me about the purpose of my unique contribution?

____

Complete "Apostles."

Day 3 Read 1 Corinthians 13. How can I perform my ministry in a loving way?

____

Complete "Prophets" and "Teachers."

Day 4 Read James 1–2. What does the phrase *faith without actions is dead* (2:26) mean?

____

Complete "Miracle Workers" and "Healers."

Day 5 Read James 3–5. After nearly nine months with my group, how have I experienced James 5:13-20 being carried out?

____

Complete "Helpers" and "Administrators."

Day 6 Read 1 Corinthians 1:17-31 and John 13:1-20. What is the message and reminder in these two passages?

____

"Recording Commitments"; list names of others and their gifts you have identified.

Day 7 Rest and prayer.

PRAYER

Pray daily before study:

"Teach me, LORD, what you want me to do,
and I will obey you faithfully;
teach me to serve you with complete devotion"
(Psalm 86:11).

Prayer concerns for this week:

THE BIBLE TEACHING

NOTES, REFLECTIONS, AND QUESTIONS

No one, not even the person most committed to Jesus Christ, sees himself or herself clearly and accurately. That is why we place ourselves in the company of fellow Christians. Often others see our spiritual usefulness better than we see it ourselves.

We have two goals this week:

1. To *identify*, by ourselves and in the group, our personal talents, our gift to the fellowship.
2. To *commit* ourselves, with the encouragement of the group, to serve God in a specific way in the days ahead.

Others in the group will be waiting to receive your thoughts about their gifts, trusting your judgment and your spiritual insight. Spend as much time thinking and praying about their gifts as about your own. They too will be ready to decide their specific ministry for the days ahead.

In addition to studying the Bible passages, think about the needs of your congregation and the hurts of the world. Think carefully about children and their needs, about youth and ways to reach them, about adults and their pain. Think of physical, spiritual, financial, and emotional needs of people you know. Think of the least, the last, and the lost; the wealthy and the self-satisfied. Remember the sick, the poor, and people who live without faith or hope. Think of individuals like the Samaritan woman who are cut off from the community.

Think of ways you can encourage and assist others to use their gifts to serve God.

Biblical Guidance

We need first to remember some things we have learned. Look up the following Scripture references to refresh your memory:

- God works in unusual and surprising ways to accomplish spiritual tasks. Remember Sarah and Abraham (Genesis 18:9-15).
- Sometimes God uses weakness to show that power belongs to God. Remember what Paul said in 1 Corinthians 1:26-29.
- God can do much through people who willingly turn themselves and what they have over to God. Remember Barnabas, the "One who Encourages" (Acts 4:36-37).
- God does not reveal the divine will to the curious but to the obedient. Remember Peter (John 21:15-19).
- Talent is varied. So are gifts and graces. You are uniquely a part of the body of Christ. No one can take your special place. Remember 1 Corinthians 12:27-31.
- Leadership in the church requires unusual humility and a willingness to serve without glory. Remember Jesus' washing of the disciples' feet (John 13:1-17).
- No one has enough power to achieve spiritual ministry by herself or himself. You will need God's help. Remember what Paul said in Philippians 4:13.

How do you determine what your "gifts" are? Older people know through experience what they enjoy, what "they are good at," what others compliment them on, what gives them a long-range sense of satisfaction, what seems to be helpful or useful to other people, and what God seems to be pushing or pulling them to do.

Young people are often feeling their way. Lacking a great deal of experience, they can experiment. They can try new things, sometimes working alone, sometimes with supervision. Many an excellent teacher began as an assistant. Many disciples are asked to be helpers and turn into prophets and preachers.

Sometimes persons receive or discover new gifts when they find themselves in new situations. The death of a loved one may show a person to be a healer through the consoling of other family members. Discussion of a social issue at school or with friends may cause someone to respond as a prophet. Through a talk with a Christian friend, someone may sense the call to be an apostle.

Gifts of the Holy Spirit differ from talents. Talents are God-given, natural, a part of being born. Gifts are received through the gift of our salvation in Christ. Both talents and gifts can be used to serve God.

Gifts are also different from "the fruit of the Spirit" (Galatians 5:22-23, RSV). "The fruit of the Spirit" is for every disciple and grows with varying degrees in each disciple. "The Spirit produces love, joy, peace, patience, kindness, goodness, faithfulness, humility, and self-control" (5:22-23). Let these qualities grow in you like wildfire.

Gifts are tasks or offices or special abilities, given by the Holy Spirit to strengthen the church. The Holy Spirit distributes these gifts differently to each disciple. Many gifts are listed in Romans 12 and 1 Corinthians 12, but we will focus on only seven. They are gifts to be apostles, prophets, teachers, workers of miracles, healers, helpers, and administrators (those who direct) (1 Corinthians 12:28-31). (We discussed speaking in tongues in our study of Corinthians.)

Apostles

Apostles are given to the church to exercise general oversight and leadership. A person called to apostolic ministry shows what we call "gifts and graces." Included should be signs of spiritual power to lead others to Christ, to encourage, and to build others up in faith and love. Pastors are apostles responsible for preaching the word, maintaining order, and administering the sacraments. Paul said that he was called to be an apostle.

Do you feel that you are being called into the full-time apostolic, ordained ministry of the church? If so, how can you act on this call?

____

Are there other persons in the group who show evidence of this gift and who, you believe, are being called to be apostles? Name them.

____

____

Prophets

A prophet is one who speaks for God. The spiritual gift is to receive and communicate a message of God to the people. Such disciples may witness quietly in private conversations. They may testify, speak, or preach in public. Some become lay speakers; others give lay testimony. Some prophets are social activists, writing or speaking a Christlike word on public issues. Some may serve in political life, in community service, or in school organizations. Even though they may receive criticism, prophets express a biblical truth in a mixed-up, selfish world.

Prophets may focus on advice, encouragement, and comfort (Isaiah 40:1-2) or on conviction, confrontation, and social change (Acts 4:19-20).

As you think about the group, which persons, if any, seem suited to be prophets?

____

____

What forms might their ministry take?

____

____

Do you have the gift of speaking for God?

____

In what ways might you use that gift?

____

____

Teachers

While it is true that not everyone should be a teacher (James 3:1), the church always needs Christlike teachers. Some people who are professionally trained can be inadequate to teach in the church or can be great teachers. Some people who have no formal training are gifted teachers.

Keep in mind the variety of teaching. Some teachers are excellent as storytellers, information givers, teachers of songs, others as leaders of sharing in small groups.

Jesus is called the great Teacher. He gave knowledge, but he also trained disciples. Learning and training in the faith go together.

Do you think God is calling you to be a teacher in the church?

____

If so, what skills do you already have?

____

What training would you need?

____

Which age groups would you feel comfortable teaching?

____

Do you think some members of the group may have the gift of teaching? Name them. (If you think of an age group for which they may be especially called to teach, mention that.)

____

____

If asked to serve in the teaching ministry of your church, would you be willing?

____

Miracle Workers

Some people seem gifted to perform miracles, signs, and wonders. Peter's prayer restored Tabitha to life (Acts 9:36-41). Sometimes tormented individuals are released from fear or guilt or grief by people who work wonders. In the early church it was a miracle when Jewish Christians and Gentile Christians sold everything and shared it "according to what each one needed." Many wonderful things took place, called "miracles and wonders" (2:43-45).

In a group, sometimes gifted people work wonders, speaking a soft word to ease tension, showing a fresh way to overcome a seemingly impossible situation, introducing an interested friend to grace. Such Christians can serve as sensitive leaders. Some people pray for others and invite them to come to Christ. A miracle worker speaks the word of *peace*. Some Christians, with a word, a deed, or a gift, mobilize the whole church for action. They become "miracle workers."

Have you spotted someone in the group who is a worker of miracles? Name the person and give an example of his or her "miracles."

____

____

Do you possess the gift of miracle worker?

____

Healers

Some people walk into a sick room, and patients feel better. Countless Christians testify that the prayers of the church helped heal them, sometimes with laying on of hands, receiving Holy Communion, or anointing with oil (James 5:13-16). Have you ever felt the healing power of God when people were praying for you?

____

Doctors, nurses, aides, psychologists, paramedics can be spiritually gifted as well as technically trained. Some have healing in their hands, their voice, their compassion.

Healing of the soul is the ministry of some. Remember that illnesses can result from unresolved grief, guilt, or unfounded fear. God uses special persons to heal the soul and thereby heal the body.

Healing or reconciliation between persons or groups is a powerful spiritual force. By sharing the love of Jesus with others, persons can help others be healed of their pain and disappointments. Persons who can heal relationships are good listeners. They care about other people's feelings.

Remember also that even people with the gift of healing do not heal every time (2 Corinthians 12:7-9). Healings do not always depend on the sick person's faith or on the faith of the persons praying (John 9:3).

Identify persons in your group who might be healers. The gift is similar to miracle workers, but don't worry. We are not concerned about sharp definitions; we are praying for spiritual power.

Has God used you in the ministry of healing?

When?

How might God use you as a healer?

If you believe you have the gift of healing, might you consider a health-related career? What possibilities come to mind?

Helpers

No gift is more important to the church. "Helping" lubricates the gears, making church life active, abundant, and joyous. The seven Greek-speaking Jews who took over the feeding of the widows were helpers (Acts 6:2-6).

Everyone is a helper at times. But a gifted helper says yes even at great sacrifice or inconvenience. Willingness to serve in this manner is a precious spiritual gift.

Are you an especially gifted helper?

Indicate some places where you could be unusually helpful.

Who in the group stands out as a Barnabas, always willing to help?

How might your church encourage more youth to be helpers?

Administrators (Those Who Direct)

The gift of administration is the ability God gives to certain members of the body of Christ to understand the goals and to make and carry out the plans to accomplish those goals. Ability to organize a team; grace to inspire, encourage, and delegate; willingness to hold people accountable with courtesy—these are the talents and gifts of administration.

Many people do not think of themselves as especially spiritual. Yet they direct church groups wisely in matters of planning, finance, and service and relief programs. The abilities to listen, to communicate clearly, and to make decisions are necessary signs of this gift. Jethro helped Moses become a better administrator (Exodus 18:13-26). Peter wisely turned the feeding of the widows over to men "who are known to be full of the Holy Spirit and wisdom" (Acts 6:3). Church leaders are expected to be good administrators (1 Timothy 3:1-7). A church youth council member is as important as a Sunday school teacher.

If a congregation or a church group is to work smoothly, some gifted people must organize and administer. Who in your group may have the gift of administration?

Do you think God is calling you to be one who directs some of the work of the church?

Where might you offer your administrative gifts in the church?

Recording Commitments

List each person in your group and record the gifts you identified for him or her. In the group you will discuss together each person's thinking about the gifts for ministry. At that time you will do two things: (1) Write down the general consensus about each person's gifts (persons may have several) and a planned place where each can serve in the months ahead. (2) Then make your own decision, advised by the group, and write down your commitment.

Name (Others)	Gift or Gifts	Planned Place of Service

The group understands my gift(s) to be

____

____

I think my gift(s) is (are)

____

____

I plan to give myself in a special way this coming year to

____

____

____

REMEMBRANCE

"The Lord Jesus on the night when he was betrayed took bread, and when he had given thanks, he broke it, and said, 'This is my body which is for you. Do this in remembrance of me.' In the same way also the cup, after supper, saying, 'This cup is the new covenant in my blood. Do this, as often as you drink it, in remembrance of me.' "

—1 Corinthians 11:23-25, RSV

34 A Last Supper Together

OUR HUMAN PROBLEM

We so easily forget who we are. We so easily forget what God has done, is doing, and will do. So often we try to go it alone. We neglect the Word of God, the food of God, the people of God.

ASSIGNMENT

The Scripture readings this week will be "remembrance" passages that fortify understanding of the peculiar covenant people and we who are joined to the covenant people, forgiven and freed by Christ Jesus and set apart for God's ministry to the world.

Day 1 Genesis 12:1-3 (blessed to be a blessing); 17:1-21 (a covenant people)
Day 2 Leviticus 2:11-16; Matthew 5:13 (a sign of covenant, saltiness)
Day 3 Jeremiah 31:31-34 (a new covenant); 2 Corinthians 3:1-6 (on human hearts)
Day 4 Matthew 5–7 (the Sermon on the Mount, a special kind of people)
Day 5 Hebrews 9 (arranger of the new covenant)
Day 6 Isaiah 6 (a call to ministry); read and respond to "The Bible Teaching."
Day 7 Rest and prayer.

PRAYER

Pray daily before study:

"Your constant love is better than life itself,
and so I will praise you.
I will give you thanks as long as I live;
I will raise my hands to you in prayer.
My soul will feast and be satisfied,
and I will sing glad songs of praise to you"
(Psalm 63:3-5).

Prayer concerns for this week:

REMEMBRANCE

Day 1 Blessed to be a blessing, a covenant people

Day 4 Sermon on the Mount, a special kind of people

Day 2 A sign of covenant, saltiness

Day 5 Arranger of the new covenant

Day 3 A new covenant, on human hearts

Day 6 A call to ministry, "The Bible Teaching"

THE BIBLE TEACHING

NOTES, REFLECTIONS, AND QUESTIONS

In the closing time together, we will remember. We will recall, in liturgical form, phrases of God's Word that we have studied. Some words are so much a part of your subconscious memory that you will hardly notice them. Others will cause you to think, Aha! I remember from Genesis, or Leviticus, or the Psalms, or the words of Jesus. We will close our DISCIPLE study by remembering, by making covenant together, by committing our lives to Christian work and witness, and by eating the meal of grace. We will focus on three spiritual realities when we worship together.

Covenant

By now you know that we walk by faith, not alone but within a covenant community. We have joined a salvation history throng marching across the centuries in conversation with God. After being in this covenant group for nine months, think of some times when, because of this group, you were able to be stronger in your faith.

In the beginning God called Abraham and Sarah to be a pilgrim people, to bring blessing to the world (Genesis 12:1-3). The covenant had signs: land, descendants, circumcision, tithe, sabbath. Later, with Moses, the covenant had enslavement and deliverance, law and liturgy. Always the covenant meant promise and hope.

Obedience is the heart of human response. Covenant is not contract. God calls an obedient people. When they disobey, everything falls apart. Isaiah was called to tell this to a people who would not listen, a hard duty (Isaiah 6:1-10). As the forms of sacrifice became superficial, as keeping the law became legalistic, as religion became ritual without righteousness, the prophets prophesied a new inner covenant. The new covenant would require a circumcised heart.

> "My sacrifice is a humble spirit, O God;
> you will not reject a humble and repentant heart"
> (Psalm 51:17).

Jesus Christ has become for us that new covenant, putting us right with God and offering the sacrifice once and for all, the arranger of the new covenant (Hebrews 9:15-28). Now as a covenant people we live in promise: "For there is no permanent city for us here on earth; we are looking for the city which is to come" (13:14). That city is the new Jerusalem where God and the covenant people will dwell together (Revelation 21:1-6). The Holy Communion or Eucharist ("the Thanksgiving") is the common meal the covenant people eat together, remembering and waiting (1 Corinthians 11:23-26).

Communion

We have learned that our faith is not a solitary faith; we live it out together. Just as ancient Hebrews ate thanksgiving sacrifices, just as they ate the Passover meal together, together we eat the bread remembering Jesus' broken body and drink the wine remembering Jesus' blood of sacrifice. In sharing Holy Communion, something happens among us; the barriers are broken down. Read Ephesians 2:14-16. How does remembering Jesus' broken body and his blood of sacrifice help you break down barriers?

____

____

____

At the same time we remember the death of Jesus Christ, we also celebrate his resurrection, knowing that Christ is with us as we share in Holy Communion. Christians know by experience and by God's Word that Christ is present as we eat together in faith. Read Revelation 3:20.

We eat a meal of grace. We come as we are, from the "country roads and lanes" (Luke 14:23). We are the least, the last, and the lost. God provides the food and all that it means. All we do is eat in faith, believing and remembering. God counts it as righteousness. We are sorry for our sins, eager to be changed, and hopeful of God's future.

The meal is sign and symbol of covenant community. It is food for the journey, sustenance for our pilgrimage of faith.

Commitment

When Isaiah was called, he responded, "I will go! Send me!" (Isaiah 6:8). So will we.

We know now from Scripture that to be God's people means to do God's work. We must be distinctive, peculiar, a people set apart. As we reread Matthew 5–7, we were reminded how different from the world we must be. Jesus taught, "You are like salt for all mankind" (Matthew 5:13). What does that phrase mean? Our peculiarity is a sign of God's work. Our saltiness is symbol and seal of what God is doing through us to save a lost world. In the Old Testament salt symbolizes the covenant relation. When people in the Near East eat salt together, they are bonded in friendship. So when we share our saltiness with others and with God, we share covenant.

God was not satisfied only to restore Israel after captivity; God gave Israel a mission:

> "I have a greater task for you, my servant. . . .
> I will also make you a light to the nations—
> so that all the world may be saved" (Isaiah 49:6).

Our Lord stood on the mountain and gave his post-Resurrection command to his disciples: "Go, then, to all peoples everywhere and make them my disciples" (Matthew 28:19).

NOTES, REFLECTIONS, AND QUESTIONS

The Covenant Service

The practice of holding special services for making and renewing covenants goes back to such Scripture passages as Deuteronomy 26:17-18 and Jeremiah 31:31-34. This covenant service draws also upon the rich tradition of Puritan literature. Although across the years the service has been revised from its early Presbyterian, Baptist, and Methodist beginnings, the covenant prayer has changed little.

Order of Worship

GATHERING

GREETING

Dearly beloved, the Christian life to which we are called is a life in Christ, redeemed from sin by him, and through him consecrated to God. Upon this life we have entered, having been admitted into that New Covenant of which our Lord Jesus Christ is mediator, and which He sealed with His own blood, that it might stand for ever.

On one side the Covenant is God's promise that He will fulfill, in and through us, all that He declared in Christ Jesus, who is the Author and Perfecter of our faith. That His promise still stands we are sure, for we have known His goodness, and proved His grace in our lives day by day.

On the other side we stand pledged to live no more unto ourselves, but to Him who loved us and gave Himself for us, and has called us to serve Him that the purpose of His coming might be fulfilled.

From time to time, we renew our vows of consecration, especially when we gather at the Lord's Table: but on this day we meet expressly, as generations of our forebears have met, that we may joyfully and solemnly renew the Covenant which bound them and binds us to God.

Let us then, remembering the mercies of God, and the hope of His calling, examine ourselves by the light of His Spirit, that we may see wherein we have failed or fallen short in faith and practice, and, considering all that this Covenant means, may give ourselves anew to God.

HYMN
"O for a Thousand Tongues to Sing"

PRAYER OF ADORATION
Let us pray:
Let us worship our Creator, the God of love;
God continually preserves and sustains us;
we have been loved with an everlasting love;
through Jesus Christ we have been given complete knowledge of God's glory.
You are God; we praise you; we acknowledge you to be the Lord.
Let us glory in the grace of our Lord Jesus Christ.
Though he was rich, for our sakes he became poor;
he was tempted in all points as we are,
but he was without sin;
he went about doing good
and preaching the gospel of the kingdom;
he accepted death, death on the cross;
he was dead and is alive for ever;
he has opened the kingdom of heaven
to all who trust in him;
he sits in glory at the right hand of God;
he will come again to be our Judge.
You, Christ, are the King of Glory.
Let us rejoice in the fellowship of the Holy Spirit,
the Lord, the Giver of Life.
Through the Spirit we are born into the family of God,
and made members of the Body of Christ;
the witness of the Spirit confirms us;
the wisdom teaches us;
the power enables us;
the Spirit will do far more for us than we ask or think.
All praise to you, Holy Spirit.

SILENT PRAYER

LORD'S PRAYER

FIRST LESSON
Isaiah 49:1-10

PSALM OR ANTHEM
Psalm 8

SECOND LESSON
Colossians 2:1-7

GOSPEL
Luke 14:12-24

SERMON
[Let each person tell what the DISCIPLE study has meant in his or her spiritual development.]

HYMN
"Come, Let Us Use the Grace Divine"
[This hymn may be read in unison or sung to the tune of "Amazing Grace."]

CONFESSION OF SIN
Let us humbly confess our sins to God.

O God, you have shown us the way of life
through your Son, Jesus Christ.
We confess with shame our slowness to learn of him,
our failure to follow him,
and our reluctance to bear the cross.
Have mercy on us, Lord, and forgive us.
We confess the poverty of our worship,
our neglect of fellowship and of the means of grace,
our hesitating witness for Christ,
our evasion of responsibilities in our service,
our imperfect stewardship of your gifts.
Have mercy on us, Lord, and forgive us.
Let each of us in silence make confession to God.

SILENCE
Have mercy on us, Lord, and forgive us.
Have mercy on me, O God, according to your steadfast love;
In your abundant mercy blot out my transgressions; thoroughly wash my iniquity from me, and cleanse me from my sin.
Create in me a clean heart, O God, and put a new and right spirit within me.
Now the message that we have heard from God's Son and that we announce is this: God is Light, and there is no darkness in him.
When we live in the Light—and he is the Light— then we have fellowship with one another, and the blood of Jesus his Son purifies us from every sin.
If we say that we have no sin, we deceive ourselves, and there is no truth in us.
But if we confess our sins to God, he will keep his promise; he will forgive us all our wrongdoing.
Amen. Thanks be to God.

COLLECT
Let us pray:
Father, you have appointed our Lord Jesus Christ as Mediator of a New Covenant;
Give us grace to draw near with fullness of faith and join ourselves in a perpetual Covenant with you, through Jesus Christ our Lord. Amen.

THE COVENANT
In the old Covenant, God chose Israel
to be a special people and to obey the Law.
Our Lord Jesus Christ, by his death and resurrection,
has made a New Covenant with all who trust in him.
We stand within this Covenant and we bear his name.
On the one side,
God promises to give us new life in Christ.
On the other side, we are pledged to live,
not for ourselves but for God.
Today, therefore, we meet to renew
this Covenant that binds us to God.
(The people stand.)
Friends, let us claim the Covenant God has made
with his people
and accept the yoke of Christ.
When we accept the yoke of Christ,
we allow Christ to guide all that we do
and all that we are,
and Christ himself is our only reward.
Christ has many ways for us to serve him;
some are easy, others are difficult.
Some receive applause; others bring only reproach;
some we desire to do because of our own interests;
others seem unnatural.
Sometimes we please Christ and meet our own needs;
at other times we cannot please Christ
unless we deny ourselves.
Yet Christ strengthens us and gives us the power
to do all these things.
Therefore let us make this Covenant with God our own.
Let us give ourselves completely to God,
trusting in his promises and relying on his grace.

I give myself completely to you, God.
Assign me to my place in your creation.
Let me suffer for you.
Give me the work you would have me do.
Give me many tasks,
or have me step aside while you call others.
Put me forward or humble me.
Give me riches or let me live in poverty.
I freely give all that I am and all that I have to you.
And now, holy God—Father, Son, and Holy Spirit—
you are mine and I am yours. So be it.
May this Covenant made on earth
continue for all eternity.
Amen.

CONCERNS AND PRAYERS
[Let opportunity be given for prayers for others.]

THE PEACE
[Stand and greet each other with appropriate signs of love and peace.]

OFFERING
[Let the bread and wine be placed before the minister.]

THE GREAT THANKSGIVING
The Lord be with you.

And also with you.

Lift up your hearts.

We lift them to the Lord.

Let us give thanks to the Lord our God.

It is right to give our thanks and praise.

It is right, and a good and joyful thing,
always and everywhere to give thanks to you,
Father Almighty, Creator of heaven and earth.
You formed us in your image
and breathed into us the breath of life.
When we turned away, and our love failed,
your love remained steadfast.
You delivered us from captivity,
made covenant to be our sovereign God,
and spoke to us through your prophets.
And so,
with your people on earth
and all the company of heaven
we praise your name and join their unending hymn:

Holy, holy, holy Lord, God of power and might,
heaven and earth are full of your glory.
Hosanna in the highest.
Blessed is he who comes in the name of the Lord.
Hosanna in the highest.

Holy are you, and blessed is your Son Jesus Christ.
Your Spirit anointed him
to preach good news to the poor,
to proclaim release to the captives
and recovering of sight to the blind,
to set at liberty those who are oppressed,
and to announce that the time had come
when you would save your people.
He healed the sick, fed the hungry,
and ate with sinners.

By the baptism
of his suffering, death, and resurrection,
you gave birth to your Church,
delivered us from slavery to sin and death,
and made with us a new covenant
by water and the Spirit.
When the Lord Jesus ascended,
he promised to be with us always,
in the power of your Word and Holy Spirit.
On the night in which he gave himself up for us
he took bread, gave thanks to you, broke the bread,
gave it to his disciples, and said:
"Take, eat; this is my body which is given for you.
Do this in remembrance of me."

When the supper was over he took the cup,
gave thanks to you, gave it to his disciples, and said:
"Drink from this, all of you;
this is my blood of the new covenant,
poured out for you and for many
for the forgiveness of sins.
Do this, as often as you drink it,
in remembrance of me."

And so,
in remembrance of these your mighty acts
in Jesus Christ,
we offer ourselves in praise and thanksgiving
as a holy and living sacrifice,
in union with Christ's offering for us,
as we proclaim the mystery of faith.

Christ has died, Christ is risen, Christ will come again.

Pour out your Holy Spirit on us, gathered here,
and on these gifts of bread and wine.
Make them be for us the body and blood of Christ,
that we may be for the world the body of Christ,
redeemed by his blood.

By your Spirit make us one with Christ,
one with each other,
and one in ministry to all the world,
until Christ comes in final victory
and we feast at his heavenly banquet.

Through your Son Jesus Christ,
with the Holy Spirit in your holy Church,
all honor and glory is yours, Almighty Father,
now and for ever.

Amen.

BREAKING THE BREAD
The minister breaks the bread . . . while saying:

Because there is one loaf,
we, who are many, are one body,
for we all partake of the one loaf.
The bread which we break
is a sharing in the body of Christ.

The minister lifts the cup . . . while saying:

The cup over which we give thanks
is a sharing in the blood of Christ.

GIVING THE BREAD AND CUP
The bread and wine are given to the people, with these or other words being exchanged:

The body of Christ, given for you. **Amen.**
The blood of Christ, given for you. **Amen.**

PRAYER AFTER COMMUNION
Let us give thanks to the Lord.
Lord, we give thanks for the gift of this holy meal.
We praise you that you sent your Son
that through him
we might be reconciled completely to you.
Christ sacrificed himself.
We offer the sacrifice of our lives.
Let all that we do be a response
to the sacrifice Christ made for us. Amen.

HYMN: "A Charge to Keep I Have"

DISMISSAL WITH BLESSING
May the God who established a Covenant
with those who seek to enter the kingdom
be always present with you.
Amen.
May Jesus Christ, who sealed the new Covenant
with his sacrifice on the cross, bring you peace.
Amen.
May God's Holy Spirit guide your life.
Amen.
Go in peace to serve God and your neighbor
in all that you do.
Amen. Thanks be to God.
